GAMES TO IMPROVE YOUR CHILD'S ENGLISH

by

Abraham B. Hurwitz
Professor of Creative Recreations
Yeshiva University

and

Arthur Goddard
Chairman, Academic Subjects
The New York School of Printing

A Fireside Book
Published by Simon and Schuster

CONTENTS

PART THREE: SCORING THE GAMES

PART FOUR: WORD LISTS, BIBLIOGRAPHY AND INDEXES

To children, who all learn through play,
This book has useful things to say.

PART ONE

To the Parent

We learn from our parents.—Alcaeus.

1

HOW GAMES
MAKE LEARNING FUN

THIS BOOK PROVIDES you with a wide variety of educational games, of varying degrees of difficulty, that you can play with your child to help him master the most important learning tool of his life, his language.

The impulse to play games is part of your child's nature. Play is what he does in his free time. It is one of his ways of investigating the world on his own, of growing up and developing a personality. Whether at home, in the playground, or on a trip, what a child learns in his games adds to and is incorporated into his school instruction. His games awaken the eagerness to learn, to think, to imagine, to listen, to create, and to express his ideas.

We Americans are basically fun-oriented, and we want even our education to be entertaining. With games it is easy to overcome a child's indifference or even hostility to the work involved in studying, memorizing, or reviewing, and to transform these negative attitudes into a lifelong love of learning.

The games in this book are what teachers call motivational devices. That is, they give your child incentives to further and continued learning that allows him to proceed on his own and at his own pace, as far as he can go. They make learning what are generally regarded as "dry" subjects, like spelling and grammar, a pleasure. At the same time, the challenge of competition provides the child with an additional stimulus and spurs him to extend his verbal abilities as far as he can.

Here, then, is a simple and effective way for you to teach and for your child to learn; and the pleasure that you will take in playing these games with each other will make both the teaching and the learning easy and fruitful. For what is agreeably learned is long remembered. Indeed, play is one of the most delightful ways in which you and your child can enjoy each other. For you, there is the experience of sharing the fun of learning, of joining in the games, of spending hours in close companionship with your child. As for him, he looks forward eagerly to playing new games with you, and in later years his memories of you will be associated with the happy times he had in your company.

2

WHAT THESE GAMES TEACH

THE PURPOSE of this book is to help you to teach your school-age child the proper use of words.

You can best appreciate the value of the games if you think of the language skills we all need in everyday life and of the problems created by inability or ineffectiveness in speaking and writing. Have you ever wondered how some people always seem to have at their instant command just the words they need in every situation? And have you noticed how those with verbal power—the power to articulate their thoughts and desires clearly, to argue convincingly, to describe precisely, to tell a story interestingly—generally command respect and gain positions of prestige and influence? On the other hand, think of the needless embarrassments and difficulties that commonly arise from errors in spelling ("Is it *ie* or *ei?*" "With two *l*'s or one?") or usage, from grammatical mistakes (*"Who* or *whom?" "Me* or *I?"*) and lack of clarity in communication.

These games have been devised to give your child the confidence that comes with proficiency in the use of his mother tongue and to spare him awkward moments of doubt, hesitation, or error in expressing himself verbally.

What's learned with pleasure is learned full measure.

The intellectual challenge offered by each game can easily be graduated in difficulty. By means of the numbered variations suggested after many of the games, you can simplify or complicate them indefinitely to adapt them to any degree of verbal ability, to any level of intelligence, and to every type of interest. At their simplest, the games constitute what educators call a "readiness program" for the school child in the early grades or for the beginner. At their most complex, they will test adults with a rather high degree of linguistic skill.

These are not the kind of verbal puzzles that, once the answers have been filled in, have fully served their transient purpose of entertaining or amusing and then hold no further interest. On the contrary, each game is a source of a potentially endless series of possible "plays," including variations, refinements, and complications that challenge the participants' ingenuity, resourcefulness, imagination, and creativity. Indeed, the games in this book are so flexible that they can be adapted to all school subjects and played at home, in a classroom, at a recreation center, or in a car; and they can be selected and shaped to meet the needs of the individual child, his friends and classmates, adult groups, clubs, and even larger audiences. There are, in fact, virtually no limits, save those of the players' time, patience, and inventiveness, to the myriad "moves" that can be made in every game.

Moreover, the wealth of possible variations in each game is matched by the diversity of topics and techniques of play, so that your child need never feel bored. There are passive games and active games; "trigger-situation" games and dramatic games; card games and pencil-and-paper games; dictionary games and treasure hunts; word games and sentence games; rhyming games and riddles; and some that defy any precise classification.

These games are an excellent substitute for the many time-killing toys and purposeless pastimes that often fill a child's leisure hours. Games of dice, cards, checkers, dominoes, hopscotch, bingo, lotto, pointer-spinning, etc., all popular with children, have here been given an educational purpose and value. What your child will learn from the games in this book, besides specific factual information about words and sentences, is, first of all, a set of *basic mental skills* whose utility extends far beyond the sphere of language. He will, in fact, learn:

—— to concentrate

—— to see relationships and analogies

—— to be accurate

—— to form intelligent hypotheses

—— to follow directions

—— to compare and categorize things, ideas, places, people, and words.

These abilities, developed early in childhood, will stand a person in good stead in any situation throughout his life. They are basic in that they are generally applicable to any subject or problem and useful in every type of circumstance.

But, in addition, these games will help your child to develop a number of *specifically linguistic skills:*

—— to spell

—— to define

—— to use a dictionary

—— to add new words to his vocabulary

—— to learn the meanings of common roots for the building of words

—— to pronounce words correctly

—— to express his ideas in coherent sentences and paragraphs

—— to punctuate

—— to recognize verbal incongruities and nuances of meaning

—— to use figures of speech and verbal imagery.

Some of the teaching, of course, is indirect; that is, it simply promotes verbal facility. Thus, words that the child has seen or heard but never used himself become parts of his active vocabulary as he plays the games.

Language mastery, then, is the tool that these games will put into the hands of your child. They will teach him how to use his native tongue rightly, skillfully, and effectively. Played in their various forms over a period of years, they will promote mental development by providing both a favorable environment for learning and the intellectual nourishment required to sustain it.

3

HOW TO USE THIS BOOK

"Where do I begin?"

You may begin anywhere. The arrangement of the games in the text is not to be taken as fixed. Because of their variety, they lend themselves to any desired sequence, depending on the subject or skills to be stressed.

"In what order should I play the games?"

You may set up your own sequences and combinations, your own program for increasing your child's vocabulary and verbal power.

You will find that there are a number of things that vary in all of these games:
(1) skills taught
(2) number of players (one, for independent play; two, three, or larger groups)
(3) method of play
(4) level of maturity

The skills taught are described at the beginning of each game. For example, under the heading WORD WHEEL, we are told that "This game builds vocabulary by training the players to group words in logical categories." We know then that this game is primarily designed to broaden vocabulary and ability to see relationships, and that spelling and pronunciation are secondary skills here.

You will see at a glance just how many players each game is best suited for, as we have included this information under the heading of each game.

The method of play is described within the game itself.

The level of maturity is also listed in the heading of each individual game. Under GHOST, for example, we find the words "All Levels." This tells you that any age-group, and any combination of age-groups, can play this game.

"How do I use the word lists?"

At the back of this book, you will find four word lists: Common Homonyms, Common Prefixes, Common Roots, and Common Suffixes. These lists are designed to serve as a supplemental pool from which to draw additional material for the games when the players have exhausted their own vocabularies. For example, the list of Common Homonyms will provide additional sets of words for the players of HOMONYM WAR, a word-matching game, while the lists of Common Prefixes, Common Roots, and Common Suffixes will provide the tools for a game like WORD WHIRL, which uses a spinning pointer to teach your child to form new words from their simplest elements.

"How can I tell whether a game is suitable for the maturity of the players?"

It is very difficult to classify any of these games according to the precise age for which they are ideally suitable.

In the first place, children of the same age are not always equally mature. They differ in experience, schooling, rate of intellectual growth, and exposure to verbal stimulation.

Besides, most of these games, as you will discover, can be profitably and enjoyably played at more than one level of maturity. Games that may prove tough or challenging for nine-year-olds can be easy and interesting for children of twelve or over and may often be fun even for adults, especially if the level of difficulty is "escalated" in ways described in the text.

In fact, you will find that many of these games are ideal for families. Here the spread in ages and verbal knowledge is actually an advantage, because older and younger children can enjoy playing together, and you can join in the fun as well.

Therefore, instead of indicating the suitability of these games in terms of particular ages or age groups, we have preferred to describe them in terms of the following broad categories:

Elementary—chiefly for children in the primary grades of elementary school.

Intermediate—for children in the upper terms of elementary school and in junior high school, including the first term (ninth year) of high school.

Advanced—for senior high school students and adults.

Elementary-Intermediate—a range including both.

Intermediate-Advanced—starting at a higher level than the foregoing and extending through and beyond high school.

All levels—admitting of the broadest possible range by means of escalating devices described in the text.

We must emphasize that these levels of maturity, although based on our best judgment and experience as educators, are to be interpreted somewhat flexibly, because neither their upper nor their lower limits are by any means precise. Children differ too much from one another to fit neatly into such categories. You yourself will soon find from experience where your own child is to be placed, and you will be pleasantly surprised as you watch him advance from one level of maturity to the next as he gains verbal facility and knowledge through playing the games.

Meanwhile, if you should find a particular game either too easy to be challenging or too difficult to encourage your child's effort, you can adjust it to your needs. You make a game easier by relaxing its rules or by using extremely simple words as examples; and you can make a game harder by following the suggestions that we have included in almost every one. Then too, in adding variations to many of the games, we have tried to carry the level of difficulty a little higher each time. Hence, it is generally advisable to begin by playing the first game in a series before trying any of the variations.

You will note that we have not included any games for the preschool child or the child in the nursery or kindergarten. But children from six to eight, at the elementary level, although they may not be able to spell all the words they know, can read and hear rhymes. So when you play a game with them, you can write down on a blackboard the words they supply in the little rhyming and other games we have prepared for this group.

In general, we think the most elementary games are the rhyming games at the beginning and some of the alphabet games in Chapter 6. On the other hand, the games suitable for the broadest range of abilities are generally those classified as best for large families, groups, or parties. These have been grouped separately, for your convenience, at the end of each chapter.

"What materials do I need for these games?"

For many of these games you will need no materials at all. If you do need, for example, cards or colored paper or a timer, you will find these items listed just under and to the right of the title of the game.

"How do I prepare the materials?"

Naturally, you will want to have ready in advance whatever materials are needed for playing and scoring a game.

Suppose, for example, that the game requires you to prepare cards with words or letters of the alphabet. A simple method of doing so is to take an old deck of playing cards and paste on the front of each card a detachable sticker on which the letter or word can be printed in black ink with a felt marking pen. (Excellent for this purpose are self-adhesive file folder labels like those sold under the trade name Permagrip.) Another method of preparing for a card or a domino game is to use three-inch-by-five-inch cards cut up into one-inch squares on each of which a letter or a word can be placed. Out of fifteen such cards you can make squares for two hundred and twenty-five letters or words. The task of placing these on the squares can be made into a learning activity in itself if the child is encouraged to cut the letters or words out of old newspapers and magazines.

Or suppose the game calls for writing a letter of the alphabet on each square. In order to be sure that the ratio of the different letters selected for the game will approximate the frequency with which they are used in forming English words, you can use the following formula, based on scientific studies, for every two hundred cards:

Vowels: E—15; A—10; I—10; O—10; U—10.

Consonants: S—10; T—10; H—10; C—10; P—8; B—8; R—8; D—8; M—8; G—8; L—8; N—8; F—8; W—8; J—5; K—5; Y—5; V—5; X—2; Z—2; Q—2.

Include in every deck a few blank cards as "jokers wild" that can stand for any letter or word.

In the directions for playing each card game, you will find exact information concerning the number of cards to prepare and the kinds of letters or words to use.

To prepare for dice games, you may use wooden or plastic blocks. You can make the dice attractive by covering them with differently colored paper and writing the words, letters, or syllables, as required, on detachable stickers.

A wheel and a spinning pointer, such as is called for in WORD WHIRL, WORD WHEEL, and similar games, is easily constructed with a compass or plate and a pin. First draw a circle or concentric circles, as required, on a piece of paper. Then insert the words, letters, roots, prefixes, suffixes, or syllables as directed for the game. Next mount your chart firmly on a piece of cardboard. Stick a pin or a two-pronged paper fastener through the center, and over this slip either a safety pin or a paper clip bent into the shape of a pointer. You now have a spinner for your word game.

For vocabulary and spelling games in which words are varied and built by the addition of prefixes, suffixes, or syllables, you can use shallow boxes or box lids to make simple tachistoscopes. These are devices which expose through a "window" only one word, syllable, or letter at a time as strips of tagboard or heavy paper are pulled through a slit, as illustrated below. You can use two different prefixes, suffixes, or syllables with the same box by turning it around and pulling through another list of words, letters, or syllables.

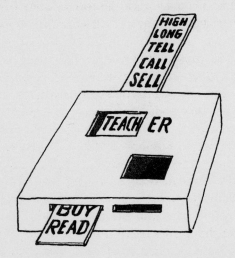

"How can I teach?"

Let the games do the teaching!

It is quite understandable that you may have some doubts

concerning your ability as a teacher, especially if you feel a little rusty about the subject matter or if you think these games require some pedagogic skill on your part. Do not allow yourself to become so much concerned about your child's learning that you let anxiety charge the atmosphere. Though the ultimate goal is educational, the emphasis should always be on play rather than on teaching. Especially at the beginning, the spirit of fun and recreation should prevail if you are to win and hold your child's interest. After all, games are contests, not tests.

"How do I go about playing the games?"

Establishing rapport and capturing attention, particularly in these days of television and other distractions, may not always be easy. If the child is watching a program on television and is obviously absorbed in it, he should not be pressed to play a vocabulary game. Of course, if you can find a point of contact between the game you have in mind and what he is watching or doing, you may be able to lead him to play with you.

Begin with a favorite game, and then, having aroused the child's interest, channel it toward any specific game you have in mind. You might start with a joke, a conundrum, or an amusing story. As an aid to you in gaining attention at the outset, there are numerous small items of "spice" in the form of a line or two of humor—a "teaser," a piece of verbal drollery, a pun, a tongue twister, a linguistic oddity, or a riddle—to set the mood of relaxation and keep everything in a light vein. Some of these also illustrate or emphasize a point, demonstrate a fact, and aid the memory.

Of course, you should first read the description of the game yourself and become familiar with its possible variations.

Next, prepare your materials, if any are needed.

It is best to begin by naming the game and explaining it slowly and clearly, but only as much as is needed to start playing. Keep the rules brief at first. Other rules can be added as the game progresses, after the child has mastered its basic pattern.

"How can I hold the child's interest?"

A child's cooperation and span of attention will increase in proportion to the pleasure and sense of achievement he derives from playing the game successfully. It should not be so difficult that he cannot meet its challenge, because he will soon become frustrated and lose interest. On the other hand, be careful not to make the game so easy that your child will be bored. Make an effort to fit the game to the maturity, background, ability, and interests of the child or the group.

Be sure to join in the game yourself. Your active participation and enthusiasm cannot fail to prove infectious. On the other hand, if the child sometimes prefers to play the game only with his peers, you may serve as umpire or scorekeeper, or an older child in the group may do so under your supervision.

If a child has fallen into the habit of giving up quickly, he can be encouraged or even given hints. If he cannot find the answer, he should simply be told what it is and allowed to continue. He should be praised for his successful efforts and reminded of past successes if he tends to become discouraged.

Another good way of arousing and holding interest is to involve other children who are enthusiastic about playing the game. In group games, it is important to select those that involve most of the players most of the time. Children lose interest when they have to wait too long for their turn. If necessary, divide the players into groups according to their ability to play. Choosing children on the basis of their readiness is generally preferable to having them take turns, be-

Men must be taught as if you taught them not,
And things unknown proposed as things forgot.—POPE.

cause they are then on the *qui vive* as they seek to be called upon.

If a child makes a mistake, do not let him become a "drop-out" from the game for long. "Losers" should be included at the first opportunity and given a chance to redeem themselves. Letting other children help the losers increases their sense of security and personal worth.

Mistakes should be promptly corrected, and all questions should be answered simply, clearly, and patiently. A child's questions are requests for help and clues to what he wants to learn. It is when he is having his questions answered that he is adding to his knowledge.

In order to keep the game moving, a time limit should be set for each answer. One way of making the passage of time evident is to have an hourglass egg timer show visibly that "time is running out." A stop watch, a gong, a disk bell, an electric timer such as is used for cooking, a clock or even a wrist watch may also serve the same purpose. The tempo can be speeded up or slowed down, or the time limit can be changed, according to the abilities of the players.

In a group of more than four, "surprise" timing may be tried. A ball, a beanbag, or a similar object is thrown to the player who is to respond; and he must do so when he catches it. Since no one knows to whom the ball will be tossed next, everyone is kept on the alert.

"How do I score the games?"

To enhance the fun of these games, we have included in Chapter 8 a variety of suggestions for turning the scoring into games in themselves. In the sections entitled "Games to Score Games," "Scoring Group Games," and "Matching the Players," you will find an abundance of devices to vary your methods of keeping score and tallying results.

"Do these games really teach?"

All the games in this book have been tested. No matter

how inexperienced you may be at playing games, you can count on these to do their job of entertaining and teaching. Some of them are classics that have been played for generations, though they lend themselves to being kept up to date with fresh material; and even the newer games have been tried countless times with all kinds of children.

Using the Indexes

The Index of Games will help you to locate games you have enjoyed playing and wish to find again. The Index of Skills Taught will enable you to find just the game you need to correct your child's weaknesses, or that corresponds to his interests.

Do not try to judge the value of a game simply by reading its description. After all, these games were designed for children, not adults, even though adults may enjoy playing some of them. Let your child be the judge. The fun is in the playing, not in the telling or the reading, and only after you have tried a game will you be able to appreciate its worth.

Have fun!

PART TWO

Games to Play

4

GAMES WITH RHYMES

FROM THE MOMENT your child begins to play "ring-around-a-rosy" or "all around the mulberry bush," he is ready for you to start him on his way toward learning new words and expressions and gaining facility with language through games.

Children are fascinated with the rhyme and rhythm of verse and love to sing over and over again rhyming nonsense syllables. They like to experiment with words and the sounds of words, with consonances and assonances and echoes and alliterations and jingles and cadences.

The games in this chapter, beginning at the elementary level, take advantage of this natural delight in rhymes and the music of verse to encourage creativity, experimentation, and resourcefulness in the use of words and to give the child a sense of mastery over the materials of language.

A rhyming dictionary is a useful book to have at hand. Either of those mentioned in the bibliography can be consulted in preparing for some of the games. It's also fun to use it to make up new words for a well-known song and then to

By changing a single letter, make a rhyme that turns a place for storing money into a place for storing gasoline.
Turn BANK into TANK.

sing or play the tune with a group of children. Once they get into the spirit of the game, they can be encouraged to compose their own lyrics and parodies.

I. Ready Rhymes

The games in this section are all designed to put rhymes on the tip of your child's tongue, to teach him how to construct rhymes, and to acquaint him with the various spellings of the same rhyme sounds.

RHYME PING-PONG

ELEMENTARY   *Clock or timer*
2 *only*

You can begin playing this game with your child to familiarize him with simple rhymes and later make it gradually more difficult as he develops skill and maturity.

Set a time limit, and start at a slow pace. You can later adjust the speed of the rhyme volley as desired.

Begin with easy rhymes made from words familiar to the child, so that he gains a sense of achievement right from the outset. For example, you might say "Boy." Now, within a given time, the child must toss back a rhyme for *boy*—say, *toy*. Next it is your turn—or, if another child is playing the game, his turn—within the same time limit to call out still another word rhyming with these two—e.g., *joy*, *enjoy*, etc. The idea is to see how long the players can go on doing this before exhausting their stock of ready rhymes. The winner is the player who lasts the longer.

To start with, many simple words can be made to rhyme with such words as *bat*, *bet*, *gum*, *blow*, *play*, *bear*, *hole*, *ball*, *bone*, *hot*, and *zoo*.

At a later stage, children can be shown that what counts is not the spelling but the sound of the word. Thus, *what* rhymes with *hot*, but *though* and *rough* do not rhyme.

RHYME TIME   VAR. 1

ELEMENTARY   *Paper and pencil*
2 *or more*   *Clock or timer*

In this variation each player, within a given time, has to think of as many words as possible that rhyme with the given word.

The question is put in the form, "How many words can you find that rhyme with ———?" and each player writes down his list until the time is up. The player with the longest list wins.

Another way of scoring the game is to give one point for each rhyme listed and one extra point for any rhyme not thought of by any other player.

For a number of interesting and more advanced variations of this game, in which more than two can participate, see KATE, BETTER LATE THAN NEVER, GATEWAY, GREAT WORDS, HOW DO I RATE?, ICEMAN, and NATIONS (pages 92–98).

RHYME WHIRL   VAR. 2

ELEMENTARY-INTERMEDIATE   *Clock or timer*
2 *or more*

Besides teaching children a wide variety of rhymes and rhyming words, this variation improves reading by aiding in the recognition of common consonant blends. It also calls for attention to the differences and similarities in the sounds of words.

Using a compass or plate, draw two concentric circles proportioned as shown here. Around and within the circumference of the outer, larger circle write a number of consonant blends like BL, BR, CL, CR, DR, FL, FR, GL, GR, CH, KN, PL, PR, SC, SCH, SH, SL, SR, ST, STR, SW, TH, THR, TR, SN, SM, WH, etc. Then, around and within the circumference of the inner, smaller circle write a number of simple rhyme endings like

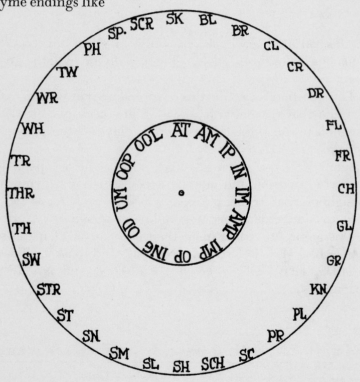

AT, AM, IP, AND, OP, ING, IM, OWN, ANCE, UM, OD, OOP, OOL, AZE, INK, ANK, OKE, OCK, UN, ITE, IPE, ICK, ACT, IKE, IDE, etc.

Next, cut out the center disk neatly with a razor or a sharp knife and mount the remaining outer rim of the larger circle on a piece of cardboard. Finally, insert the center disk, likewise backed up by a piece of cardboard to give it some stiffness, in its place by means of a two-pronged paper fastener pushed through the center, so that the inner disk can be freely twirled.

The players take turns twirling the center disk to line up rhyme endings with different consonant blends. Each player is free to choose any one of the combinations that simultaneously line up if it makes a word. For example, suppose that a player lines up IM with TR, to make TRIM. Within a given time, he must name as many words as he can that rhyme with *trim*—say, *slim*, *him*, *grim*, *gym*, *whim*, *prim*, *brim*, *skim*, *vim*, *hymn*, *limb*, *rim*, etc. As can be seen from these examples, what counts is the rhyme, not the spelling. Thus, words like *praise*, *prays*, and *maize* could be cited as rhymes for *glaze* on the rhyme whirl.

A player receives one point for each rhyming word he names within the given time limit. If, after twirling the disk, a player cannot find any combination that makes a word, he loses his turn to the next player. If he chooses a combination that has been previously used, he may not repeat rhymes already given. The one with the greatest number of points wins the game.

Having in reserve a number of additional center disks with more rhyme endings can help to vary the game and make it more difficult.

Add one letter to a word meaning a part of the body and get a rhyming word that's a sign of sorrow.
EAR plus T = TEAR.

Change a barrel into a job by changing one letter and getting a rhyme.
Turn CASK to TASK.

RHYME WHEEL   VAR. 3

ELEMENTARY-INTERMEDIATE   *Blackboard and chalk*
2 or more   *Clock or timer*
                              Wheel and spinning pointer

In this variation the players go one step further by building rhymes from given endings found by twirling a pointer on a wheel like that shown below.

Here only one circle is needed. Around and within its circumference you can place rhyme endings of varying difficulty—e.g., END, ABLE, IPE, ACT, ICK, IF, ORN, ORT, AWL, OOL, EAK, OKE, etc.

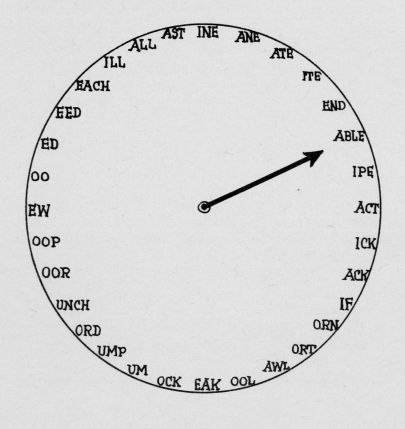

Each player, in turn, gets one spin. He must then name as many words as he can, within a given time, that contain the rhyme with the sound of the ending to which the spinner points. For example, if he gets OKE, he might say "Joke, cloak, croak, smoke, poke, spoke, and oak" before time is up. Each of these words would then count as one point in his credit. They would all be written down on the blackboard for the other players to see.

Now, if he or another player again spins the pointer to OKE, no credit could be given for any of the words already listed. New rhymes would have to be thought of—perhaps *yolk, folk, revoke, soak, broke,* and *woke.* In this way, all the players are put on their mettle and learn new words and rhymes from one another.

Finally, after every player has just about exhausted his stock of rhymes for the endings shown on the wheel, the list under each should be looked at by all and compared with the lists under these endings to be found in a rhyming dictionary. Thus, everybody can learn new words and rhymes.

BLENDS AND ENDS   Var. 4

INTERMEDIATE   *Blank cards (playing-card*
2 *or more*   *size)*

This variation likewise develops basic reading skills by familiarizing the players with common initial consonant blends as they appear in words that rhyme.

First prepare twenty-six cards by writing on each a different consonant blend. Any twenty-six of the following may be chosen: BL, BR, CH, CL, CR, DR, DW, FL, FR, GL, GR, KN, PL, PR, QU, SC, SCH, SCR, SH, SHR, SL, SM, SN, SP, ST, STR, SPR, SW, TH, TR, THR, TW, WH, SQU, SK, and PH. Add a joker.

Then prepare thirty-four cards with common rhyme endings like AT, AM, IP, OP, OPE, ING, IM, OWN, ANCE, UM, OD, OOP, AZE, IZE, ID, IDE, AME, AND, INE, AD, UMP, IMP, OO, INK, AWL, IVE, AY, AVE, ATE, ANK, IPE, ILE, ALE, and IRE. These are good endings for the blends, but others could be substituted in alternative decks. Add a joker to this pack too.

Shuffle each pack separately. Deal each player four cards from the deck of consonant blends and lay the deck of rhyme endings face down on the table.

Now each player, in turn, draws one card from the top of the deck of rhyme endings. Let us say that the first player, holding a hand with PR, ST, BL, and GR, draws the card with AND. He can lay down GRAND, STAND, and BLAND, using the same rhyme-ending card for all three consonant blends. These now appear face up on the table next to him, and he holds one card in his hand. At least *two* consonant blends must always be laid down for each rhyme ending.

The next player, drawing a card from the top of the rhyme-ending deck, follows the same procedure if he can find in his hand at least two consonant blends that will fit the rhyme ending he draws. If he cannot do so, he adds the rhyme-ending card to his hand, perhaps forming a single word with it and a consonant blend, and the next player follows. A single word being held can be played as soon as another consonant blend that makes a word to rhyme with it appears in his hand.

If a player lays down his complete hand or all his consonant blends, he gets a chance to draw four more cards from the deck of consonant blends. The game proceeds in this fashion until all the cards in the pack of consonant blends are used up. (This may happen before all the cards in the other deck are used, of course.)

Points are scored by counting the number of rhyming words laid down by each player and subtracting the number of cards left in his hand at the end of the game. No credit is given for a single word, like FLOP, in a player's hand.

The jokers are "wild" and can be treated as any letter combination desired, whether as consonant blends or rhyme endings.

BLENDS AND ENDS CASINO   VAR. 5

INTERMEDIATE   *Blank cards (playing-card*
2 *or more*   *size)*

This variation, which makes use of materials like those in BLENDS AND ENDS, is played like the familiar card game known as casino. It develops the reading skills of the players by acquainting them with frequently occurring consonant blends appearing in words that rhyme.

First prepare a set of seventeen cards by writing on each *two* consonant blends—e.g., BL, BR; CH, CL; CR, DR; FL, FR; GL, GR; PL, PR; SH, SCH; SC, SK; SCR, SL; SM, SN; SP, SPR; SHR, ST; STR, SW; TH, THR; TR, TW; KN, PH; and SQU, WH. To these add seven cards by writing *two* consonants on each—e.g., B, C; D, F; G, L; M, N; P, R; S, T; and W, H. This will give you twenty-four cards of consonants and consonant blends. You can, of course, vary the pairs of consonant blends and consonants appearing on each card in any way you like; you need not use just the combinations suggested here.

Next prepare a set of twenty-eight cards by writing on each a common ending that could be used for making rhymes. If the ending can be spelled in different ways, write all the variants on the same card. For example, the cards might be prepared thus: OR, ORE, OAR; OUR, OWER; IME, YME; INK; ANK; EW, UE; OON, UNE; EEL, EAL; AY, EIGH; AIN, ANE; OOT, UTE; ERE, EAR, EER; AIL, ALE; ULE, OOL; AIR, ARE, EAR; ITE, IGHT; AMP; IMP; IP; IFE; AW; ACK; IN; INE, EIN; EEZE, EASE; EW, OO; OWN, ONE;

UB. (Note that in cases where the same spelling, such as EAR, may be pronounced in different ways, as in *gear* and *wear*, the card on which that spelling is written always contains at least one other variant spelling—e.g., ERE or AIR—to indicate the sound of the rhyme intended.) Naturally, other rhyme endings could be used or substituted in the deck in subsequent rounds.

Putting the two sets together will produce a deck of fifty-two cards. If you want to start by making the game very easy, you may substitute three or four jokers for any of the rhyme-ending cards. Then, in successive rounds, you can replace a joker at a time with one of the cards you removed from the deck. However, it is always a good idea to keep at least one joker in the deck.

After the cards are thoroughly shuffled, the players are dealt four cards each, and four cards are laid face up on the table. It is generally a good idea for a player, when his cards are dealt to him, to separate in his hand the rhyme-ending cards from those with consonants and consonant blends.

If the first player has in his hand a card that, with one on the table, will make *two* words that rhyme—e.g., in the deck described above, STR, SW in his hand, and AIN, ANE on the table—he may take in the card from the table, match it with the card in his hand, display the combination to the other players, call out the rhyming words (i.e., STRAIN and SWAIN), and place both cards face down in a pile in front of him. In fact, a player may take in from the table, with the same card from his hand, as many cards as will make, with it, *two* rhyming words. For example, if AY, EIGH were also on the table, the same player could take this card in too with his STR, SW card to make STRAY and SWAY. And, of course, a rhyme-ending card in one's hand, like IP, can be matched with any consonant or consonant-blend card or cards on the table—say, CH, CL—if two rhyming words (here CHIP and CLIP) can be made by combining both cards.

As always, a joker is "wild" and may be treated as any consonant, consonant blend, or rhyme ending desired.

Suppose, however, that a player has *two* cards in his hand which, together with one card on the table, could make two rhyming words—say, CR, DR and SC, SK in his hand, and AMP on the table. Although neither one of the two cards in his hand will make two rhyming words with AMP, both together would. In that case, he may put either one, CR, DR or SC, SK, on the table over AMP and say either "Building CRAMP" or "Building SCAMP." This announcement means that he has in his hand a card with which he can take in that "build" when his turn next comes. If a player has *three* cards in his hand that, together with the card on the table, will form *three* rhyming words, he can build on his build the next time his turn comes to play.

Any player, however, when his turn comes, can take in a previous player's build if he has the right card to form the rhyming words; or he can build on his own; or he can take in a card from the table with a card from his hand to form two rhyming words; or he can take in more than one card from the table. If he can do none of these, he places a card face up on the table. He can do this at any time except when he has a build of his own waiting.

After a player has used up the first deal of four cards each, he is given another hand of four cards, but no more cards are dealt out face up on the table.

The play continues in this way until all the cards in the deck have been dealt out. Any cards taken in by a player are always added to the pile in front of him. The player who is the last to take in a card or cards from the table also takes in whatever other cards may still be left lying there.

Score is kept by counting the number of cards in one's pile. The winner of the round is the player with the most cards. If several rounds are played, after every round a record should be kept of the score of each player so that totals can be added up at the end.

By changing just one word in a rhyming pair and keeping the rhyme, show the effect of air pollution on a lovely metropolis.
It can turn a PRETTY CITY into a GRITTY CITY.

How do you turn bad medicine into good by changing the first word of a rhyming pair and keeping the rhyme?
Turn a POOR CURE into a SURE CURE.

How would you turn a soft-drink establishment into a trading center by switching the first word of a rhyming pair and keeping the rhyme?
Turn a POP SHOP into a SWAP SHOP.

What rhyming pair of words describes a shy suitor?
SLOW BEAU.

How do you tame an unruly child by changing one letter in a rhyming pair and keeping the same rhyme?
Turn a WILD CHILD into a MILD CHILD.

RHYMES FOR THE BIRDS
What birds fill out the rhymes in this little verse?
Jabbering noisily the livelong day
Is the bold and lively ———.
You can see a little ———
Hopping on the branches narrow.

MORE RHYMES FOR THE BIRDS
What words fill out the rhymes in this little verse?
The sharp-clawed, wide-eyed, wise old ———
Preys on insects, mice, and fowl.
That lovely song in the trees you heard
Was the morning carol of a woodland ———.

STILL MORE RHYMES FOR THE BIRDS
As you stroll at dawn in the quiet park,
You can faintly hear the twittering ———.
High in the sky on your springtime walk
Hovers the watchful prairie ———.

RHYME DICE

INTERMEDIATE   *Dice*

2 *or more*

This game familiarizes the players with common rhymes that may be formed by words whose endings are spelled in various ways.

Mark each of the six sides of four, five, or six cubes with a different word that rhymes with some other word on another cube. For example, if four cubes are used, the words *climb*, *thyme*, *dime*, and *crime* would appear on four different cubes, not on the same cube. Since each cube has six faces, you will need six different rhyme endings. If five cubes are used, each of the thirty words should rhyme with four others. So far as possible, try to find rhyming words that differ in their spelling of the rhyming sound.

Here is one possible set of thirty such words, of many that could be found: *news, fuse, ooze, whose, zoos; watt, swat, pot, kumquat, apricot; word, third, heard, absurd, bird; mind, dined, blind, twined, kind; blaze, praise, phrase, maize, ways; shoal, pole, roll, control, mole.*

When two play, each is given, to begin with, two cubes. The other cubes are then held in reserve until, after several rounds, the players exchange or replace their cubes.

If the first player, on his first throw, turns up two words that rhyme, he scores one point and gets another chance to throw the dice. If the two words he turns up do not rhyme, his opponent throws his own dice.

If just three cubes are used, the same three can be thrown by each player. In that case, one point is earned for throwing a rhyming pair, and two points for throwing a rhyming triplet.

Still another way of playing the game is to let each of the two players throw the same four cubes at one time. The following scoring possibilities then emerge: no rhymes—lose turn; a pair of rhymes—one point; three rhyming words—two points; four rhyming words—three points; two pairs of rhyming words—four points.

If three play, each gets two cubes, which they can exchange in later rounds. Or the players may throw any number of the same cubes at one time.

RHYME CONCENTRATION

ALL LEVELS   Blank cards (playing-card
2 only   size)

This card game can be used to review familiar rhymes and to introduce new rhymes and rhyming words. True to its name, it requires concentration and a retentive memory.

Prepare a deck of cards arranged in matched pairs (or even triplets and quadruplets) of rhyming words. The rhymes and the words to be selected for the cards will depend on what is to be taught or reviewed and the level of difficulty desired. They may include such easy and obvious matches as *pore* and *sore*, *dear* and *clear*, *life* and *wife*, *tea* and *sea*, and *rose* and *pose*; or, at an intermediate level, such words as *tough* and *puff*, *plough* and *now*, *crude* and *stewed*, and *taught* and *thought*; or even such difficult combinations as *hurrahed* and *façade*, *guitar* and *bazaar*, *quadruped* and *watershed*, *hypotenuse* and *introduce*, *cryptic* and *triptych*, and *criminal* and *subliminal*. Triplets and quadruplets can contain words of different degrees of difficulty—e.g., *spoon*, *hewn*, and *commune* or *quicker*, *liquor*, *knicker*, and *vicar*.

The number of cards in the deck will depend on the players' ability to concentrate. Too much of a strain is placed on the memory of each player if more than forty-eight cards are used. This number, divisible by two, three, and four, lends itself to various combinations of pairs, triplets, and quadruplets. However, extra sets of cards with different rhyming words can be kept in reserve for later rounds.

Shuffle the cards and spread them out face down on the table. The first player picks up two cards at random and shows them to his opponent. If the cards match—i.e., if they make a rhyme, like *gamble* and *ramble*—the first player lays them face up on his side of the table and scores one point. He then gets another chance to find a matching pair. If he fails to do so, he must return one of the cards he has picked up, after showing both to his opponent, face down, to its former place on the table. He keeps the other card in his hand and, when his turn next comes, draws only one card.

The second player now picks a card from those lying face down on the table and shows it to his opponent. He then tries to recall the wording and the position of the card that was put down by his opponent in order to determine whether the word on it will rhyme with the one on the card in his hand. If he remembers that they do not rhyme, he may choose any other card. If, either through good memory or good luck, he succeeds in getting a rhyming pair of words, he lays both cards, face up, on his side of the table, scores a point, and gets another chance to find a matching pair. Whenever a card is drawn from the table, it must be shown to the other player in order to give him a chance to memorize its wording and position in case it is laid down again and is later wanted.

The game proceeds in this way until the last card has been drawn from the table, whether at random or because a player recalled its wording and location. The winner is the player with the highest score.

When playing with rhyming triplets or quadruplets, if a player draws a card that rhymes with a pair laid down previously by his opponent, to form a triplet, he may take his opponent's pair, add his own rhyming word, put the whole triplet on his own side of the table, and draw again. Similarly, his opponent may win back the triplet if he can draw the rhyming card that makes it a quadruplet. If a player draws a card that rhymes with any pair or triplet on his own side of the table, he adds it to his collection and draws again. In each case, the player adds a point to his score.

The game can be made increasingly difficult by inserting sets of harder rhyming words in successive rounds. If the deck is enlarged, it is a good idea to write on the back of each card a number (1, 2, 3, etc.) to help the players to associate it with the word on its face.

RHYME DOMINOES

ELEMENTARY-INTERMEDIATE   *Blank cards (playing-card*
2 *or more*   *size)*

This is a delightful way of reviewing common rhymes and introducing the players to new ones. Although this game is best for two, it can be played by three or even four.

Prepare twenty-eight cards by marking each off with a horizontal line through its center when it is held long side up, so that the space is divided equally into two halves.

Now in each half of every card write in a word to match the arrangement of the numbers on a set of dominoes so that the same number is always represented by a word with the same rhyme ending. To match the rhymes with the numbers, proceed as follows:

To match the domino with 0-0, prepare a card with, let us say, *gun* and *sun*. Now every 0 will be represented by a word that rhymes with these.

1-1 might correspond to *fat* and *cat;* 1-0 would then be a word rhyming with *fat* (say, *mat*) and a word rhyming with *gun* (say, *pun*).

2-2 might correspond to a new rhyme—let us say, *hand* and *band*. Then 2-1 could be *sand* and *sat;* and 2-0, *strand* and *fun*.

3-3 could be *hope* and *rope;* 3-2, *dope* and *land;* 3-1, *slope* and *brat;* and 3-0, *mope* and *done*.

4-4 might be *sink* and *drink;* 4-3, *think* and *soap;* 4-2, *ink* and *gland;* 4-1, *brink* and *hat;* 4-0, *mink* and *bun.*

5-5 could be *gum* and *slum;* 5-4, *strum* and *rink;* 5-3, *drum* and *grope;* 5-2, *crumb* and *bland;* 5-1, *thumb* and *that;* and 5-0, *dumb* and *run.*

6-6 might be *tan* and *man;* 6-5, *ban* and *glum;* 6-4, *than* and *blink;* 6-3, *fan* and *cope;* 6-2, *span* and *fanned;* 6-1, *pan* and *pat;* and 6-0, *can* and *won* (or *one*).

These examples are given only to demonstrate the principle to be followed in constructing the "dominoes." Naturally, other rhymes or rhyming words, more or less difficult, could be substituted for the ones listed here, but the organization of the rhyming words should follow this pattern.

Shuffle the cards thoroughly and lay the deck face down on the table.

If there are two players, each in turn draws a card until he has seven; three or four players draw five cards each. If a player finds that he has in his hand cards that can be matched with one another—i.e., cards with words that rhyme—he puts them down, when his turn comes, face up on the table with the rhyming words adjacent to each other, whether in a straight line or at right angles. The next player may lay down one or more cards from his hand, either independently or to match any rhyme at either end of a set that has already been laid down by the first player. If a player cannot form such a match, he has to draw a card from the top of the deck and keep on doing so until he finds a rhyme. The object of the game is to be the first to get rid of all the cards in one's hand.

There are several ways of making this game more complicated. Neither the rhyme endings nor the rhyming words need to be as simple as the ones given here. Moreover, *pictures* (e.g., of the sun, a mat, a rope, a hat, a thumb, a man, a can, a cat, a drum, etc.) can be substituted for some or all of the words, thus requiring the players to associate words with visual clues.

HINK PINK

INTERMEDIATE-ADVANCED   *Clock or timer*

2 *or more*

This game can be played endlessly, begun and dropped and picked up again. It calls for verbal ingenuity and imagination.

For rhyming pairs of one-syllable words, a player says, "I have a Hink Pink"; for two-syllable words, "I have a Hinky Pinky"; and for three-syllable words, "I have a Hinkety Pinkety." He then gives a brief description of his Hink Pink or Hinky Pinky or Hinkety Pinkety. Within a given time limit, the other players have to guess the answer, which must consist of two rhyming words of one, two, or three syllables respectively.

For example, suppose a player says, "I have a Hink Pink. It's an enormous flatboat."

Well, that's easy. It's a *large barge*, of course.

Here are a few more Hink Pinks:

Homely girl	Plain Jane
Angry father	Mad dad
Bashful lad	Coy boy
Fat fish	Stout trout
Angry employer	Cross boss
Tiny sphere	Small ball
Girl from Switzerland	Swiss miss
Antagonism	Ill will
Obese feline	Fat cat
Bulky burner	Thick wick

And here are some Hinky Pinkies:

Happy captain	Chipper skipper
Happy canine	Jolly collie
Sole rhyme	Single jingle
Convenient confection	Handy candy

Agreeable rustic	Pleasant peasant
Kitchen knife	Butter cutter
Odorous vagabond	Fragrant vagrant

Obviously, Hinkety Pinkety makes greater demands on the players' verbal knowledge and skill. Here is a good one to start with:

Evil cleric	Sinister minister

And one more for good measure:

Happier canine	Merrier terrier

Think of the amusing ways one might describe a *resident president*, an *airier area*, a *quieter rioter*, a *fiery diary*, a *judicial official*, a *rotary notary*, or a *crueler jeweler*.

Once the Hinky Pinky or Hinkety Pinkety bug bites you, you'll never be the same. Advanced players may even want to try three-word Hinky Pinkies like *Baker, take her! Pick her, vicar! Eye her, friar! Tie her, prior! Cure it, curate! Pastor passed her, Sister hissed her, Mister missed her, Picket, pick it! Kick her quicker! Sailor, bail her! Slam her hammer! Bend her fender! Lend her splendor, Spoil her broiler, Serve her fervor, Suit her suitor, Shoot her tutor, Lick her liquor, He's in season, Place in basin, Kiss us, Mrs., Hoist her oyster, Dole her dolor, You're fewer, You're truer, Vow her power, Nectar wrecked her, Heed her, speeder!* etc. Real enthusiasts for this sort of thing may go on from here to construct four-word Hinky Pinkies like *Let her pet her*.

WHAT'S MY RHYME?

INTERMEDIATE

3 or more

This is an excellent game for learning rhymes and building vocabulary.

Essentially, the game is a battle of wits between one player and all his opponents. He begins by saying, "I have a word that rhymes with ————," and mentions a word—say, *SAT*.

Now the other players take turns asking him questions about the word, but without naming it. For example, he may be asked, "Is it a feline?" He, in turn, must guess what word his questioner has in mind and mention it in his answer. Thus, he might answer, "No, it's not a cat." The dialogue might then continue in this vein:

PLAYER 3: Is it something you step on?

PLAYER 1: No, it's not a mat.

PLAYER 2: Is it a rodent?

PLAYER 1: No, it's not a rat.

PLAYER 3: Is it something used for storage?

PLAYER 1: No, it's not a vat. (Perhaps he had this word in mind to begin with, but he decides at this point to retreat to another word that he knows and that has not yet been mentioned. For if he says, "Yes, it is a vat," the person who identified the rhyme, in this case Player 3, scores a point and gives the next rhyme. So Player 1 tries to hold his position as long as he can.)

PLAYER 2: Is it used in a game?

If Player 1 cannot guess what word Player 2 is referring to, his questioner must tell what word it is (in this case, BAT) and then, after scoring a point, give the next rhyme.

Since no rhyming word may be repeated in a question, the person proposing the rhyme has to have a good vocabulary of rhymes in order to be able to match all those offered by his combined opposition. In this particular game, Player 1 might have retreated from *hat*, *flat*, *slat*, and *brat* to *gnat*.

The game is scored by crediting one point to any player whose word cannot be guessed by his opponent, one point to the person proposing the initial rhyme for each rhyming word of his opponents that he succeeds in guessing, and two points to the opponent who guesses his word when he finally runs out of words to fall back upon.

Of course, this game can be played with words of more than one syllable, too.

WHAT'S THE NAME OF THE GAME?
Down the alley balls go rolling;
Ninepins fall as we go ———.
With flashing stick the goalie stocky
Strikes the puck in a game of ———.

USE CLUES!
The batter swings and hits the ———.
It quickly soars above the ———.

What rhyming pair of words describes a morose pal?
GLUM CHUM.

How do you make a rhyme to turn a swindler into a generous fellow by changing just two letters?
Change CHEATER to TREATER.

A TERRIBLE MISS-TAKE!
A mister kissed a miss;
A mister kissed her.
A miss missed her kiss;
A miss missed her mister.
And Mister missed his Miss.
Did Mister kiss his Miss?
No, Mister missed her.

FLOWER POWER
With thorns along the hedges grows
The fragrant, wild, familiar ———.
Its yellow petals holding up
Stands the graceful ———.

I have a Hinky Pinky. It's a shrewd nurse.
CANNY NANNY.

I have a Hinky Pinky. It's a cautious scholar.
PRUDENT STUDENT.

MATCH MY RHYME

ELEMENTARY-INTERMEDIATE   *Clock or timer*
3 or more

In this game, the players must likewise be quick with a rhyme, but they must also have retentive memories.

The first player mentions a word that begins with A—say, ABLE.

Now the next player must say any word that rhymes with it, such as *fable*. Each player thereafter must do the same, within a given time. In this case, they might proceed with *table*, *label*, *gable*, *sable*, and *stable*.

A player scores one point for each rhyming word he adds to the list. If he misses, he may challenge the preceding player to match his rhyme. If the preceding player can do so, he scores an extra point; if he cannot, he is penalized two points. Anyone else who can think of a rhyme that has not been mentioned so far scores two points.

When the possibilities of a given word seem to have been exhausted, a rhyming dictionary may be consulted to see whether the players missed any rhymes. Then another word, this time beginning with B, can be tried, and so on.

FISHING FOR RHYMES

ELEMENTARY-INTERMEDIATE   *Blank cards (playing-card*
2 or more   *size)*

This game will teach children to recognize rhymes, acquaint them with common ones, and build their vocabulary.

A deck of cards must first be prepared. Each card is to have on it a different word, but the words selected should form rhymed sets of two, three, or more. Naturally, they should be suited to the interests and maturity of the players and should include some new vocabulary for them.

At least fifty-two cards—i.e., twenty-six pairs of rhymes—should be used. Extra sets of cards can be reserved to increase the difficulty in successive rounds after the players have become familiar with the easier, one-syllable rhymes.

The cards are thoroughly shuffled, and five are dealt to each player, one at a time per round, the remainder being placed face down on the table.

Beginning with the player on the dealer's left, each player, in turn, one at a time, asks any other player for a card that rhymes with a particular word he already has. He says, "Please give me a word that rhymes with ————."

If the player addressed has one or more cards with such a word, he must give them all to the one who asked for them. The latter may then continue to ask any other player for the cards he wants as long as he is successful. If he cannot get the card he wants from the player he addresses, he is told to "Go fish," and he must draw the top card from the deck lying face down on the table. If this card completes a set of rhymed words, he may lay it down, and he gets another chance to draw, until he is unable to obtain a rhyming set. Then the turn to play passes to the next player at the left.

As a player succeeds in obtaining sets of rhymes, he shows them to the others and lays them face down in front of him. When there are no more cards left in the deck, the round is over, and the player with the most sets of rhymes wins. Ten points are scored for winning each round.

If a player has a card that is called for but denies having it when asked, he is penalized one point for each player in the game.

———————————

Read this three times, each time faster than before:

Spilled oil soils. Spilled oil spoils. Spilled oil spoils soils. Oiled soils spoil. Soil spoils oil. Oil-spilled soil spoils. Oil-spilled soil soils. Oil-soiled soil spoils.

RHYM-O

ELEMENTARY-INTERMEDIATE   *Blank cards (bingo or*
3 or more   *lotto size)*
                                                   Small slips of paper
                                                   Small colored
                                                       cardboard squares

This game, which is very similar to bingo, is an excellent way of teaching rhymes. At the same time, it familiarizes children with common homonyms—i.e., words like *sole* and *soul* that have the same sound but different spellings and meanings. The materials needed require some preparation by the parent or teacher.

Each participant receives a card like the one shown below.

R	H	Y	M	O
UM	IM	OME	UN	OR
UN	OME	IM	UM	IM
UM	UN	OR	IM	OME
OR	UM	IM	OME	UM
IM	OME	UM	OR	UN

In this particular game, the rhyme endings UM, IM, OME, UN, and OR have been used, but any others that can become part of several rhyming words can be selected. Of course, aside from the top line, all the cards are different in the arrangement of the rhyme endings.

Slips of paper or cardboard are then prepared, each containing a letter of the word RHYM-O followed by a word containing one of the rhyme endings selected for the game. Thus, for UM, words like *slum, dumb, some, sum, thumb, come, crumb, chum, plum, plumb,* and *hum* might be prepared and written on cards like R-SLUM, H-DUMB, Y-SOME, M-SUM, etc. For IM, one could match the letters of RHYM-O with words like *him, slim, skim, trim, brim,* and *whim.* For OME, there could be cards with words like *home, roam, foam, tome,* and *loam.* For UN, one could make up cards with words such as *gun, sun, son, shun, won, one, done, run, spun, pun, ton, tun,* and *fun,* just to show the many different ways in which the same sound can be spelled. Similarly, for OR, there could be cards with words like *boar, bore, core, lore, four, for, fore, door, floor, sore, soar,* and *store.*

From a box into which these slips have been placed, one is picked and read to the players. Let us say that the slip selected reads O-GRIM. All the players now check their cards to see whether they have a box labeled IM in the row below the letter O. (On the particular card shown here, it is the second box from the left in the top row.)

The players have been given a set of small colored cardboard squares of the same size as the boxes on the card. Whoever has a box with a rhyme ending that is in accord with the word that has been read and is in the right row writes the word on one of these colored squares and places it over the corresponding box on his card.

The game proceeds in this way until one of the players has covered a whole row (five boxes) horizontally, vertically, or diagonally. He then calls out "RHYM-O!" and steps up to have his card checked. Of course, he gets no credit if he puts COME in the OME box or makes a similar mistake. Thus, RHYM-O is not simply a game of chance; it calls for a knowledge of spelling, vocabulary, homonyms, and rhymes, as well as a certain amount of good luck.

One way of making the game more instructive and interesting is to prepare the slips of paper with rhyme endings rather than words. Thus, a slip might read O-IM. In that case, a player with an IM box in his O row would have to think of a rhyming word himself, spell it correctly on his colored cardboard square, and then cover the corresponding box on his card.

If the game is played in this way, it should proceed in accordance with the rules of lotto rather than bingo; that is, in order to win, a player should be required to cover *all* the boxes on his card. And in that case, of course, he may not use the same word twice; for every new IM, for example, he has to think of a *different* rhyming word.

Repeat this three times, each time faster than before:

With his stiff slit tights and fast fists he's fit first for fist fights. His stiff tights, fit tight, slit in his first fast fist fight. Fast tiffs with tight fists and stiff tights are fit fights for first slights. His stiff fist fits tight and slightly slits tight tights in fast fist fights. He's stiff from fits, tiffs, and fist fights. This tight-fisted stiff fits tight, all right!

Repeat this three times, each time faster than before:

To soothe her suitor she too sued her tutor.
Two sooty suits and two two-suiters suit her tutor.
To suit her suitor two too sooty tutors shoot her.

What Hinky Pinky describes Madame Defarge in Dickens' Tale of Two Cities?
BITTER KNITTER.

Say this three times, each time faster than before:

Arresting a resting radish-relishing wrestler she'd shadowed, she rashly rushed and dashed to shards a reddish radish dish and shaded red a sad dish of rationed shad she'd shared.

II. Jocular Jingles

Once your child has a stock of ready rhymes, he is ready to use them in making verses.

The games in this section teach him how to add to rhyme two other R's: rhythm and reason.

CON-VERSE

ELEMENTARY-INTERMEDIATE   *Clock or timer*
2 or more

This game calls for nimble wits and a ready fund of rhymes.

The object is to keep the ball of conversation—or perhaps we should call it "conversification"—rolling by responding, within a given time limit, with a rhyme to anything said or asked by another player. In other words, the players carry on a conversation—of sorts—in rhyme.

It might begin like this:

PLAYER 1: How are you?
PLAYER 2: As good as new.
　　　　　 Where did you go?
PLAYER 1: Out in the snow.
　　　　　 What did you do?
PLAYER 2: I tied my shoe.

One point is scored for each appropriate line. If a player cannot think of one, he may challenge the preceding player to supply one of his own. If the preceding player cannot do so, he is penalized two points.

Extra points could be earned by adding a line with a third or even a fourth rhyme. The game can be further complicated by introducing rhymes of more than one syllable, like *bottom* and *got 'em*.

RHYTHMIC RHYMES   VAR. 1

ALL LEVELS
2 or more

This variation carries the players the next step along the road toward versifying. It teaches them to keep their rhymes within a definitely established rhythm.

Only two can play at a time. If more than two are present, they may take turns playing with the winner of each match.

The two players sit facing each other. Simultaneously, and with an even rhythm, they first clap their hands once, then slap their thighs, next snap the fingers of the left hand, and finally snap the fingers of the right hand. They keep this up in perfect rhythm together, in a slow tempo at first, while they carry on the game of CON-VERSE described above, but trying this time to work the rhyme exactly on the beat in order to coincide with the snapping of the fingers of the right hand, and making the number of syllables in the response exactly match the number in the first line so as to produce a perfect couplet.

The pace should be kept slow at the beginning, until the players gain facility. They take turns proposing the first line, and they may agree on the number of rounds of claps permitted before a response must be given. It is not necessary to keep strictly to the pattern of a conversation, with questions and answers. A player can tell a story, make a humorous comment, or add anything relevant that he can think of in the time allotted.

Here is how the game might start:

PLAYER 1: I go to school.

PLAYER 2: I'm not a fool.

I ate some bread.

PLAYER 1: It tastes like lead.

You hurt your shin.

PLAYER 2: I still can grin.
     I had a fight.
PLAYER 1: But you're all right.
     You can't beat me.
PLAYER 2: Just wait and see!

The game goes on until one of the players misses. He may then challenge his opponent to supply a rhyming verse to match his own line. If he does so, he scores a point; if not, he is penalized two points. One point is scored by each player for every rhythmic rhymed response.

Difficulty can be added by increasing the number of syllables in each line or in the rhyme. Here, for example, is one such beginning:

PLAYER 1: You look somewhat thinner.
PLAYER 2: I came late for dinner.
     But I'm not a sinner.
     I can be a winner.
     I make my lines all rhyme.
PLAYER 1: But not within the time.

AD-VERSE   VAR. 2

ALL LEVELS
2 or more

This variation can be played endlessly. It provides further practice in simple versifying.

The first player begins by telling a little story in rhymed verse, the last line of which ends with a reference to something present, absent, found, lost, bought, sold, etc. The next player must then add two rhymed lines to the story, picking it up in the first line with a reference to the object previously mentioned and introducing a new object in the second line. The game proceeds in this way until the chain is broken by a player's failure to supply the "missing link." In that case, he may challenge the preceding player to do so. If his AD-

VERSary can, he scores two points; if he cannot, he is penalized two points. One point is scored for each added link in the chain.

Here is how one such chain of rhymes began:

PLAYER 1:   I went downtown
                    To see Mr. Brown.
                    He gave me a nickel
                    To buy a pickle.

PLAYER 2:   The pickle was sour;
                    So I bought a flower.

PLAYER 1:   The flower was dead;
                    So I got some bread.

PLAYER 2:   The bread was stale;
                    So I bought a pail.

PLAYER 1:   The pail was small;
                    So I got a ball.

PLAYER 2:   The ball was hard;
                    So I bought some lard.

PLAYER 1:   The lard was thick;
                    So I found a stick.

Children will carry on a game like this indefinitely, meanwhile thinking up a host of rhymes.

RE-VERSE   VAR. 3

INTERMEDIATE-ADVANCED   *Paper and pencil*
2, 4, or any even number   *Clock or timer*

This variation teaches children the rudiments of versification and encourages creativity.

Each player is allowed time to work out a couplet, that is, two rhyming lines, according to a definite rhythmic pattern —say, eight syllables alternately unaccented and accented— and any rhyme he wants. For example, with this pattern, and using the AT rhyme ending, a player may write:

> Be sure, when you put out the cat,
> To give his head a little pat.

Other players, with other rhyme endings and rhythm patterns, will work out different couplets.

Now, each player, dividing his paper in half horizontally, writes in the lower part just the rhythmic pattern of unaccented and accented syllables in each line, followed by its last word. Thus, the player with the couplet above would write:

> ∪ ′ ∪ ′ ∪ ′ ∪ ′ (cat),
> ∪ ′ ∪ ′ ∪ ′ ∪ ′ (pat).

If there is any punctuation at the end of the first line, it is also inserted.

Each player now detaches the lower half of his paper with this sketch of his couplet and exchanges it with his opponent.

Within the same time that was given for the original couplets to be written, the players must "re-verse" the rhythmic patterns they have been given—i.e., they must try to think of words that might fill out the couplet according to the given rhythm and rhyme and still make sense. For example, another player, given the pattern shown above, might fill it in thus:

> It's fun to own a pussy cat,
> And treat him to a gentle pat.

The game can be made more difficult by requiring all the players to adhere to a particular rhythmic pattern—e.g., trochees (′ ∪), iambs (∪ ′), dactyls or waltz time (′ ∪ ∪), anapests (∪ ∪ ′), or various combinations of them—and by extending the length of the line from eight to ten or even twelve syllables.

By changing only one letter, can you turn a waterfowl into a large animal that rhymes with it?
Turn GOOSE into MOOSE.

III. Group Games

Though some of the games in this chapter can be played by only two, most can involve three or more. However, certain games with rhymes are best suited for larger families, their friends, or children's parties. Here are a few.

RHYME GRAB BAG

ALL LEVELS
Large families or groups

Paper and pencil
Blank cards (playing-card size)
Clock or timer

This is a good game for familiarizing children with common rhymes and teaching them to versify.

With the aid of a rhyming dictionary, prepare about fifteen or twenty sets of rhyming cards. Some sets might consist of more than two rhyming words, and the rhyme sound should, if possible, be spelled in different ways—e.g., *moan, flown,* and *shone; shine, sign,* and *stein; applaud* and *gnawed; comb, roam,* and *home; what, hot,* and *yacht; do, who, sou, gnu,* and *grew; watch* and *scotch; though, so, sew, know, owe, trousseau, toe, depot, apropos,* and *cocoa; snore, soar, nor,* and *four; right, spite,* and *neophyte; sour* and *power;* etc.

Write each word on a separate card, mix up the cards, and throw them helter-skelter into a box or bag. Each player, in turn, draws a few cards at random. The number drawn will depend on the number of players and the total number of cards prepared. The game might begin with no more than four cards to each player, but it should be possible, at later stages, or with more advanced and experienced players, to increase the number to six or eight.

Each player must then compose a poem, within a given time, using all the words on his cards to end the lines of couplets each of which would end its other line with any word he can think of that rhymes with it. If he draws two rhyming words, he must make one couplet with them. The player with the best poem wins.

Another way of playing the game is to allow each player, in turn, to draw only one card. When all have drawn, each takes his turn in pronouncing the word on his card. If anybody, when his turn comes, finds that he has drawn a card that rhymes with a word already pronounced, he pronounces the word on his card and wins the rhyming card from the other player. Thus, if Player 1 draws PLEASE, and Player 4 draws FREEZE, the latter, when it is his turn to play, may take the first player's card from him. And if Player 5 has drawn SEIZE, he can then take both words from Player 4.

If no words drawn rhyme, or after all players have had a chance to take rhyming words from one another, a second round of drawings is begun. Now some players may have two or more cards. Any rhymes a player has in his hand he is entitled to keep unless some other player whose turn comes after his has a word that rhymes with his; in that case, he loses all his words that rhyme with the other player's. For example, a player with GIRAFFE and CARAFE will lose both to a succeeding player who has a card with STAFF on it.

The game continues in this way until all the rhymes have been matched up. The player with the most cards wins.

Further difficulty can be added to the game at this point, if desired. Each player, with the rhymes in his pile of cards, can be required, within a reasonable time, to make up a jingle. The player who succeeds in incorporating the greatest number of his rhymes in his verse scores the highest.

The game can be made more demanding and instructive if a definite rhyme scheme is required. For example, extra

points may be given for a jingle that conforms to the pattern
A B A B—i.e., with the third line rhyming with the first, and
the fourth line rhyming with the second. Still further complications may be added by giving a higher score to any jingle that conforms to some particular rhythmic pattern—for
example, a waltz rhythm of three beats with the accent on
the first. In that case, the rhythm may be beaten on a drum
or a tin can, clapped, or tapped out with the feet.

RHYME CLIMB

ALL LEVELS
Large families or groups

This game builds rhymes by easy steps. Because it "climbs,"
it is best scored by means of FIREMAN UP THE LADDER
(page 322). The more players, the better.

The players agree on an ending that will make many
rhyming words—say, EEZ. The first player may start with
peas. The next may move to *tease*. The third may suggest
fleas. A fourth may go to *breeze*. A fifth may hit upon *trees*.
A sixth may think of *bees*.

Each player scores as many points as there are letters in the
rhyming word he mentions. So the object of the game is to
"climb" up the letter ladder of rhyme by building big words.
Instead of confining the range of suggestions to words like
these, *seize*, and *cheese*, the players are impelled to try for
words like *isosceles*, *parentheses*, *aborigines*, etc.

Good rhyme endings for this game, which can lead to a
number of big words, are *eev*, *ox*, *oom*, *oo*, *oot*, *act*, *ake*, *af*,
ack, *ess*, and *ide*.

*What three-word Hinky Pinky gives good advice to Hansel and
Gretel when they enter the house of the witch?*
SHOVE IN OVEN!

RHYME MIME

INTERMEDIATE-ADVANCED
Large families or groups

This is essentially a game of charades that develops the ability to think of rhymes and promotes creativity.

Each player thinks of two rhyming words whose meanings could be represented in pantomime. Then each in turn mimes his rhyme before the other players. A player who guesses one of the words wins two points; if another player then guesses the other rhyming word, he wins one point. Anyone who guesses both rhyming words wins four points.

Thus, a player may perform the "business" of opening a bottle and drinking and then eating as clues to the familiar expression "wine and dine."

Among the many rhyming words suitable for use in this game are *ship* and *trip*, *hot* and *pot*, *slob* and *snob*, *jaw* and *claw*, *snore* and *sore*, *hose* and *clothes*, *pose* and *doze*, *sweep* and *sleep*, *peep* and *leap*, *pet* and *fret*, *sing* and *sting*, *drink* and *slink*, *squint* and *sprint*, *bite* and *fight*, *sew* and *throw*, *sign* and *shine*, and *spin* and *grin*. As can be seen, the game offers many possibilities for hilarity.

DUMB CRAMBO

INTERMEDIATE-ADVANCED
Large families or groups

This well-known game is a variation on RHYME MIME, above. It teaches children rhymes, builds vocabulary, and encourages originality and inventiveness.

The players are divided into two evenly matched teams. With one team out of the room, the other decides on some verb—preferably one with which many words rhyme—that can be acted out or pantomimed. Suppose, for example, that they choose the word FIGHT. When the other group returns, they are told that the word rhymes with MIGHT. Once more the other group leaves the room to decide among themselves what they think the word is. Suppose they think the word is WRITE. When they return, without speaking they act out this word, some by making silent scribbling motions, others by pantomiming the use of pen or pencil, etc. The other group must then decide whether the correct verb has been guessed. If it has not been, they shake their heads. Neither side may say a word.

The game proceeds in this way until the correct word has been guessed and acted out. Then the ones that chose the word clap their hands, and it is their turn to leave the room while their opponents select another word.

RHYME MY NAME

ELEMENTARY-INTERMEDIATE   *Clock or timer*
Large families or groups

This game sharpens the players' ability to think of rhymes. It can be played by any number; the more, the better.

The first player calls out the name of a boy or a girl. Within six seconds, the next player must use the name in a rhyme. If he cannot do so, he may challenge the first player to say what rhyme he had in mind. Points are earned by meeting challenges, supplying rhymes, and then thinking up new names to be used in rhymes.

Here is how one such game began:

PLAYER 1: Jack
PLAYER 2: Is back. Kate.
PLAYER 3: Is late. Bridget.
PLAYER 4: Bridget's a fidget. Jean.
PLAYER 5: Is clean. Hannibal.
PLAYER 6: Hannibal's a cannibal. Jonas.
PLAYER 1: Jonas'll phone us. Gussie.
PLAYER 2: Is fussy. Paul.

PLAYER 3: Is tall. Roger.
PLAYER 4: Roger's a dodger. Nancy.
PLAYER 5: Is fancy. Hal.
PLAYER 6: Hal's a pal. Jerry.
PLAYER 1: Jerry is merry. Jim.
PLAYER 2: Jim's slim. Mary.
PLAYER 3: Mary is wary. Jason.
PLAYER 4: Jason's a mason. Luke.
PLAYER 5: Luke's a duke. Giles.
PLAYER 6: Giles smiles. Mabel.
PLAYER 1: Mabel is able. Hattie.
PLAYER 2: Hattie is natty. May.
PLAYER 3: May is gay. John.
PLAYER 4: Is wan. Mark.
PLAYER 5: Mark's dark. Anne.
PLAYER 6: Anne's tan.

VERSE 'N VERSE

INTERMEDIATE   *Paper and pencil*
Large families or groups

Although this game does teach the players rhymes, it can be
played just for laughs.

Each player writes a line of verse, either original or from
memory. The slips of paper are then folded so that the next
player to whom they are passed cannot see the line.

Now the fun begins. Each player passes his slip to the
person at his right, telling him only the last word in the line
he has just written. The next player then has to supply the
next line, to rhyme with the last word of the previous line.
Then once again the papers are passed, with the players telling one another only the last word of the line they have just
written.

When all the papers have made a complete circuit, the
slips are unfolded, and the verses are read aloud.

5

VOCABULARY-BUILDING GAMES

Words are the pegs to hang ideas on.
—HENRY WARD BEECHER

IT IS WIDELY RECOGNIZED that an extensive vocabulary is more likely to accompany success than any other single characteristic so far isolated and measured. And no wonder! For power over words is, essentially, a command of ideas. It is the power to persuade, to reason, to argue, to explain. Ultimately, it is the key to mastery over things and the minds and hearts of men.

Scientific studies of children's language show a prodigious growth in vocabulary during the first six years of a child's life. From the helpless state of infancy, in which needs are communicated only by crying, the child, by the age of six, has acquired a speaking vocabulary of approximately 2,500 words and a vocabulary of understood words estimated at 20,000. Yet this is only the beginning of a potential growth that matches, at every stage, that of the mind itself.

A good way of building a child's vocabulary is to find some subject or situation that will hold his interest and let him follow it up by discovering the words appropriate for it. After all, the normal way of learning new words is in a variety of contexts, and that is the way the child learns them in these games.

For almost all of them a good dictionary is essential. Children should look upon the dictionary as their friend in need and should be shown early how to use it to find the word they are looking for. These games introduce children to the dictionary, accustom them to using it, and build positive attitudes toward it as a useful aid.

I. Visual Aids to Word Knowledge

Each of the games in this section is based on the principle that vocabulary-building depends quite as much on seeing how words look as on hearing how they sound and understanding what they mean.

WORD SQUARES

ALL LEVELS
2 *only*

Paper and pencil

This game will not only improve vocabulary but will promote better spelling.

Each player, to start with, draws a square divided into twenty-five boxes, five in each row.

Now the first player, visualizing some five-letter word written in the boxes either vertically, horizontally, or diagonally, or even backward, calls out any letter in the word and writes it in its appropriate box, but without showing his chart to his opponent. Let us suppose that, thinking of the word PLANT, the first player calls out the letter A and writes it in the third box of his upper horizontal row, as shown in the illustration on page 70.

His opponent may place this letter in any box he pleases on his own chart to form part of a word he has in mind. Thus, thinking of START, he may place the A in the third box from the top in the first vertical row at the left. Now it is his turn to call out a letter—let us say, T—and to place it in its appropriate box for the word he wants, as shown. The same letter may be called out more than once, and every letter called out must be put in some box or other.

The game continues back and forth in this way, with each player trying to form as many words as possible with the letters he and his opponent call out, until all the boxes have been filled.

PLAYER 1   **PLAYER 2**

		A		
		T		

T				
A				

Five points are scored for each five-letter word; four for a four-letter word; three for a three-letter word; etc. Credit is likewise given for words within words. For example, the word *never* (counting five points) contains within itself the words *ever* (worth an additional four points) and *eve* (valued at three more points), so that a total of twelve points can be scored with this one word. Naturally, players should try to form words of this type in order to get the most out of every letter. The player scoring the highest wins.

The game can be made more difficult by increasing the number of boxes or by having someone call the letters for both players.

SQUARE WORDS   VAR. 1

INTERMEDIATE-ADVANCED   *Paper and pencil*
2 *or more*

This variation, at a somewhat more advanced level, also teaches spelling and vocabulary.

Each player, after drawing a square of sixteen boxes on his paper, writes in the boxes of the top horizontal line and also in those of the first left vertical line a four-letter word agreed on by all—let us say, ODOR.

O	D	O	R
D	A	R	E
O	R	A	L
R	E	L	Y

C	A	P	E
A	V	I	D
P	I	L	E
E	D	E	N

Now each player has the task of "squaring off" this word by fitting into the other boxes letters to make a square of words that are the same horizontally and vertically—i.e., whether read from left to right or from top to bottom. The first player to produce such a square wins the game.

An example of a winning square starting with the word ODOR is shown in the accompanying illustration. A few other squares, built on different words, are also shown on the following page.

S	T	O	P
T	A	M	E
O	M	E	N
P	E	N	T

L	E	A	N
E	L	S	E
A	S	K	S
N	E	S	T

After a few rounds with four-letter words, you might try raising the level of difficulty by inviting the players to square off a five-letter word in twenty-five boxes. In that case, instead of starting with a particular word agreed on by all, let each player independently experiment with his own and see who can work out a word square first.

Just to show that it can be done, here is one based on the word PLANT.

P	L	A	N	T
L	O	S	E	R
A	S	S	A	Y
N	E	A	R	S
T	R	Y	S	T

In the example of a squared-off five-letter word shown opposite, a different word square could have been formed from the same initial word, TAMER, by substituting AFIRE for AGILE, thereby turning ELECT to ERECT. And a change of only two letters in the initial word, to make it BAKER, turns MITES to KITES. Thus, the possibilities of making twenty-five-box word square are really quite numerous.

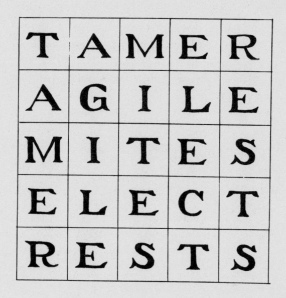

What word in the English language has no vowels?
HMMMM.

Why are a, e, and u considered the handsome vowels?
Because you can't have beauty *without them.*

What is that which you can keep even after you have given it to someone else?
Your word.

Build a word meaning a chart or graph by changing the color of a metric unit of weight.
DIAGRAM!

BOXING MATCH   VAR. 2

INTERMEDIATE-ADVANCED   *Paper and pencil*
2 *or more*

The "boxing" in this variation, which can be played by two
or more, consists in putting into their appropriate boxes, in
the sixteen- or twenty-five-box chart used in the preceding
games, any arrangement of letters that will make a word
square. In short, this variation reverses the procedure of
SQUARE WORDS.

Each player first independently works out on his own
paper, with any words he can think of, a word square of the
kind exemplified in the preceding variation. He then scram-
bles the words and gives them to his opponent, who must reconstitute them into a square. The first to do so wins the
boxing match.

For example, the words NEARS, LOSER, TRYST, PLANT,
and ASSAY, used in SQUARE WORDS, above, if given in
that order to one of the players, would have to be fitted into
a square as shown in the illustration on page 72.

SQUARE DEAL   VAR. 3

INTERMEDIATE-ADVANCED   *Paper and pencil*
2, 4 *or any even number*   *Blank cards (playing-card
                                 size)*

This variation represents the next step in "escalating" the
difficulty of word squares.

First each player works out a word square on his own paper
with any words he chooses. Because of the difficulty of this
variation, it is best to start with four-letter words arranged
in sixteen boxes. The player then writes a definition of each
word on a separate card, shuffles the four cards, and gives

them to his opponent in exchange for the latter's set of definition cards. Winning the game then involves two additional steps: first, thinking of four-letter words that fit the definitions, and then arranging the words into a square.

For example, suppose the definitions given are: "To remain quiet," "Affects with pain," "A fruit," and "A Great Lake." The words are REST, AILS, PEAR, and ERIE, arranged as in the illustration below.

After the players have gained some facility with sixteen-box squares, they can graduate to twenty-five-box arrangements of five five-letter words, and the really ambitious can take a postgraduate course with a thirty-six-box square of six six-letter words.

P	E	A	R
E	R	I	E
A	I	L	S
R	E	S	T

What word do you associate with a visit to Egypt?
SENILE.

WORD BLOCKS   VAR. 4

INTERMEDIATE-ADVANCED   *Paper and pencil*
2 *only*

This is a variation of WORD SQUARES. Again, the players
learn vocabulary and spelling while they are having fun.

As before, each divides a square into twenty-five boxes, five
across and five down. This time, however, the first player
calls out a consonant, which he and his opponent are free to
place in any box in their respective squares. Then each selects
any vowel he wants and puts it wherever he likes in his
square without telling his opponent what vowel it is or where
it is being placed. Now the other player must call out a consonant, and again each places it wherever he wishes in his
own square together with whatever vowel may seem appropriate. The game continues in this way until one of the
players spells a five-letter word horizontally, vertically, diagonally, or backward.

After both players have developed some facility in building words in this way, the game can be continued until all
the boxes in each square have been filled. The winner is then
the player who has succeeded in blocking in the most words.
If several rounds are played, a numerical score for each
player can be calculated by adding up the total number of
letters used to form the words in his square.

LETTERBOXES   VAR. 5

INTERMEDIATE-ADVANCED   *Paper and pencil*
2, 4, *or any even number*

This is the most challenging of all the variations of WORD
SQUARES. It can be elevated to any level of difficulty desired to teach both spelling and vocabulary. But it should

not be attempted until all the players have gained facility in constructing word squares by playing all the preceding variations a number of times.

Each player begins by independently squaring off any four-letter word he chooses. He then collects all sixteen letters used in his square, sorts them, and exchanges them with his opponent for the latter's set of letters. Now each player must somehow reconstitute his opponent's word square from the letters comprising it by putting them in their correct "letterboxes." The first to do so wins the game.

Here, for example, is the word square constituted of the letters A A A, E E E, L L, M M, N N, P P, S S:

It is a good idea for a player, when exchanging his letters with his opponent, to arrange them beforehand, as above, in strictly alphabetical order to avoid giving any clues as to the words they might compose.

Of course, this game becomes really intriguing when it is played with twenty-five letters to square off a five-letter word.

What word is made up only of vowels?
AYE.

To what question can you never truly answer No?
"What does Y-E-S spell?"

By spoiling an alcoholic beverage build a word that means a border or edge.
MARGIN!

What is the most important thing in the world?
The letter e *because it is first in* everybody *and* everything.

What three words are most often used?
I DON'T KNOW.
Correct.

Why are the abbreviations of degrees tacked on to a man's name?
To show that he is a man of letters.

How do you write out "Mrs." in full?
"Mistress." But this old title of courtesy for a married woman is now always contracted to "Mrs." and pronounced "misiz."

Love Poem

O, MLE, what XTC
I always feel when I U C;
I U's 2 rave of LN's I's;
4 LC I gave countless sighs;
4 KT, 2, and LNR,
I was a keen competitor;
But each is a non-NTT,
4 U XL them all, U C.

Spell "mousetrap" in three letters.
C-A-T.

What word has five A's and no other vowel?
ABRACADABRA.

What is the coldest place in a theater?
Z-row.

What word has six I's?
INDIVISIBILITY.

II. Vocabulary-Building
Graphs and Charts

With the games in this section the child passes from the recognition or construction of common abbreviations to the formation of complete words.

ABBREVIATION CROSSROADS

ELEMENTARY-INTERMEDIATE   *Graph paper and colored*
2 *or more*   *pencil*
                                           Clock or timer

This game teaches children the meaning of common abbreviations.

A sheet of graph paper is prepared as shown on the following page.

The first player closes his eyes and puts his pencil point on the paper. If he hits a line, he misses his chance, and it is the next player's turn to try. If he hits a box, he must try to make as many meaningful abbreviations as he can with the six letters with which that box is aligned vertically, horizontally, and diagonally.

For each letter in his abbreviations he scores one point. Succeeding players follow the same procedure. If a player hits a box that has already been marked, he gets two additional chances to hit an empty box. The game ends either within a set time or when all the boxes have been marked.

A dictionary should be readily available to settle disputed points.

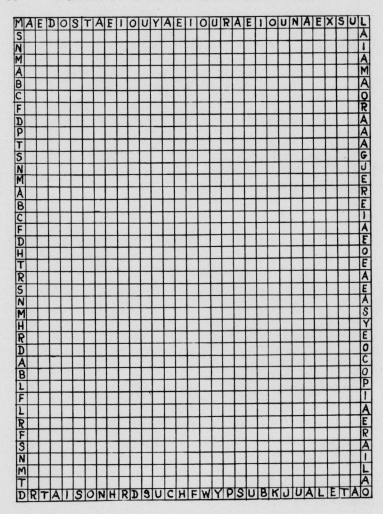

What is the difference between a light fog and a gentleman?
One is a mist; the other is a mister.

What five-letter word can lose four without changing its sound?
QUEUE.

ABBREVIATION GRAB BAG VAR. 1

ELEMENTARY-INTERMEDIATE *Small slips of paper*
2 *or more* *Clock or timer*

In this variation the letters, each written on a small card or slip of paper, are thrown helter-skelter into a hat or bag. Each player then picks six letters out of the hat, as in a lottery, and does the best he can, within a given time, to form as many abbreviations as possible with them.

ABBREVIATION DICE VAR. 2

ELEMENTARY-INTERMEDIATE *Paper and pencil*
2 *or more* *Dice*
Clock or timer

The same purpose can be served by putting the letters on dice, one on each of the six faces of each die, or matching the numbers on the dice with letters. Then the players "shoot the dice" and try, within a given time, to form abbreviations with whatever letters they throw. Each player should be allowed three throws to accumulate six letters, which he can arrange as he wishes on his paper.

Why are two t's like hops?
Because they make beer better.

Why is the Isthmus of Panama like the first u *in CUCUMBER?*
Because it's between two seas.

What odd number, when beheaded, becomes even?
Seven.

BULL'S-EYE

INTERMEDIATE-ADVANCED   *Paper and pencil*
2 *or more*   *Graph paper and colored*
                                   pencil
                               Clock or timer

This game is played in essentially the same way as ABBRE-
VIATION CROSSROADS, but it teaches spelling and vocabulary as well. The graph paper is prepared as in the accompanying illustration.

Here the player who hits a box must try, within a given
time, to form as many English words or abbreviations as he
can from the combinations of twelve letters with which the
box is aligned vertically, horizontally, and diagonally. He is
free to arrange the letters in any order he wants. Scoring is
the same as in ABBREVIATION CROSSROADS, except that
two points are gained for each letter of any word or abbreviation of six letters or more.

For instance, ALBANY, A.L., B.A., ANY, A.B., NAB, BAN,
and LAB (which by no means exhaust the possible words
and abbreviations that may be obtained with these six letters) would be scored thus:

For each letter in ALBANY, two points: 12
One point each for every letter in the other words and
abbreviations—A.L., B.A., ANY, A.B., NAB, BAN, LAB: 18
                                                         —
                                          Total: 30

In this game, proper names may be counted as words. In
other versions of the game, credit may also be given for forming prefixes, suffixes, and roots.

RD	DA	AF	SS	RA	DA	UN	AM	RE	SE	AR	US	PA	QU	CI	UN	SS	CO	MA	NA	EX	LI	ML	MA	ME	TA	ME	PA	NA	MS	SA	ST
AC																															BM
BA																															QR
AD																															JK
DA																															ST
AF																															MM
EX																															AL
BE																															UN
AM																															ST
LA																															LM
AS																															SJ
KE																															CK
MA																															AS
FA																															ZE
SS																															BJ
LI																															AM
FR																															XY
ME																															TA
SP																															IM
HA																															AR
ML																															FM
TA																															CO
IA																															UN
SM																															TL
IC																															SA
TA																															ZO
IM																															CI
RA																															US
PA																															RE
IN																															NA
QU																															SS
RA																															LA
UN																															EX
IS																															SF
PA																															MA
SE																															FR
US																															ME
RE																															IN
NA																															MS
UN																															SS
SA																															SE
AM	LA	AM	DA	CI	IA	CA	AM	AS	FR	HA	CC	AF	CP	CO	AM	IN	BA	GS	BE	FI	CO	LO	IS	AC	EX	AD	FR	GS	FA	EX	ER

HIT OR MISS   VAR. 1

INTERMEDIATE-ADVANCED   *Paper and pencil*
2 *or more*   *Graph paper and colored*
                                  pencil
                               Clock or timer

This variation of BULL'S-EYE is played by using different
combinations and arrangements of the same or other letters
on the graph paper to suit any desired purpose and allowing
the players the greatest possible leeway, within the time
limit, in interpreting the letters they strike.

Thus, a player is encouraged to be as creative as he can
with them. He may, for examples, use initials like JFK, TR,
FDR, LBJ, etc., to represent the names of famous people. He
may make words from letters, like *teepee* (from TP), *cutie*
(from QT), *empty* (from MT), etc. He may use Latin abbreviations like *e.g.*, *ibid.*, *i.e.*, and *ff.* Or he may use the letters to stand for government agencies like the FBI or com-
panies like RCA.

In this game, twelve additional points are given for using
all the letters.

CRISSCROSS   VAR. 2

ELEMENTARY-INTERMEDIATE   *Graph paper and colored*
2 *or more*   *pencil*
                               Clock or timer

In this variation, which makes use of graph paper prepared
in either one of the ways shown in the accompanying charts,
the players learn both spelling and vocabulary.

Let us first consider the simpler, three-letter version, which
can be played by children at the elementary level. The players are given the first of the accompanying charts and, for a

start, are asked to insert a particular vowel—say, A—in every box in which it could, in combination with the letters aligned with the box, make one word or more, whether reading from the side across or the top down. For example, in the chart shown here, the first vertical column would read: PAR, TAR, and WAR. Additional credit could be earned, beyond the one point for each of these words, if the child could find the words RAN, RAP, RAT, and RAW in this set. The second vertical column would offer the possibility of BAN (and its complement, NAB) and BAT (as well as TAB). Other words that could be formed with the combinations shown here are CAN, CAP, SAC, CAT, CAW, PAD, SAD, WAD, MAN, MAP, MAT, TAM, TAD, MAW, FAN, FAT, NAG, GAP, SAG, GAS, TAG, GAT, WAG, LAP, PAL, and LAW. If proper names are allowed, SAM and DAN could be added to this list.

The child making the largest number of words in a given time wins the game.

After the possibilities of one vowel have been exhausted, another can be proposed.

	R	B	C	D	M	F	G	L
N								
P								
S								
T								
W								

The game can be made more complicated by adding a line of letters at the bottom horizontally and at the right side vertically, to give a total of four letters for each box, plus the vowel. Thus, if K were placed at the right side opposite N at the left, words like RANK, BANK, DANK, and LANK could be formed with the vowel A in the top row, and RINK,

MINK, and LINK with I. And if T were placed at the bottom opposite R at the top, words like RANT, STAR, TART, and WART could be formed in the first vertical row with the vowel A. The other letters at the bottom and the side can be filled in as desired.

Another way of adding difficulty to this game is to permit particular vowel combinations—say, AI—rather than single vowels and to give extra credit for using all the letters available in a given box.

At the intermediate level a chart like the one below may be used. Possible words with A formed with this chart would

	ND	CH	NK	ST
BL				
BR				
SC				
TH				

be BRAND, BLAND, BLANK, and BLAST, to say nothing of words included in them, like BRAN, BAND, LAST, LAND, BANK, and LANK. This version of the game, too, can be complicated by adding other letter combinations at the bottom and at the right and by permitting the insertion of particular combinations of vowels—say, EA to make BREAST. And, of course, the chart can be enlarged.

Indeed, the game admits of gradation from easy charts built with whole syllables to a more advanced stage in which the players build words with a chart consisting of prefixes, roots, and suffixes. (For suggestions, see BIG DEAL, page 105.)

What kind of sense has no meaning?
Nonsense.

What kind of gate is a substitute?
A surrogate.

What kind of gate is made of variegated stone?
Agate.

How do you date by being obliging?
Accommodate.

What kind of nation protects your health?
Vaccination.

What word is made shorter by adding a syllable to it?
SHORT.

Where can you find written down word for word everything you said in your last conversation?
The dictionary.

What is the difference between a participant in a spelling bee and a wizard uttering an incantation?
One spells a word; the other words a spell.

If flammable *means "capable of being easily ignited," what does* inflammable *mean?*
The same thing! The prefix in *here means "thoroughly, completely." So anything marked* inflammable *can be easily ignited. The opposite of* flammable *and* inflammable *is* nonflammable.

What is the difference between continuous *rain and* continual *rain?*
A continuous rain is uninterrupted; rain is continual when it keeps on recurring day after day.

What is the difference between practicable *and* practical?
Practicable means "usable, possible, workable" and can be applied to things and ideas, but not persons. Practical means "experienced, useful, not theoretical" and can be applied to persons as well as things and ideas.

III. Roots and Affixes

A great many words in our language are formed by the addition of *affixes* to a relatively small number of Greek and Latin *roots*. For example, the word *importer* is composed of three parts: a *prefix* (*im*, meaning "into"), a *root* (*port*, meaning "carry"), and a *suffix* (*er*, meaning "one who"). The addition of other affixes to the same root results in the formation of words like *exportation*, *deportation*, *support*, *reporter*, *transportation*, etc.

A child takes a giant step forward in building his vocabulary as soon as he gains facility in recognizing or forming new words composed of roots and affixes whose meanings are already familiar to him. The games in this section are designed to acquaint him with these verbal building blocks and to provide practice in constructing words with them.

WORD WHIRL

INTERMEDIATE-ADVANCED   *Paper and pencil*
2 *or more*   *Wheel and spinning pointer*
    Clock or timer

This game improves vocabulary by teaching the meaning of common prefixes, suffixes, and roots and by providing practice in word-building with them.

Draw three concentric circles, divide them into sectors, and fill them in as shown in the accompanying illustration. Write the suffixes in the outermost arcs, the prefixes in the middle areas, and the roots in the sectors nearest the center.

Mount the chart firmly on a piece of cardboard, and stick

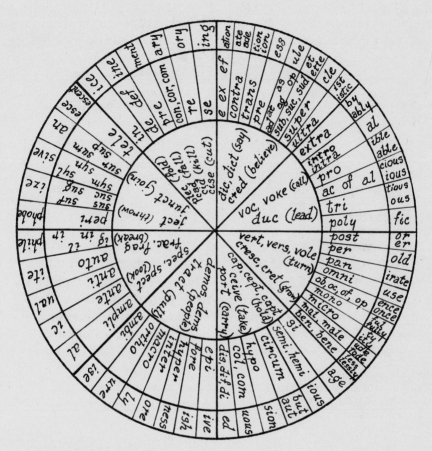

a pin in the center. Over this slip either a safety pin or a
paper clip bent into the shape of a pointer.

Each player, in turn, gets three spins. The first is used to
find roots; the second, to locate a prefix; and the third, to get
a suffix. Given these three elements, the player must make
up as many words as he can within a given time. He may
use any variant form of a root, prefix, or suffix that is listed
with it on the chart.

Let's say, for example, that a player gets the roots VOC,
VOKE, and DUC; the prefix E, EX, EF; and the suffix IBLE or

ABLE. He can gain one point for each of the words EVOKE, EVOCABLE, VOCABLE, and EDUCABLE. If he cannot think of one of them, any other player who does can gain a point.

Additional roots can be found by consulting the list appended at the back of this book. They may be inserted by making up a new center disk. If a separate center disk is constructed, it can be twirled to line up with different prefixes and suffixes.

DON'T MISS A WORD!

Intermediate-Advanced   *Clock or timer*
2 *or more*

This is one of several games with affixes that are played like SILLY SYLLABLE (page 244). It adds words to the players' vocabulary at the same time that it teaches them spelling.

The first player, thinking of a word beginning with the prefix MIS, provides a clue to its meaning by asking a question in the form "What sort of Miss . . .?" The next player must then, within a given time, guess what the word is. If he does so, he must think of another word beginning with MIS and likewise provide the succeeding player with a clue to its meaning. The game proceeds in this way, with players dropping out as they are unable to guess the word or think of new words beginning with the same prefix. The winner is the player who survives this process of elimination.

Here is how the game might begin:

Player 1 : What sort of Miss hates all mankind?
Player 2 : A misanthrope. What sort of Miss is an error?
Player 3 : A mistake. What sort of Miss hurts business?
Player 1 : Mismanagement. What sort of Miss hates women?
Player 2 : A misogynist. What sort of Miss is not a Miss at all?

PLAYER 3: A mister. What sort of Miss gets you into trouble with the law?

PLAYER 1: A misdemeanor. What sort of Miss destroys a nation?

PLAYER 2: Misrule. What sort of Miss prompts a kiss?

PLAYER 3: Mistletoe. What sort of Miss is out of place?

PLAYER 1: A misfit. What sort of Miss flies through the air?

PLAYER 2: A missile. What sort of Miss has the wrong name?

PLAYER 3: A misnomer.

Although all the words used here are nouns, the game can also be played with verbs beginning with the same prefix if the question is put in the form "How do you miss when you . . .?" For example, a game might proceed in this way:

PLAYER 1: How do you miss when you steal money?

PLAYER 2: Misappropriate. How do you miss when you lead someone astray?

PLAYER 3: Misguide. How do you miss when you lose things?

PLAYER 1: Mislay. How do you miss when you lead someone astray?

PLAYER 2: We had that already. Misguide.

PLAYER 1: No. Misdirect. How do you miss when you waste money?

PLAYER 3: Misspend. How do you miss when you don't understand?

PLAYER 1: Misconstrue or misunderstand. How do you miss when your orthography is all wrong?

PLAYER 3: Misspell.

What is the difference between an illusion *and a* delusion?

An illusion *involves belief in what seems to the senses, the mind, or the imagination to be real or true, like an optical* illusion. *A* delusion *involves the inability to distinguish between what only seems to be and what actually is, real or true, like the* delusion *that one is being persecuted.*

THE EGGS-ACT WORD   VAR. 1

INTERMEDIATE-ADVANCED   *Clock or timer*
2 *or more*

This variation teaches the players the meaning and spelling
of a number of words beginning with the prefix EX when it
is pronounced "eggs."

The procedure is the same as in DON'T MISS A WORD
except that the question must be put in the form of "What
kind of eggs . . .?" in order to provide a clue to the answer
in each case.

Here is how a game might begin:

PLAYER 1: What kind of eggs are looked at carefully?
PLAYER 2: Examined. What kind of eggs are too high in
price?
PLAYER 3: Exorbitant. What kind of eggs are ranked very
high?
PLAYER 1: Exalted. What kind of eggs are full of cheer?
PLAYER 2: Exhilarated. What kind of eggs are overrated?
PLAYER 3: Exaggerated. What kind of eggs are all worn
out?
PLAYER 1: Exhausted. What kind of eggs are irritated?
PLAYER 2: Exasperated.

Other words that could be used in this game are *exuberant*,
exempt, *existing*, *exonerated*, *exemplary*, *exultant*, etc.

KATE   VAR. 2

INTERMEDIATE-ADVANCED   *Clock or timer*
2 *or more*

In this variation the players learn words ending in CATE.
Since most of these are verbs, the questions are put in the
form "How can Kate . . .?" Otherwise the procedure is the
same as in the preceding variation.

Here, for example, is the way one game might proceed:

PLAYER 1: How can Kate spread her knowledge?

PLAYER 2: Educate. How can Kate keep the wheels turning?

PLAYER 3: Lubricate. How can Kate point the way?

PLAYER 1: Indicate. How can Kate tell a lie?

PLAYER 2: Prevaricate. How can Kate stop breathing?

PLAYER 3: Suffocate. How can Kate give each his fair share?

PLAYER 1: Allocate. How can Kate find things?

PLAYER 2: Locate. How can Kate chew her food?

PLAYER 3: Masticate. How can Kate reproduce?

PLAYER 1: Duplicate.

A similar procedure can be followed with words like *abdicate, fabricate, dedicate, extricate, adjudicate, advocate, communicate, excommunicate, authenticate, eradicate, complicate, equivocate, confiscate, inculcate, desiccate, bifurcate, placate, rusticate, domesticate, reciprocate, vacate, syndicate, prognosticate, vindicate, implicate, intoxicate, pontificate,* and *predicate.*

BETTER LATE THAN NEVER   VAR. 3

INTERMEDIATE-ADVANCED   *Clock or timer*

2 *or more*

This variation can be played when the possibilities of KATE appear to have been exhausted. It teaches the players the meanings of words ending in LATE. The same procedure is followed as in the preceding games, but here the clue must be given in the form of a question that defines a verb ending with these letters.

Thus, the game might begin in this way:

PLAYER 1: Am I too late to make a pile?

PLAYER 2: Accumulate. Am I too late to raise the ante?

PLAYER 3: Escalate. Am I too late to imitate?
PLAYER 1: Emulate. Am I too late to figure?
PLAYER 2: Calculate. Am I too late to kiss?
PLAYER 3: Osculate. Am I too late to tickle?
PLAYER 1: Titillate.

Other LATE words that can be used in this game, according to the abilities of the players, are *elate, circulate, annihilate, formulate, congratulate, assimilate, expostulate, contemplate, simulate, dissimulate, stimulate, ejaculate, gesticulate, flagellate, coagulate, adulate, correlate, relate, dilate, oscillate, scintillate, percolate, articulate, inflate, deflate, ventilate, desolate, insulate, vacillate, collate, capitulate, recapitulate, tabulate, granulate, stipulate, inoculate, translate, isolate, postulate, interpolate, speculate, legislate, populate, manipulate, perambulate, modulate, plate, mutilate, peculate,* and *ululate.*

GATEWAY   VAR. 4

INTERMEDIATE-ADVANCED   *Clock or timer*
2 *or more*

In the GATE way to word mastery the players learn words ending in these letters. Following the same pattern as the preceding games, the play might begin thus:

PLAYER 1: What is the gateway to making a pile?
PLAYER 2: Aggregate. What is the gateway to clearing the air?
PLAYER 3: Fumigate. What is the gateway to inflicting punishment?
PLAYER 1: Castigate. What is the gateway to wrinkling metal or cardboard?
PLAYER 2: Corrugate. What is the gateway to stirring people up?
PLAYER 3: Instigate.

Other words for this game would include *irrigate, delegate, relegate, promulgate, segregate, arrogate, interrogate, investigate, subjugate, litigate, propagate, conjugate, navigate, mitigate,* and *obligate.*

GREAT WORDS VAR. 5

INTERMEDIATE-ADVANCED *Clock or timer*
2 *or more*

This variation is the GRATE way to build vocabulary and is modeled on the preceding games. The questions are put in the form "What is the great way to . . .?" and the answers would include words like *immigrate, emigrate, migrate, integrate, disintegrate, denigrate,* etc. The game can be played as a follow-up to the first four variations.

HOW DO I RATE? VAR. 6

INTERMEDIATE-ADVANCED *Clock or timer*
2 *or more*

In this variation the question "How do I rate . . .?" is put by each player to the next one in a form that will provide a clue to a word ending in RATE. In all other respects this variation is played exactly like the preceding ones.

For example, the game might proceed in this way:
PLAYER 1: How do I rate when I'm angry?
PLAYER 2: Irate. How do I rate when I go into details?
PLAYER 3: Elaborate. How do I rate when I swing?
PLAYER 1: Vibrate.

The game can be carried on with such words as *invigorate, ameliorate, exaggerate, operate, cooperate, separate, berate, aspirate, evaporate, suppurate, expectorate, calibrate, corroborate, incorporate, eviscerate, dehydrate, liberate, lacerate, macerate, obliterate, proliferate, tolerate, reverberate, re-cuperate, underrate, overrate, sequestrate, enumerate, illus-trate, remonstrate, prate, incarcerate, reiterate, inaugurate, saturate, lucubrate, prostrate, ulcerate, orate, moderate, re-generate, generate, penetrate, narrate, perpetrate, orchestrate, crate, consecrate, desecrate, accelerate, concentrate, adulter-ate, commiserate, celebrate, commemorate, frustrate, arbi-trate, incinerate,* and *perforate.*

Enthusiasts may proceed to still other variations, along the same lines, like HOW DO YOU DATE? (*intimidate, invali-date, liquidate, inundate,* etc.) and even HOW DO YOU MATE? (*intimate, amalgamate, sublimate, estimate, ani-mate, decimate, cremate*).

ICEMAN   VAR. 7

INTERMEDIATE   *Clock or timer*

2 *or more*

This is an ICE way to learn some new words and their spell-ing. It is played like the preceding variations except that the cue is given by asking "What kind of ice . . .?"

Here is how a game might begin:

PLAYER 1: What kind of ice would the world be better off without?

PLAYER 2: Vice. What kind of ice is used as a seasoning?

PLAYER 3: Spice. What kind of ice is seen at weddings?

PLAYER 1: Rice. What kind of ice is easier to give than to take?

PLAYER 2: Advice. What kind of ice do cats relish?

PLAYER 3: Mice. What kind of ice do you gamble with?

PLAYER 1: Dice.

Among other words that can be used in this game are *lice, twice, thrice, slice, splice, device, gneiss, paradise, pre-cise, sacrifice, price, trice,* etc.

What is the difference between impassable *and* impassible?
Impassable *means "incapable of being passed over or crossed";* impassible *means "incapable of feeling or suffering."*

What is the difference between admittance *and* admission?
Admittance *is permission to enter;* admission *may mean either something admitted as true or the right to enter and enjoy the privileges of membership or of being admitted.*

What kind of eggs are used as specimens?
Examples.

What key is the hardest to turn?
A donkey.

When does a public speaker steal lumber?
When he takes the floor.

Name a carpenter's tool you can spell forward and backward in the same way.
Level.

What fruit is on every penny?
A date.

What room can no one enter?
A mushroom.

Why is a crossword puzzle like a quarrel?
Because one word leads to another.

Why is a member of parliament like a shrimp?
Because he has M.P. at the end of his name.

What is the longest word in the English language?
The longest word in Merriam-Webster's unabridged dictionary (third edition) is PNEUMONOULTRAMICROSCOPICSILICOVOL-CANOCONIOSIS. It is the name of a disease of the lungs, occurring in stonecutters and miners, caused by the habitual inhalation of very fine silicate and quartz dust and minute particles of natural glass.

NATIONS   VAR. 8

INTERMEDIATE-ADVANCED   *Clock or timer*

2 or more

The large number of words ending in NATION can be pleasantly learned by playing this game. The question is put in
the form "What kind of nation . . .?"

The game might begin in this way:

PLAYER 1: What kind of nation changes constantly?

PLAYER 2: Alternation. What kind of nation never
changes?

PLAYER 3: Stagnation. What kind of nation is hellish?

PLAYER 1: Damnation. What kind of nation is fanciful?

PLAYER 2: Imagination. What kind of nation is tyrannical?

PLAYER 3: Domination. What kind of nation is disrespect-
ful?

PLAYER 1: Insubordination. What kind of nation is sloth-
ful?

PLAYER 2: Procrastination. What kind of nation is royal?

PLAYER 3: Coronation. What kind of nation is youthful?

PLAYER 1: Rejuvenation.

The words used will naturally reflect the knowledge and
abilities of the players. On the one hand, the game can be
played with such common words as *fascination, donation, in-
dignation, assassination, examination, determination, resig-
nation, carnation, elimination, extermination, discrimina-
tion, intonation, hibernation, inclination, nomination,* and
contamination. But with more advanced groups more difficult
words can be introduced, such as *abomination, indoctrina-
tion, dissemination, assignation, machination, ordination,
alienation, incarnation, denomination, designation, profana-
tion, culmination, germination,* and *recrimination.* To these
could be added, for really advanced players, such words as
vaticination, fulmination, rumination, and *predestination.*

INTERNATIONAL SMORGASBORD

INTERMEDIATE-ADVANCED	*Paper and pencil*
2 *or more*	*Clock or timer*

This game adds to the child's vocabulary by showing him how to build words with prefixes, roots, and suffixes. It also teaches spelling.

The name of the game is derived from the fact that Greek and Latin affixes and roots are the "dishes" listed, as in a Chinese menu, in three columns, A, B, and C (prefixes, roots, and suffixes). The object of the game is to combine these "dishes" to form a complete "meal."

Each player is given the same "menu"—e.g., the one shown below.

A	B	C
IN (IM)	DIC (DICT)	ION
CON (COM)	VOC	IVE
PRO	DUC (DUCT)	ATOR
PER	VERT (VERS)	ABLE
DE	TRAC (TRACT)	IBLE
PRE	JUNC (JUNCT)	ER
RE	CEP (CEPT)	OR
EX	SPEC (SPECT)	ATION
TRANS	CRED	MENT
POLY	JEC (JECT)	FY

Selecting a "dish" from each column to make a single "course," the players compete to see who can make up the longest "meal,"—i.e., construct the greatest number of words within a given time.

Among the words that could be constructed with the "menu" shown here are: INCEPTION, RECEPTION, PER-CEPTION, CONCEPTION, INVOCATION, REVOCATION, CONVOCATION, PROVOCATION, INCREDIBLE, PREDIC-TION, CONDUCTOR, REDUCTION, INDUCTION, DE-

TRACTOR, DETRACTION, CONTRACTOR, CONTRAC-
TION, EXTRACTION, RETRACTION, PROTRACTOR, IN-
SPECTION, CONJUNCTION, EXCEPTION, EXTRACTIVE,
PERCEPTIVE, RETRACTABLE, INTRACTABLE, INVER-
SION, CONVERSION, REVERSION, PERVERSION, DEJEC-
TION, REJECTION, INSPECTOR, etc. Naturally, all words
must be spelled correctly.

Other affixes and roots that could be used to vary or to add
to the "menus" include: *aceous, ortho, omni, cide, ness, circum, hypo, amphi, auto, bi, hyper, rupt, greg, mono, script,*
etc. Lists of prefixes, roots, and suffixes, with their meanings,
can be found appended at the back of this book.

COLORFUL WORDS

INTERMEDIATE-ADVANCED	*Paper and pencil*
2 *or more*	*Blank cards (playing-card size)*
	Clock or timer

This game familiarizes the child with the meaning of common prefixes, roots, and suffixes and with the many words
formed from them.

Prepare three packs of at least twenty cards each. On the
cards of one pack place detachable stickers on each of which
should be printed in red ink a prefix, together with any of
its variants having the same meaning—e.g., *di, dif, dis.* On
each of the stickers attached to the cards in the second pack
should be printed in blue ink a root, together with all its
synonymous variants, if any—e.g., *am, ami, amic.* And on
each of the stickers attached to the cards in the third pack
should be printed in green ink a suffix and any variants of
it having the same meaning—e.g., *ance, ancy, ence, ency.*
The roots and affixes may be selected, according to the maturity and abilities of the players, from the lists appended

at the back of this book. As long as all three packs contain an equal number of cards, more cards may be added to each pack as needed. The game may be made easier by adding a few jokers to each pack.

Shuffle the cards in each pack and lay all three packs on the table face down, with the prefixes at the left, the roots in the center, and the suffixes at the right. Turn up the top card of the root pack and place this card face up in front of the pack.

The first player now turns up the top card of the prefix pack and the top card of the suffix pack. He has one minute to make as many words as he can with all three cards. He scores ten points for a word made with all of them (prefix, root, and suffix) and five points for a word made with either a prefix and a root or a root and a suffix. Thus, he may get credit for calling out any word or words he finds within the largest word he can form.

He lays face up before him the cards needed for whatever words he can form with them. For each letter he has to add to or drop from those on the three cards to form his word he loses one point. Any extra card or cards not needed or used to form a word he places face up in front of its appropriate pack, whether prefix or suffix, to start a discard pile. If he can make no word at all, all three cards are placed face up in front of the packs from which they were drawn.

Suppose, for example, he turns up the prefix *a* and the suffix *ation*, and the root is *voc*, *voke*. He could score ten points for completing the word *avocation* and an additional five points for finding and calling out the word *vocation* within it. He would then have the right to turn up three more cards, one from each pack. If, in the minute allotted to him, he makes only the word *vocation* and discards the *a*, he scores only five points.

Now his opponent or the next player has a minute to make any new words with the materials already exposed—i.e., the word formed by the first player and any discarded prefix or suffix. Thus, if he picks up the discarded *a* and uses it to make the word *avocation* by placing it in front of the first player's turned-up word *vocation*, the second player puts the entire word face up in front of him. Now the first player loses the five points he had earned for the word. They go to the second player, who has had altogether two minutes to think of the word *avocation* and so earns just half of what he would have received for the same word if he had been the one to draw the prefix and the suffix originally and had formed the word in a minute.

The second player next proceeds to turn up another root, prefix, and suffix. With these he might build a new word or, if he turns up, say, the suffix *al*, he might add it to his own word, to form the word *avocational*. Or another player, in his turn, might deprive him of *avocation* by adding *al* to it if it is discarded or turned up later. If the additional prefix or suffix is picked up from one of the face-down packs, the player using it will receive ten points, whether he adds it to a word of his own already formed or to a word of another player which he takes for that purpose. But if the additional prefix or suffix is picked up from the top of either of the face-up discard piles, the player using it will get only five points, whether he adds it to a word of his own already formed or uses it to take another player's word. In either case, a player losing a word to another loses also whatever he originally earned for the lost word. Hence it is important to keep score after each move involving the formation of a word.

After the first player has had his turn, it may happen that a root is discarded, along with the prefix and the suffix he turned up. In that case, the next player may turn up another root and is permitted to combine both to form a word, if that is possible—e.g., *telescope, monograph, monochrome, phonograph*, etc. (Although combining forms like *tele, mono,* and *phon* usually serve the same function as prefixes and are included as such in some lists, we have preferred to classify them as roots in the list appended at the back of this book.)

Naturally, words so formed may be further altered by the addition of appropriate suffixes, if they are turned up. The player who combines two roots in this way may then have a chance to turn up another root, as well as a prefix and a suffix, to start the process again.

Only the top card of a discard pile may be drawn by a player, and then only to build a word, when his turn comes, by adding to one already laid down, either by himself or by another player.

The game ends when all the roots have been turned up.

WORD CASINO

INTERMEDIATE-ADVANCED	*Paper and pencil*
2 *or more*	*Blank cards (playing-card size)*

This adaptation of a popular card game provides practice in building words with prefixes, roots, and suffixes.

Prepare a deck of fifty-two cards by pasting on each a detachable sticker with a different prefix, root, or suffix. There should be, in all, sixteen prefixes, sixteen suffixes, and twenty roots, or, if you wish to make the game easier, eighteen roots and two jokers. The roots and affixes may be selected, according to the abilities of the players, from the lists appended at the end of this book. Different forms of the same root or affix should be included together on the same card. For convenience, the prefixes, roots, and suffixes may be distinctively colored, as in COLORFUL WORDS, above.

After shuffling the cards thoroughly, deal the players four cards each and lay four cards face up on the table.

The object of the game is for each player, when his turn comes, to form as many words as he can by using just one card from his hand and as many cards as possible from the table.

Suppose, for example, that a player holds the root GRAM, GRAPH, GRAPHY in his hand, and among the cards on the table are PHON, PHONE, PHONO and TELE. He can pick up both roots from the table, pronounce the words TELE-GRAM, TELEGRAPH, TELEGRAPHY, PHONOGRAM, and PHONOGRAPH, and place all three cards in a pile face down in front of him. (Note that he cannot make the word TELE-PHONE because it does not include a root or an affix from his hand.) For each of these words he receives as many points as the number of cards he used to form it—i.e., in this case, 5 words x 2 cards each, or 10 points.

Another method of taking in cards from the table is by "building." Suppose a player has in his hand the prefix TRANS and the suffix ATION, and the root PORT is on the table. When his turn comes, he may lay down the suffix ATION next to the root PORT and say "Building TRANS-PORTATION." This announcement means that he has in his hand the prefix needed to complete this word when his turn comes next. However, he runs the risk that, before his turn comes again, some other player may take in his build with a prefix like IM, EX, or DE. On the other hand, by his build he deprives any other player of the possibility of using PORT with a prefix like RE, COM, SUP, or DIS.

It is also possible for a player, in some cases, to build on his own build if he has the right cards. For example, he may first add ATE to the root MEDI, to build IMMEDIATE, and then add IM to build IMMEDIATELY, if he has the necessary cards in his hand.

When a player cannot form a word with any card in his hand, he puts a card on the table, and it is then open to capture by the next player.

After a player has used up the first deal of four cards, he is given another hand of four cards, but no more cards are dealt out face up on the table.

The play continues in this way until all the cards in the deck have been dealt out. Any cards taken in by a player are always added to the pile in front of him. The player who is last to take in a card or cards from the table also takes in whatever other cards may still be left lying there. For these, if they do not make words, he receives only one point each.

BIG DEAL

INTERMEDIATE-ADVANCED
3 *or more*

Blank cards (*playing-card size*)

This game improves vocabulary by teaching the meaning of common prefixes, suffixes, and roots and by providing practice in word-building with them.

The deck, prepared in advance by parent or teacher, consists of sixty-eight cards in all: sixteen with prefixes (seven with RE, three with PRE, two with MIS, and four with UN), forty-two roots (three each of VIEW, HEAT, TELL, CALL, COVER, SPELL, EVEN, UNDERSTAND, FAIR, COIL, FORM, CLAIM, TAKEN, and WRITTEN), and ten suffixes (five each of ED and ING).

After the cards are shuffled, seven cards are dealt to each player, and the rest of the pack is laid face down on the table. The object of the game is to build as many words as possible by putting together prefixes, roots, and suffixes. To this end, each player, in turn, draws a card from the pack and, if necessary, discards an unwanted card, as in rummy. When a player feels that he has accumulated enough points, he calls "Stop!" All the players then put their cards on the table and count their points according to the following schedule:

For calling "Stop!"	2 points
For any good combination of prefix and root (UNCOVER, for example)	6 points
For any good combination of root and suffix (COVERING, for example)	8 points

For any good combination of prefix, root, and
    suffix (RECLAIMED, for example)   20 points
For the highest score in the round   5 points

For unused prefixes, roots, and suffixes left in one's hand,
points are subtracted according to the following schedule:

Prefix	5 points
Root	2 points
Suffix	1 point

However, no more than the total number of points gained
may be subtracted from any hand.

The winner of each round deals the next one.

A total of 250 points wins the game.

A good way of keeping score for this game is KEEPING
OUT OF THE RED (page 324).

With the particular combination of prefixes, roots, and suffixes shown here, almost ninety different words can be
formed. Some roots, such as FORM, with which as many as
twelve different words can be built, are good to retain in one's
hand, while others, like FAIR, from which only three words
can be built, should be discarded.

The game can be made more difficult if other prefixes,
roots, and suffixes are added or substituted. Actually, what
served as roots in the basic game are really complete words.
In modified games, children can be introduced to such common roots as *duct, fer, ject, junct, mit, port, script, spect,
tract,* and *vert.* With these can be included such prefixes as
im, trans, con, sub, de, ex, and *pro,* as well as suffixes like
ive, ion, er, or, able, ible, and *ly.* At a still more advanced
stage, cards may be introduced with *contra, ante, post, anti,
bi, super, sect, vise, dict, fract,* and *ist.* These can be mixed
with the others in suitable proportions to make various words
familiar or new to the children.

What part of London *is in* France?
The letter n.

Using the seven letters EEERRSV, make four words, each of seven letters, with three E's, two R's, one S, and one V.
RESERVE, REVERSE, REVERES, and SEVERER.

A feeling all persons detest,
Although 'tis by everyone felt,
By two letters fully expressed,
By twice two invariably spelt.
What is the word?

ENVY (NV).

What kind of nation is the goal of all travelers?
Destination.

Why should a stupid fellow who is about to take an examination study the letter p?
Because it can make any ass pass.

What two words contain the first six letters of the alphabet?
FABRICATED and BIFURCATED.

Mention two compound words that contain six consecutive consonants.
LATCHSTRING and CATCHPHRASE.

When does the blacksmith start a fight in the alphabet?
When he takes A poke R and makes A shove L.

Why is the letter o *like a neatly kept house?*
Because it is always in order.

Why is u *the jolliest letter?*
Because it is always in the midst of fun.

Why is a scandal like the letter w?
Because it makes ill will.

IV. New Versions of Old Favorites

Two old favorites among vocabulary-building games are CATEGORIES and GHOST. But for each of these we have a number of variations that offer you the opportunity of "escalating" them to higher and higher levels by a series of pleasant and easy gradations.

CATEGORIES

INTERMEDIATE-ADVANCED   *Paper and pencil*
2 *or more*   *Clock or timer*

This is the classic game for building vocabulary. It is an ideal way of encouraging a youngster to notice the things around him and to learn their names. By training him to group items logically in their correct classification, this game also contributes to the development of an orderly mind.

Since a premium is placed on knowing unusual words not likely to be thought of by other players, almost everybody who participates learns some new words when the results are pooled and the answers are compared.

First, each player is asked, in turn, to name a category, such as fruits, flowers, vegetables, animals, birds, fish, colors, fabrics, tools, boats, trees, gems, countries, authors, meats, etc. As these are named, each player lists them vertically on a sheet of paper.

Then they agree on some word of five letters—say, HANDS. This is written across the page, above and somewhat to the right of the vertical list of categories, to form a rectangular chart with boxes large enough to accommodate the words to be filled in.

Now, each player, within a given time, has to fill in the boxes by finding in every category a word that begins with the letter at the top of the column.

Below, for instance, is the way one such chart might look.

	H	A	N	D	S
FRUITS	HUCKLEBERRY	APPLE	NECTARINE	DATES	STRAWBERRY
TREES	HEMLOCK	ASPEN	NUTMEG	DOGWOOD	SUMAC
FLOWERS	HYACINTH	ANEMONE	NARCISSUS	DAISY	SWEET PEA
TOOLS	HATCHET	AX	NIPPERS	DIVIDER	SAW
FABRICS	HAIRCLOTH	ASTRAKHAN	NYLON	DENIM	SILK
ANIMALS	HAMSTER	ALLIGATOR	NEWT	DONKEY	SHEEP

Plenty of time should be allowed so that most of the boxes will be filled in. Then the papers are exchanged for scoring. A player reads aloud the first word on the paper before him, and the other players check to see whether it is duplicated on theirs. If the word is correct, the player who thought of it receives as many points as there are other players who did *not* have it on their papers. Thus, if five are playing the game, and only one thought of ASTRAKHAN, that word would be worth four points; but if two players had thought of it, each of them would be credited with three points for it. The same procedure is followed with each word, and the player who scores the most points wins.

With this system of scoring, a player who wanted to avoid the common word SAW which others might think of, might write, instead, *scythe, sickle, shovel, stapler,* or *spatula.* If he doesn't think of these, others might; so that, when the results are compared, almost everybody learns some new words.

Here are two of several possible variations of this game.

ONE-WORD CATEGORIES   VAR. 1

INTERMEDIATE-ADVANCED   *Paper and pencil*
2 or more   *Clock or timer*

In this variation, the players draw up, cooperatively, a rather
long list of categories—anywhere between ten and twenty.
Then a single letter is agreed upon, and every player tries,
within a given time, to write one word for each of the categories listed, all beginning with the same letter. The system
of scoring would be the same as in CATEGORIES.

CHAIN CATEGORIES   VAR. 2

INTERMEDIATE-ADVANCED   *Paper and pencil*
2 or more   *Clock or timer*

This is also known as TAIL-AND-HEAD CATEGORIES. It
fosters concentration, improves spelling, builds vocabulary,
and adds to the players' knowledge in the various areas represented by the categories chosen.

Each player sets up a chart like the one used in CATE-
GORIES, listing at the left about five or six categories and
leaving room opposite each for five words. But instead of
using the letters of some other word at the top of the columns
in the chart, he must, within a given time, form a chain with
the words he lists for each category: the second word must
begin with the last letter of the first word, and the first letter
of the third word must be the same as the final letter of the
second word; and so on.

An example of one player's chart is shown opposite.

Of course, the chain might be arranged vertically instead
of horizontally, as shown, for a start, with the transition from

Dances	minueT	TwisT	Two-steP	PolkA	Apache
Games	TenniS	SquasH	HandbalL	LeapfroG	Golf
Languages	ArabiC	ChinesE	EnglisH	HebreW	Welsh
Insects	fleA	AnT	TicK	KatydiD	Dragonfly

minueT in the first column to Tennis. In that case, it is better to require no more than four words across.

The scoring is the same as in the preceding variation.

WORD WHEEL

ELEMENTARY-INTERMEDIATE   *Wheel and*
2 *or more*   *spinning pointer*
                                  Clock or timer

This game builds vocabulary by training the players to group words in logical categories. It may be considered a rotary version of CATEGORIES (Page 108).

Draw two concentric circles, and mark them off as shown on page 112. Use the same type of homemade pointer as in WORD WHIRL.

Each player, in turn, gets two spins, the first to find the category, and the second to hit upon a letter of the alphabet.

The object of the game is to name, within a given time, as many words as possible beginning with the letter pointed to and referring to things in the designated category.

Any categories may be selected to suit the interests and maturity of the players: clothes, games, famous people, etc.

These may be inserted on a separate center disk, which can then be independently whirled.

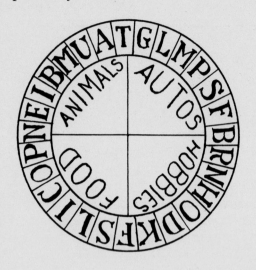

GHOST

ALL LEVELS   *Clock or timer*

2 or more

This is\ the classic word game that almost everybody has played at one time or another, though few are aware of its many possible fascinating variations.

The first player, thinking of any word of more than three letters, calls out just its first letter. Then the second player, thinking perhaps of the same word or some other word of at least four letters, adds a second letter. Each succeeding player must think of a word that begins with the letters already called out and must add one letter, but he must avoid completing any word.

Generally, only one minute is allowed for a player either to add a letter or to challenge the preceding player to say what word he had in mind. If the preceding player cannot meet this challenge, either because he really had no word in mind or because he cannot spell it correctly, he is penalized by becoming "a fifth of a ghost." If he does meet the challenge successfully, then it is his challenger who is so penalized. A player suffers the same penalty if he completes a word of four or more letters and someone else points this out.

A second penalty makes a player two-fifths of a ghost, and so on until five penalties make one a whole ghost. No surviving player may speak to a ghost during the course of the game. Anyone who does becomes a ghost too. Naturally, ghosts are free to do their best to elicit remarks from the surviving players. The winner is the one player who is left at the end.

Suppose, for example, that the first player, thinking of the word AUNT, calls out "A." The second player, thinking perhaps of AGREEABLE, will call out "G." The third player, thinking of AGATE, will call out "A." The fourth player, thinking of AGAINST, will add "I." Now the fifth player finds that he cannot think of any words other than AGAIN and AGAINST that begin with this combination of letters. For either of these he would have to add an N and thus complete a word.

As a rule, proper names, foreign words, and abbreviations are prohibited.

Here are a number of interesting variations.

BACKWARD GHOST   VAR. 1

INTERMEDIATE-ADVANCED   *Clock or timer*
2 *or more*

This is a wonderful game for training the visual memory of the spelling of words.

It is the same as GHOST, except that a player must, within a given time, compose words by inserting a letter *in front of* the ones already called out. In effect, the words are to be spelled *backward*.

Here is one possible beginning:

PLAYER 1: E
PLAYER 2: LE
PLAYER 3: BLE
PLAYER 1: UBLE
PLAYER 2: LUBLE
PLAYER 3: OLUBLE
PLAYER 1: SOLUBLE

Player 1 is one-fifth of a ghost, having made the complete word SOLUBLE. He would have been in the same difficulty if he had completed *voluble*.

SUPERGHOST   VAR. 2

INTERMEDIATE-ADVANCED   *Clock or timer*
2 *or more*

This more modern and more complicated variation is also called FORE-AND-AFT GHOST or HEADS-AND-TAILS GHOST. It is an ideal way of introducing a child to the common prefixes.

The rules are the same, except that a player may add a letter *either before or after* the ones already called out. In short, one can spell backward or forward from any point. Again, only words of four or more letters count.

In both this and the preceding variation, a knowledge of prefixes can frequently help a player to avoid adding a letter that completes a word. For example, suppose a player's turn comes when the letters FAC have been given. To avoid making the complete words FACE or FACT, he might add either an I after the C (for FACING) or an E before the F (for PREFACE). If he puts an F before the F (for EFFACE), he also successfully avoids being turned into part of a ghost.

Should this game prove too great a strain on the memory, players may be permitted to use paper and pencil to keep a record of the letters called out.

SUPERDUPERGHOST   Var. 3

ADVANCED   *Pencil and paper*
2 *or more*   *Clock or timer*

This variation challenges the players' powers of concentration and calls for a good knowledge of spelling and vocabulary. A time limit is needed for each answer.

What makes this variation different from SUPERGHOST is that a player may compose words by inserting a letter in front of, after, or *between* the letters already called out, in order to avoid completing a word, so long as he can still make some other word. Only words of five letters or more count.

Thus, suppose a player has to add a letter to FAC, as above. He can put an R between the F and the A (for REFRACT). Adding to either end might build words like *fraction* or *diffract*. But putting an E between the F and the R leads to a new word—FERACIOUS, or with another insertion, AFTERACT.

GRAPHIC GHOST   Var. 4

ALL LEVELS   *Paper and pencil*
2 *only*   *Graph paper and colored*
                                 pencil

This is a quiet variation. Like other versions of GHOST, it teaches spelling and improves vocabulary.

Use a square, like the one shown on page 116, consisting of about two hundred and twenty-five boxes, with fifteen boxes on each side.

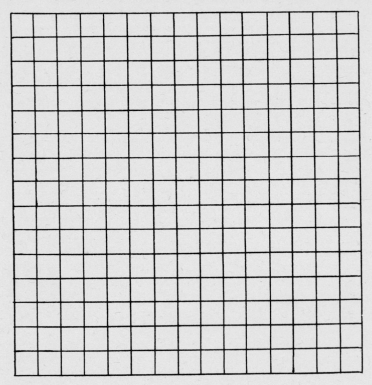

The first player, with some word in mind, writes its first letter in the box at the upper left corner. His opponent, also thinking of some word, adds the necessary letter to the one already written, proceeding horizontally. The players then take turns adding letters in this manner. A player loses one point if he cannot state the word he has in mind when he is challenged to do so. If he completes a word, he loses another point. When one of the players has lost five points, his opponent wins the game.

If SUPERGHOST is played graphically, the letters must be placed precisely in the box in which they belong, leaving space before and after for the missing letters of the word.

More difficult variations can also be tried. For example, the players might attempt to build vertically, moving downward, from the letters of a given word or part of a word written horizontally. In that case, too, SUPERGHOST can be played graphically by placing letters in the vertical row in which they belong and leaving space above and below for the missing letters of the word. If a square of fifteen boxes on each side proves too small, the grid can be extended in any direction to suit the needs of the game.

GRAPHIC GHOST can also be played by more than two players if the grid is placed on a blackboard. Then the players can take turns chalking in the letters of the words they have in mind.

<hr>

What sort of Miss contains a message?
A missive.

What is that from which the whole may be taken, and yet some will remain?
The word WHOLESOME.

Why is a man clearing a hedge at a single bound like a man snoring?
Because he does it in his leap (his sleep).

What sort of Miss spells trouble?
Mischief.

What's an intellectual crevice?
A wisecrack.

With two syllables am I said;
A bride needs me when she's wed.
My first is faithful and honest;
My second's done with needle and thread.
What am I?

Trousseau (true, sew).

V. Compounds and Combinations

THE GAMES in this section provide practice in combining words to form compounds and in building big words from smaller ones.

ENDLESS WORD CHAIN

INTERMEDIATE

2 *or more*

This is one of several games that help children to see how simple words can be combined to form compounds. It builds vocabulary, improves spelling, and teaches the use of the dictionary to determine, in case of dispute, whether a compound is spelled solid, with a hyphen, or as two separate words.

The first player begins forging the word chain by calling out a pair of words that form a compound, like *lunch box*. Now the next player must form a new compound by beginning with the last word of the previous player's compound— e.g., *box spring*. The game proceeds in this way until a player cannot think of a compound word that could be formed from the last element of the preceding player's word. Then, as in GHOST, the preceding player may be challenged to tell what word he had in mind. Thus, before calling out a compound word, every player had better be sure he can meet such a challenge from the player who follows him. If not, the penalties are the same as in GHOST. Of course, each player, after calling out a compound, must spell it correctly.

The game started here might continue as follows:

PLAYER 3: Springtime.

PLAYER 1: Time lock.
PLAYER 2: Lock step.
PLAYER 3: Stepladder.
The game lends itself to a number of interesting variations.

CONNECTOGRAPHS   VAR. 1

INTERMEDIATE-ADVANCED   *Paper and pencil*
2 *or more*

This is a visualized version of the endless word chain that permits the players to see how far each can go independently in building a series of compound words from a given word.

Each player boxes off an area—let us say, to begin with, a square with five boxes on each side. The boxes should be made large enough to accommodate words of about five or six letters each.

Now all start with the same word—say, APRIL—in the upper-left box. At a given signal, the players are to proceed filling in the remaining boxes, as far as possible, both horizontally and vertically, with an endless chain of compound words, starting from APRIL. A reasonable time limit should be set.

Here, for example, is how one might start:

APRIL	SHOWER	BATH	HOUSE	BOAT
FOOL		ROOM		TRIP
PROOF		MATE		HAMMER

What is it that, by losing an eye, has only a nose left?
Noise.

PUT-TOGETHER   VAR. 2

ELEMENTARY-INTERMEDIATE
2 or more

In this variation of ENDLESS WORD CHAIN, all the compound words formed by the players must be spelled solid—i.e., without a hyphen, as one word. If there is doubt about a player's word in this respect, the dictionary should be consulted.

The game begins with the first player calling out a word which, when added to another—either before it or after it—could make a solid compound word. Suppose, for example, that the first player calls out "Saw."

Now the next player must suggest a word which, when added to SAW—whether preceding it or following it—could form a compound word, like *hacksaw* or *sawdust*. He receives one point for building the compound and another for spelling it correctly.

If he cannot think of a compound word that could be formed from SAW in this fashion, he may challenge the first player to supply one. Failure to do so would, of course, involve a penalty of two points.

The game continues in this way, as players suggest other simple words that could form parts of such compounds as *firefly*, *bandwagon*, *wallboard*, *sidewalk*, *sandbox*, *lipstick*, etc., each of which is composed of parts that are themselves words.

WORD COMBINATIONS   VAR. 3

ELEMENTARY-INTERMEDIATE   *Blank cards (playing-card*
1 or more   *size)*

In this variation, which teaches spelling, simple words are composed from still simpler ones. It is an ideal game for a child to play by himself or with a companion.

Prepare a set of cards by writing on each a word that could form a part of a longer word—e.g., *stick*, *tar*, *be*, *off*, *ball*, *am*, *ice*, *get*, *sea*, *house*, *store*, *horse*, etc. Such words can easily be found in many words of three syllables or more, like *together*, *incapable*, *gasoline*, *lieutenant*, *diploma*, *cockatoo*, *origin*, and even in some words of two syllables, like *palled*, *fortune*, *message*, *current*, *grammar*, *brandish*, *incite*, *hermit*, *mayor*, and *season*. Just be sure that for each word on a card there is another card with a word that can combine with it.

The player or players then try to form as many new, longer words as possible by combining the cards in various ways. Thus, words that might be built with the elements listed here are *beam*, *target*, *office*, etc.

In a larger group, each child can be given a big card with only a part of a word, like *ind*. Then he must find his "mate" with the other part—the child who holds up the letters *ian*. Children who make up a complete word then line up with their cards.

The game can be further complicated if a long word, like *penmanship*, is broken up into three parts, each of which is a word in itself: *pen*, *man*, and *ship*.

SILLYGISMS   VAR. 4

INTERMEDIATE-ADVANCED   *Clock or timer*
2 or more

The fact that English spelling and pronunciation are often worlds apart causes many children much anguish in learning to write. Yet the disparity between orthography and phonology (to use the technical terms) can also be made the subject of fun and laughter. This variation, which follows the preceding game of WORD COMBINATIONS quite naturally, helps children to appreciate the humor of the situation and lightens the tension involved in learning to spell.

The best way to understand the game is to examine a typical sillygism:

"This is a pew. This is a pill. Therefore, this is a pupil."

The idea, you see, is to build up a word by putting together syllables that have the sound of other, logically unrelated words. In short, the word so constructed must *not* consist of a combination like *sawdust*, *coattail*, or *baseball*, in which two or more words are logically joined together to form a compound. No, the words should have no connection whatever, like *mop* and *pet* (*moppet*).

The first player, thinking of some sillygism, calls out only the first sentence—say, "This is an inn."

Now the second player must try to determine what word the first player had in mind or perhaps think of a word himself. If he cannot do so, he may challenge the first player to complete the sillygism. One point is earned for thinking of the complete sillygism, and one point for spelling each of the three words of which it consists. (This particular one continues as follows: "This is a turn. Therefore, this is an intern." INN, TURN, and INTERN would have to be correctly spelled.) If a player is challenged to complete his sillygism, he is penalized two points if he cannot do so. Mispronunciations are likewise penalized, like *soup*, *purse*, *stitch*, *us* (*superstitious*).

Here is how one game proceeded:

PLAYER 1: This is a pan.

PLAYER 2: This is a tree. Therefore, this is a pantry.

PLAYER 3: This is a pan.

PLAYER 1: We just had that one. It's pantry.

PLAYER 3: No, this is a nick. Therefore, this is a panic.

PLAYER 2: This is a miss.

PLAYER 3: This is a sill. Therefore, this is a missile.

PLAYER 1: This is a dome.

PLAYER 2: I can't imagine what you have in mind.

PLAYER 1: This is a minion. Therefore, this is a dominion.

(Here Player 1 thought of a three-syllable sillygism.)

PLAYER 3: This is a prod.

PLAYER 1: This is a duct. Therefore, this is a product.

PLAYER 2: This is a prude.

PLAYER 3: What do you mean by that?

PLAYER 2: These are dents. Therefore, this is prudence.

PLAYER 1: This is a sea.

PLAYER 2: This is a son. Therefore, this is a season.

PLAYER 3: No good! You have a mispronunciation. Minus one point for you! This is a seed. Therefore, this is secede.

(Here a verb has been used instead of a noun. Allowing different parts of speech adds to the instructiveness of the game.)

PLAYER 1: This is a sigh.

PLAYER 2: This is fun. Therefore, this is a siphon.

PLAYER 3: This is a sigh.

PLAYER 1: We've had that already. It's siphon.

PLAYER 3: Not this one. This is a kick. Therefore, it's psychic.

PLAYER 1: This is a tail.

PLAYER 2: This is an oar. Therefore, this is a tailor.

PLAYER 3: This is a cat.

PLAYER 1: This is tar. Therefore, this is a catarrh.

PLAYER 2: This is an ax.

PLAYER 3: This is a scent. Therefore, this is an accent.

PLAYER 1: This is a part.

PLAYER 2: This is a tea. Therefore, this is a party.

PLAYER 3: This is rust.

PLAYER 1: This is a tick. Therefore, this is a rustic.

PLAYER 2: This is a pate.

PLAYER 3: This is a run. Therefore, this is a patron.

The game can go on in this way with sillygisms like *pat* and *tee* (*patty*), *tine* and *knee* (*tiny*), *ants* and *sir* (*answer*), *sin* and *you* (*sinew*), *tack* and *tick* (*tactic*), *pray* and *sea* (*précis*), *vest* and *tree* (*vestry*), and *wind* and *doe* (*window*).

At a more difficult level the same game can be played with

sillygisms forming three-syllable words, like *fan* and *attic* (*fanatic*) or *paw* and *city* (*paucity*). Naturally, a reasonable time should be allowed for each response.

SILLYGISM RUMMY   VAR. 5

ALL LEVELS   *Blank cards* (*playing-card*
2 *or more*   *size*)

This variation enables a parent or a teacher to adjust the degree of difficulty of the game to the abilities and needs of the players. It directs attention to the correct spelling and pronunciation of words and adds to the players' vocabulary.

First, the parent or teacher prepares three cards for each sillygism: one for the word itself and two for its parts. Even a word of three syllables can usually be broken down into two parts, like *fact* and *tory* (*factory*).

The number of sets of three cards produced will depend on the number of players. If there are two, three, or four players, fifty-one cards should be used (seventeen sets); fifty-seven cards (nineteen sets) are needed when there are five players; and not fewer than sixty-six cards (twenty-two sets) if six play.

The sillygisms can vary in difficulty. Some can be quite simple indeed, like *turn* and *nip* (*turnip*), *bird* and *den*, (*burden*), *fan* and *sea* (*fancy*), and *car* and *pet* (*carpet*). Others may involve a significant change in spelling, like *guard* and *den* (*garden*), *pin* and *sir* (*pincer*), *mice* and *elf* (*myself*), *stew* and *dent* (*student*), *cash* and *shoe* (*cashew*), *cough* and *fee* (*coffee*), and *urn* and *nest* (*earnest*). A few might challenge the more advanced players: *epic* and *cure* (*epicure*), *gang* and *green* (*gangrene*), *euchre* and *wrist* (*eucharist*), *eerie* and *sip* and *pill* and *less* (*erysipelas*), *sat* and *tie* and *it* and *tea* (*satiety*), and *farthing* and *gale* (*farthingale*).

The cards are then shuffled, cut, and dealt: ten cards to each player if two play; seven cards in a three- or four-handed game; and six cards in a five- or six-handed game.

Each player must either draw a card from the top of the deck, which has been placed face down on the table, or take the card that has been placed face up beside the deck. After adding the new card to his hand, he discards one from it, laying it face up either on top of the one already face up or in its place. Only the top card may be drawn from either of the two piles.

The object of the game is to put together complete silly-gisms. These are then laid face up on the table. The first player to set out his entire hand in this fashion wins the round. One point is credited to each player for every sillygism laid out on the table. After a number of rounds, the points are totaled to determine the winner.

A more difficult variation of the same game omits from each set the card that correctly spells the complete word in the sillygism. Thus, each set consists of only two cards. A pack for two, three, or four players would then consist of fifty-two cards (twenty-six sets); for five players, fifty-eight cards (twenty-nine sets); and for six players, sixty-four cards (thirty-two sets). The object of the game now becomes to lay down an entire hand of pairs of words that, when sounded together, make up a different word. To get credit for a pair, the player would have to spell and define correctly the word he had in mind. Thus, if he laid down *cape* and *purr*, he would have to spell the word *caper* and state its meaning too.

Here is a list of words that lend themselves to the formation of sillygisms:

balderdash	syntax
catalogue	castanet
complain	pasteurize
duplicate	capitulate
forfeit	incarcerate
fortunate	logarithm

formulate

futility

hurricane

innocuous

innuendo

inventory

mandate

sedate

mistletoe

circumstance

exactly

elate

isolate

populate

manipulate

penetrate

damnation

~~~~~~

Of just three syllables I am.
Tire, drill, gun, hammer, battering ram:
My whole describes them all when blown air does the job.
My first is recent, modern, fresh;
My second's woven straw or fabric mesh;
My last's a mite that bites into your flesh.
What am I?

Pneumatic (new, mat, tick).

Why is the nose on your face like the v in civility?
Because it's between two eyes.

In the word CLOVES, why are the C and the S, although separated,
closely attached?
Because there is LOVE between them.

A patient was surprised to find the following sign in his doctor's
office:

DON'T
EAT!

But he read it wrong. The doctor explained that what it meant
was: Don't overeat!

Why is an author greater than a king?
Because he may choose his own subjects.

BRAIN STRAIN VAR. 6

ADVANCED
2 *only*

Blank cards (playing-card size)

As its name suggests, this variation is considerably more demanding than the preceding ones. Played like SPELLING CONCENTRATION (page 217), it calls for a retentive memory as well as a varied vocabulary and a knowledge of spelling.

The cards are prepared as in SILLYGISM RUMMY, above —i.e., in pairs consisting of just the two words forming the sillygism—*pore* and *shun* or *muff* and *inn*—but not the word they form (*portion* or *muffin*). Again, the sillygisms can vary from simple ones like *tar* and *tan* (*tartan*) or *ten* and *done* (*tendon*) to such difficult ones as *can* and *tickle* (*canticle*) or *thigh* and *mole* (*thymol*).

In order to avoid straining too much the memory of each player, it is best to begin with a deck of no more than forty cards, or twenty pairs. Other sets of cards, with additional or substitute pairs of words to form sillygisms, can be kept in reserve for subsequent rounds.

The cards, after being thoroughly shuffled, are spread out face down on the table. Picking up any two cards, the first player looks at them and shows them to his opponent. If the cards should happen to form a pair, like *sly* and *me*, he places them face up on his side of the table and scores one point if he can spell the word they form (*slimy*). He then gets another chance to find a pair that forms a sillygism. If he cannot do so, he returns one card to its original place on the table, face down, after showing both cards to his opponent.

Now it is the latter's turn to select *one* card from among those lying face down on the table. If, when he looks at it, he believes it forms a sillygism with the card his opponent has just laid down, the second player tries to recall where it was put. If he is successful in finding it at the first try, he lays the pair face up on his side of the table and spells the word they form. If the second player knows that his card and the card laid down by his opponent do not form a sillygism, he picks a card at random from among those spread out on the table.

The game proceeds in this way until the last card has been drawn from the table. A card picked up from the table must always be shown to one's opponent in order to give him an opportunity to memorize its location if it is later laid down again. The winner is the player who scores the most points.

If, in later rounds, the number of cards in the deck is increased in order to make the game more difficult, it is a good idea to number the backs of the cards (1, 2, 3, etc.) as an aid to the players in associating the cards with the words on their faces.

CAN YOU DO IT?   VAR. 7

INTERMEDIATE-ADVANCED   *Clock or timer*
2 *or more*

This is another variation with compound words that can be played just for laughs.

Each player, in turn, must ask a silly question involving a play on a compound word. The humor is in the realization that one part of the compound has another meaning entirely in a different context.

Here, for example, is how one such game proceeded:

PLAYER 1: Can you see a bed spread?
PLAYER 2: Can you make a pillow fight?
PLAYER 3: Can you wake a sleeping car?
PLAYER 1: Can you see a pipe dream?
PLAYER 2: Can you see a home stretch?
PLAYER 3: Can you make a bed roll?

PLAYER 1: Can you make a bell hop?
PLAYER 2: Can you see a shoe box?
PLAYER 3: Can you make a sack race?
PLAYER 1: Can you see a dress parade?
PLAYER 2: Can you see a fire escape?
PLAYER 3: Can you see a salad dressing?
PLAYER 1: Can you make a garden fence?
PLAYER 2: Can you see a nose dive?
PLAYER 3: Can you see a cake walk?
PLAYER 1: Can you make a wolf pack?
PLAYER 2: Can you see a fox trot?
PLAYER 3: Can you see a horse fly?
PLAYER 1: Con you make a whip saw?
PLAYER 2: Can you make a board walk?
PLAYER 3: Can you make a room mate?
PLAYER 1: Can you see a fish bowl?
PLAYER 2: Can you hear an ear drum?
PLAYER 3: Can you see a walking stick?
PLAYER 1: Can you blow a shoe horn?
PLAYER 2: Can you hear a cigar band?
PLAYER 3: Can you hear a tree bark?
PLAYER 1: Can you put on the gloves with a boxing match?
PLAYER 2: Can you make a jury box?
PLAYER 3: Can you see a hand spring?
PLAYER 1: Can you watch a roller skate?
PLAYER 2: Can you make a band stand?
PLAYER 3: Can you see a clam bake?
PLAYER 1: Can you see a kitchen sink?
PLAYER 2: Can you suggest clothes suitable for a dressing room?
PLAYER 3: Can you make a house hold?
PLAYER 1: Can you make a bed spring?
PLAYER 2: Can you lift a light house?
PLAYER 3: Can you make wood work?

Since this is an elimination game, a reasonable amount of time should be given for each player to think of a question.

A parachutist, on landing in enemy territory, opened his sealed orders, which read:

GROUND
GO

What did they mean?
Go underground.

What does the following sign mean?
MAN
BOARD

Man overboard!

What common expression is signified by the following?

```
 ┌─D─┐
 L   E
 └─A─┘
```

Square deal.

What is the difference between sixteen ounces of lead and a hard-working typist?
One weighs a pound; the other pounds away.

What word denoting a part of the body can make a pair with each of four other words denoting bodily parts?
HEAD. It figures in head and tail, head and shoulders, head and heart, *and* head and foot.

What common expression is signified by the following?

N af E rie E nd D

A friend in need.

BABY MOTH: *Boohoo-hoo!*
MOTHER MOTH: This is the first time I've seen a moth bawl.

Can you mention five common phrases in each of which the name of a metal figures?
Silver tongue, platinum blonde, iron will, tin-pan alley, and brass hat (or brass tacks or brass band).

ENDS AND BEGINNINGS   VAR. 8

INTERMEDIATE-ADVANCED   *Paper and pencil*
2 *or more*

This variation on ENDLESS WORD CHAIN directs attention to the features that different words have in common. It improves spelling and vocabulary.

The idea of the game is to think of a word which ends with the same syllable that begins another word. For example, *backward* ends in *ward*, which is also the first syllable in *wardrobe*. Note also that each of the syllables to which *ward* is attached is itself a word: *back* and *robe*.

The first player, if he thought of this combination, would write on his paper: BACK———ROBE. It would then be the task of the second player to determine what the missing syllable is that will make the two words intended.

If the first player's secret syllable is discovered, his opponent scores one point and must propose another, similar pair. A pair like TEM———MIT is not acceptable for TEMPER and PERMIT because the first part does not itself make a word. On the other hand, FOOT———ON (FOOTLESS and LESSON), HAND———BODY (HANDSOME and SOMEBODY, and FIRE———WAYS (FIRESIDE and SIDEWAYS) are typical examples of acceptable pairs.

VI. Word Associations, Idioms,
and Locutions

A much-used part of our language consists of "prefabricated" phrases like *kith and kin*, familiar locutions like *stars and stripes*, set formulas like *tooth and claw*, common combinations like *Venetian blinds*, widely understood allusions like *fig leaf,* generally accepted metaphors like *wallflower,* idioms like *hard and fast,* and precise turns of phrase like *a gaggle of geese.*

The games in this section help the child to gain fluency by putting such expressions—to use one of them—"on the tip of his tongue."

WHO'S ZOO?

INTERMEDIATE-ADVANCED	*Blank cards (playing-card*
2 *or more*	*size)*

This is a delightful game which teaches children the precise words to be used in referring to animals of different sex, the young of different kinds of animals, and groups of animals.

A deck of playing cards is prepared, each with a word written on it. The words are drawn from sets that can be selected from the chart below or from the dictionary to make combinations suitable for players of different levels of maturity.

Animal	Male	Female	Young Offspring	Group
hound	dog	bitch	pup	pack, cry
goat	billy	nanny	kid	flock
sheep	ram, wether	ewe	lamb	flock, drove
pig, hog, swine	boar	sow	shoat, pigling	herd, sounder, drove, drift
goose	gander	goose	gosling	flock, flight, skein, gaggle
duck	drake	duck	duckling	flight, skein
chicken	cock	hen	chick	flock
cat	tom	quean, queen	kitten	clowder, clutter

Animal	Male	Female	Young Offspring	Group
cattle	bull, ox, steer	cow	calf, bullock	herd, drove
horse	stallion, gelding	mare	colt, foal, filly	herd
bear	bear	bear	cub	sleuth, sloth
deer	buck	doe	fawn	herd
toad	toad	toad	polliwog, tadpole	knot
elephant	bull	cow	calf	herd
turkey	cock	hen	chick	rafter
whale	bull	cow	calf	gam, pod
fish	fish	fish	fry, fingerlings	school, shoal, draught
lion	lion	lioness	cub	pride
tiger	tiger	tigress	cub	
partridge	partridge	hen		covey
lark	lark	lark	lark	exhaltation
bee	drone	queen, worker		swarm
fox	fox	vixen	cub	pack, skulk

A card marked JOKER should be included in the deck.

After the cards have been shuffled and cut, they are dealt out. The number of cards in each hand will depend on the number of players and may vary from five to seven. The remaining cards are laid face down in a pack on the table.

The object of the game is to put together cards with words that go together in sets. Some of the words, like *flock, herd, cub, drove, bull, cow,* and *hen,* may be used in a number of different combinations. A player may accumulate words in his hand until he has a complete set (animal, male, female, young offspring, and group), or he may lay down combinations of two or more, face up, on the table before him, thereby risking the possibility that some other player may score by adding to his set. He may play the joker any way he wants, but he must specify the word he wishes it to represent.

Each player, in turn, first discards one card, laying it face up on the table beside the rest of the pack, before drawing a card from the top of the pile.

Ten points are credited for laying down a complete set of five. A pair counts two points; three, three points; and four, four points. The player with the greatest number of points wins the game.

WHAT'S THE GOOD WORD?   VAR. 1

ALL LEVELS   *Blank cards (playing-card*
2 *or more*   *size)*

This is basically the same game as WHO'S ZOO? except that the words are chosen from sets selected to teach the players common words and pairs of expressions (*namby-pamby, helter-skelter, hurly-burly, chitchat, dillydally, fiddle-faddle, flip-flop, harum-scarum, pitter-patter, higgledy-piggledy, shilly-shally, willy-nilly, tittle-tattle, pell-mell, hobnob, hodgepodge, hoity-toity, huggermugger, mishmash, razzle-dazzle, riffraff, wishy-washy, zigzag, tiptop,* and similar reduplicated, or "ricochet," words) as well as the specialized vocabulary or technical terms of any field, like carpentry, cooking, sewing, printing, music, coins, etc. Essentially, this is a game of word association.

You can make up your deck of cards to suit the abilities and interests of the players. For example, at an elementary level, sets may consist of combinations like *ding* and *dong, bow* and *wow, spick* and *span, hither* and *thither, safe* and *sane,* Hansel and Gretel, Jack and Jill, Tweedledum and Tweedledee, etc. At a more advanced stage, children may be given cards with *stocks* and *bonds, ways* and *means, goods* and *services*, *means* and *ends*, *mortar* and *pestle*, *hue* and *cry*, *fire* and *brimstone*, *ball* and *chain*, *tooth* and *claw*, etc.

Literature, history, and mythology can also be included: *Romulus* and *Remus*, *Venus* and *Adonis*, *Antony* and *Cleopatra*, *Gilbert* and *Sullivan*, *Sodom* and *Gomorrah*, *William* and *Mary*, *Samson* and *Delilah*, etc. Alliterative combinations, like *bag* and *baggage*, *part* and *parcel*, *sum* and *substance*, *rack* and *ruin*, *hale* and *hearty*, *vim* and *vigor*, *frills* and *furbelows*, and *thick* and *thin* also have a place in the deck. Other obvious pairs can easily be added, like *touch* and *go*, *hard* and *fast*, *pins* and *needles*, and *ham* and *eggs*.

Words can also be paired according to categories—e.g., *pencil* and *paper*, *pen* and *ink*, *shoes* and *stockings*, *pence* and *pounds*, *ounces* and *pounds* (the latter word thus being, like many others, capable of doing double duty), *hat* and *coat*, *pots* and *pans*, *hooks* and *eyes*, *stars* and *stripes*, *fox* and *hounds*, *raincoat* and *umbrella*, *fish* and *fowl* (or *fish* and *chips*), and *army* and *navy*, to name but a few. The game can even be given a geographical touch with combinations like *Irish* and *jig*, *Russian* and *dressing*, *Venetian* and *blinds*, *Egyptian* and *mummy*, *Dresden* and *china*, *Roman* and *candles* (or *holiday*), *Indian* and *summer*, *Persian* and *lamb*, *Brazil* and *nuts*, *Japanese* and *lantern*, and *Siamese* and *twins*.

Pairs can be made as easy as *corned beef* and *cabbage*, *bread* and *butter*, *mother* and *father*, *sister* and *brother*, *thunder* and *lightning*, *lock* and *key*, *ball* and *bat*, *hit* and *run*, and *cup* and *saucer*, or as difficult as *cap* and *gown*, *Scotch* and *soda*, *Grecian* and *urn*, *atom* and *electron*, and *olive* and *branch*.

Only one word should be on a card, and one card should be marked JOKER.

Although this game can be played like WHO'S ZOO? it is more instructive if it is modeled on the card game known as "Go Fish." After the cards have been thoroughly shuffled, at least five are dealt to each player. The remainder of the deck is placed face down.

If the first player finds that some of the cards in his hand make a pair or a set of three, he lays these down, face up, on the table before him. He then selects one of his remaining cards for which he thinks he knows the matching word and asks any other player for a card with that word.

Suppose, for example, that he has WISHY in his hand. He may ask, "Please give me WASHY." If the player so asked has a card with this word on it, he must give it to the player who asked for it. The latter, after putting down his pair, WISHY-WASHY, may then proceed to ask for a card with another word that he thinks will complement a word on one of his remaining cards.

If a player who is asked for a word does not have a card with that word on it, he says, "Go fish." The asking player must then draw the top card from the deck and add it to his hand. If the card makes a pair with any word in his hand, he may lay the pair down, and he gets a chance to ask for another word. If the card drawn does not make a pair, it is the next player's turn.

The game can be made more interesting if words admitting of more than one combination are included in the deck. For example, suppose Player 1, having TRUE in his hand, asks Player 2 for TRIED.

As Player 2 does not have TRIED, he says, "Go fish."

But Player 2 has FALSE in his hand, a word that can also be matched with TRUE. So when Player 1 has completed his turn, Player 2 says, "I want TRUE."

The player with the greatest number of sets to his credit wins the game. If several rounds are played, one point can be given every player for each set he has laid down in any round. The winner will then be the one who has amassed the greatest number of points after a given number of rounds.

If a player has a card that is called for but denies having it when he is asked, he is penalized one point for each player in the game.

A player who chooses to use the joker must state what

word he intends to substitute it for. Thus, if he has TOOTH in his hand, he may call the joker, if he desires, CLAW, get credit for the pair, and deprive the player who may have CLAW of a chance to use the card later.

TIMED TONGUE-TIP TEASERS VAR. 2

INTERMEDIATE-ADVANCED
2 *only*

Blank cards (playing-card size)

Clock or timer

This game has the same educational purpose as WHAT'S THE GOOD WORD? but it places the emphasis on speed in verbal association and reaction. It helps to put common expressions "on the tip of the tongue."

Prepare a deck of playing cards as for WHAT'S THE GOOD WORD? but place the complementary cards of each set in separate packs.

Now shuffle each pack separately and lay the cards face down, giving one pack to each player.

Next divide the two packs, still face down, into several stacks of five cards each. (If fifty cards are used, each player will have five such stacks.)

When the first player, with stopwatch in hand, says "Go!" his opponent scoops up one of his stacks of cards, turns them face up, and, within fifteen seconds, must call out the five words that complement those on his cards. He receives one point for each correct answer, but ten points if he gets all five answers correct within the allotted time.

Now it is the turn of the second player to hold the stopwatch and to time the first player's responses. If both players succeed in scoring ten points each, the second time around they should scoop up ten cards (two stacks) at once and see how many of them they can complement within the allotted time. In that case, they score two points for each correct answer, but thirty points if they get all ten right.

Once a stack of cards has been turned up, and the answers have been given, it is turned down again and set aside. If a player then comes upon a card in his own stack which is complementary to one that has already been turned up by his opponent, he scores only half as much for a correct answer as he otherwise would have scored. The game ends when all the cards have been turned up once.

ANIMAL MORTGAGES   VAR. 3

INTERMEDIATE   *Blank cards (playing-card*
2 or more   *size)*
                                Clock or timer

This variation on WHO'S ZOO? likewise capitalizes on children's interest in animals to teach the precise use of language.

It may be played like WHAT'S THE GOOD WORD? Two sets of cards are prepared. On each card in one set is written the name of some animal, bird, or insect: *bee, beaver, ant, spider, mole, bat, dove, rabbit, lion, dog, chicken, fox, hornet, horse, sheep, pig, bear, wolf, squirrel, cow,* etc.; and correspondingly, on each card in the other set, the name of the animal's house: *hive, lodge, hill, cote, den, web, hole, nest, stable, shed, corral, fold, sty, pen, cave, kennel, hutch, coop, aerie, vespiary, lair, burrow, mew, apiary, aviary, columbary, pound,* etc. Make one pack of both sets and shuffle the cards. The object of the game is then to match the animals with their houses.

Or the game may be played like TIMED TONGUE-TIP TEASERS. In that case, the complementary cards of each set should be kept in separate packs.

Since some words, *hole, hill,* etc., may be used as the name of the house of several different animals, the game may also be played in reverse, using cards with these names and requiring the players to mention, within a given time, as many animals as they can that may be found in such houses.

ANIMAL ANALOGIES   VAR. 4

INTERMEDIATE-ADVANCED   *Blank cards (playing-card*
2 *or more*   *size)*
                                 Clock or timer

The names of animals, birds, and insects can also be used in a game played like ANIMAL MORTGAGES or like TIMED TONGUE-TIP TEASERS, designed to teach children certain common expressions in which these names figure as metaphors or by analogy. Some typical examples of this kind of figurative speech are: *bear hug, kangaroo court, horse sense, rabbit punch, catcall, beeline, dog days, pup tent, monkey wrench, fox trot, goose step, goose pimple, pig iron, stag party, weasel words, wolf whistle, crocodile tears, holy mackerel, loan shark, cheap skate, lobster shift, cold turkey, chicken heart, eager beaver, owl car, swan song, bulldog edition, mosquito fleet, spider wheel, worm gear,* etc.

The game can be extended to include examples of the figurative use of the names of animals, birds, and insects to signify human attitudes, dispositions, temperaments, or characters, like *bee, sloth, ostrich, dove, hawk, fox, mouse, cat, hog, goat, ox, leech, lion, chicken, eagle, monkey, donkey, mule, pig, rat, sheep, skunk, wolf, snake, loon, dodo, jackal, cuckoo, owl, grouse, lark, sucker, vulture, wasp, beaver, butterfly, louse, worm,* and *scorpion,* to name but a few. This variation is best played along the lines of TIMED TONGUE-TIP TEASERS as a game of association. In that case, the cards can be prepared either with the names of the creatures or with the names of the character traits conventionally imputed to them, like *cowardice, treacherousness, bravery, laziness, gluttony, stupidity, mischievousness, conformism, wisdom, irre-*

sponsibility, parasitism, sullenness, cleverness, etc. Then the associations can be evoked either from the trait to the animal or vice versa.

ANALOGIES   VAR. 5

INTERMEDIATE-ADVANCED   *Blank cards (playing-card*
2 *or more*   *size)*
                                Clock or timer

This variation is the next step along the way toward developing in the child an appreciation of figurative language and the imaginative power needed to think of it.

The game is played like the preceding variations. But instead of restricting the words on the cards to animals, birds, and insects, or to their presumed characteristics, you can now range freely over the entire world of vegetables, minerals, and man-made things as well, selecting any words that lend themselves, by their conventional associations, to metaphorical usage. That is, you may use any words that can stand for something else than their literal meaning. For example, among the tools, the word "chisel," from its literal significance as an instrument for close cutting, has been extended in the figurative language of slang to denote sharp or unfair practices in bargaining or business. Other tools that have similarly taken on metaphorical meanings are the *bore*, the *gouge*, the *hatchet*, the *hammer*, the *drill*, the *trowel*, and the *ax*. Among the trees, plants, and flowers, words like *lily, violet, wallflower, corn, crab apple, wild oats, clover, rue, savory, laurel, birch, balm*, and *fig leaf* have likewise taken on conventional figurative associations. Ranging farther afield, think of the expressive metaphors that have been built on words like *mouthpiece, grill, peaches and cream, bilge, forge, heart, head, honey, ginger, spice, vise, pincers, scalpel, plow*, and *anchor*.

It is, of course, easier to pass, by association, from the literal word or expression, like *throw in the towel*, to its meta-phorical meaning than to proceed in the opposite direction, but the latter exercise, if performed as the culmination of all the preceding variations, will go far toward developing in the child the power to express himself vividly.

BRAINY DAZE   VAR. 6

ALL LEVELS   *Blank cards (playing-card*
2 only   *size)*

This variation can be used to review the various forms of word association—reduplications, idioms, analogies, and other common two-word locutions or compounds.

First, make up a pack of cards consisting of matched pairs of words or parts of compounds forming expressions of the kind used in the five preceding variations. As before, the words selected will depend on the level of difficulty desired. To begin with, the deck should contain no more than forty cards, or twenty pairs, in order not to place too great a strain on the memory of each player. Different sets of cards with additional or substitute pairs of words can be kept in reserve for later rounds.

The game is played like CONCENTRATION (page 151). After the cards have been shuffled, they are spread out, face down, on the table. Picking up any two cards, the first player shows them to his opponent. If the cards should happen to match, that is, if they form a pair, like *shilly* and *shally*, *beaver* and *dam*, or *beaver* and *industriousness*, he places them face up on his side of the table and scores one point. He may then have another chance to find a matching pair of cards. If he is unsuccessful, he must return one card to its original place, face down, on the table after showing both cards to his opponent.

The second player now selects one card from among those lying face down on the table. If he thinks it makes a pair with the card that was put down by his opponent, he tries to remember that card's location. If he finds the matching card on his first try, he lays the pair face up on his side of the table, scores a point, and gets another chance to draw—two cards this time. Otherwise, he must place on the table, face down, one of the two cards in his hand, after showing both to his opponent, who then gets his chance to draw a card. At all times a card picked up from the table must be shown to the other player so that he can have an opportunity to memorize its location in case it is laid down again.

The game continues in this way until the last card has been drawn from the table. The winner is the player who has scored the most points. If, in order to escalate the game, the number of cards in the deck is increased in later rounds, the players will be better able to associate each card with the word on its face if a number (1, 2, 3, etc.) is written on its back.

KEEP YOUR WORD!   VAR. 7

ALL LEVELS   *Blank cards (playing-card*
2 *only*   *size)*

This variation can likewise be used as a review of the various forms of two-word locutions, combinations, and compounds learned in playing the preceding variations. It is played like SYNONYM WAR (page 153) and WORD WAR (page 155).

The deck is prepared as in BRAINY DAZE, above, except that the number of pairs of words or parts of compounds is increased. No fewer than twenty-six pairs, or fifty-two cards, should be used, at least at the beginning. Extra sets of cards can be reserved to raise the level of difficulty in subsequent rounds.

After the cards are shuffled, the deck is equally divided between the two players. Each places his stack of cards face down in front of him.

The first player now turns up the top card on his pile and lays it face up on the table before him. His opponent does likewise. If the card he turns up forms a pair with the other, he takes the latter and adds it to his own collection. If the card he turns up does not form a pair with the other, the first player exposes a card from his pile.

The players take turns in this way, exposing a card at a time. If a player exposes a card that makes a pair with the one on top of his opponent's turned-up pile, he takes the whole pile, placing it on top of his matched pack, and he takes the lead in turning up the next round of cards. After all the cards are face up, they are turned face down again, and the game proceeds until one player has captured all his opponent's words. The deck can then be expanded with additional cards, and a new round may begin.

What is that which is bought by the yard and worn by the foot?
A carpet.

Can you mention five common phrases in each of which the word MIND figures as a noun?
I gave him a piece of my mind.
I am of two minds.
We are of one mind.
I keep an open mind.
It's a case of mind over matter.

A sign in a dairy read: YOU CAN'T BEAT OUR MILK,
 BUT YOU CAN WHIP OUR CREAM.

Can you mention five common compounds or two-word phrases each of which begins with the name of something to eat?
Salad days, cauliflower ears, goose step, pork barrel, and grapeshot.

VII. Synonyms, Antonyms, and Homonyms

The games in this section are designed to extend the range of each player's vocabulary by familiarizing him with words that have more or less the same meaning (synonyms, like *fat*, *stout*, and *corpulent*) and words that are opposite in meaning (antonyms, like *tall* and *short*). Other games provide practice in recognizing, using, and spelling words that have the same sound but different meanings and spellings (homonyms, like *sweet* and *suite*).

SYNONYM RUMMY

INTERMEDIATE-ADVANCED   *Blank cards (playing-card*
2 *or more*   *size)*

An excellent way of enlarging a child's vocabulary is to teach him the synonyms of words he already knows. This game, besides doing that, offers you the opportunity of adjusting the difficulty to the abilities of the players and of introducing the synonyms that you would like them to learn.

Prepare cards in advance with one word on each. With the aid of a thesaurus, select words that form sets of synonyms—three, four, or five words per set—and exemplify the major parts of speech: nouns, verbs, adjectives, and adverbs. At least one or two of the synonyms in each set should be new for the players, or for some of the players, and should present a certain amount of difficulty. One card should be marked JOKER.

The size of the deck will depend on the number of players and, to some extent, of course, on the number of synonyms included in each set. About sixty cards should be prepared for two, three, or four players; sixty-five for five players; and around seventy for six players.

Now shuffle, cut, and deal, and follow the rules of rummy. In a two-handed game, ten cards are dealt to each player; in a three-handed game, seven cards; and when four or more play, six cards. The next card is then placed face up, beside the rest of the deck, which is laid face down.

Each player in turn must either draw a card from the top of the deck without showing it, or take the card that is lying face up beside the deck. After adding the new card to his hand, he must discard one from it, laying it face up either on top of the one already face up or in its place. Only the top card may be drawn from either of the two piles.

The object of the game is to collect sets of synonyms. Whenever a player has a pair or larger group of synonyms, he lays these cards on the table, face up. If he uses the joker, he must state what synonym he wants it to stand for. After drawing but before discarding, any player may get rid of a card from his hand by adding it to some set of synonyms already laid down by another player.

The first to get rid of all the cards in his hand wins the game. If several rounds are played, a point is scored by each player for every card he has laid down as part of a set of synonyms; and at the end of a number of rounds, the points are totaled to determine the winner.

ANTONYM RUMMY   VAR. 1

INTERMEDIATE-ADVANCED   *Blank cards (playing-card*
2 *or more*   *size)*

This variation, which can be played after SYNONYM RUMMY, above, is based on it and played like it, except that the cards are prepared in sets of antonyms, which the players then have to match up after the cards are shuffled and dealt.

In this variation, too, you have a chance to select the antonyms to suit the maturity and interests of the group, to introduce new words, and to extend the vocabulary of the players with different parts of speech.

This game can be made as easy or as difficult as one wishes. Easy combinations might include *thin* and *fat*, *long* and *short*, *big* and *little*, and *up* and *down*. On the other hand, relatively difficult combinations can be set up, like *quench* and *ignite*, *incarcerate* and *liberate*, *inculpate* and *exonerate*, and *repudiate* and *acknowledge*.

SYNONYM MATCH   VAR. 2

INTERMEDIATE-ADVANCED   *Clock or timer*

2 *or more*

This variation, besides adding synonyms to the child's vocabulary, strengthens what may be called "verbal readiness"; that is, it increases the verbal resources he has at his command for immediate recall and use.

The first player calls out a word for which he knows at least one synonym. The next player must, within a given time, "match" the word by providing any synonym of it, and as many more as he can think of. He receives one point for each synonym he calls out. If he cannot think of any, he may challenge the first player to state what synonym he had in mind. Any failure in this respect is penalized one point, to discourage the introduction of words that have no synonyms. A player fails to score a point if he is unable to think of a synonym, and he is penalized one point if he responds with a word that is not a synonym of the word proposed by the preceding player.

The object is to squeeze as many synonyms out of the original word as possible. If a player can think of only one or two, his opponent may add a few points to his score by thinking of some others. How far this process goes will depend, of course, on the abilities of the players and on the words they choose to begin with. If, for example, *fat* is the first word called out, the players might suggest *chubby*, *beefy*, *stocky*, *thick*, and *heavy-set* before breaking down. A more advanced group might be able to go on to *portly*, *rotund*, *paunchy*, *obese*, *corpulent*, etc.

A good way of keeping score for this game is to use the device of FIREMAN UP THE LADDER (page 322).

When the possibilities of a given word have been exhausted, a new one, preferably of a different part of speech (noun, verb, adverb, etc.), can be proposed.

A thesaurus should be kept handy to settle any disputed points.

ANTONYM MATCH   VAR. 3

INTERMEDIATE-ADVANCED   *Clock or timer*
2 *or more*

This is the counterpart and natural continuation of the preceding variation. After the players have provided the synonyms of a word, they can learn its antonyms and extend their vocabulary still further, especially as there may be several synonyms of the antonyms.

The game is played in the same way as SYNONYM MATCH, except that the players have to match antonyms.

Thus, if *fat* (to take the preceding example) is the given word, the appropriate response might be *thin*. Now the next player might suggest an antonym of *thin* (i.e., a synonym of *fat*), without using the word *fat*. In this way, the game builds on SYNONYM MATCH. For example, *chubby* might be matched by *lanky*, *paunchy* by *slender*, *beefy* by *slim*, *obese* by *lean*, and *portly* by *gaunt*.

At a more advanced level, this game can be used to teach children the prefixes that turn words into their antonyms: *ir*, *de*, *a*, *mis*, *dis*, *in*, *im*, *un*, etc., making words like *disappear*, *disservice*, *unmistakable*, *irreparable*, *decontrol*, *indi-*

visible, and *amoral.* The problem then becomes one of deciding whether to say *unsanitary* or *insanitary*, *immobile* or *unmobile,* and so forth. Similarly, children learn how to add suffixes like *less* (*hopeless*) and *ful* (*hopeful*) to form antonyms.

As with SYNONYM MATCH, different parts of speech can be used.

An appropriate method of keeping score for this game is HIGH MAN ON THE PYRAMID (page 327).

HOMONYM RUMMY

INTERMEDIATE-ADVANCED   *Blank cards* (*playing-card*
2 *or more*   *size*)

Many children have difficulty in distinguishing among homonyms—words that sound alike but are spelled differently and have different meanings, like *to, two,* and *too* or *there, they're,* and *their.* This fascinating game helps them to learn to use and spell homonyms correctly.

The cards, prepared by parent or teacher, should consist of sets matched according to meaningful combinations of words that have homonyms. (A list may be found in the appendixes.) Thus, corresponding to *mown* might be a card with *lawn* written on it, while its counterpart set might consist of one card with *moan* and another with *agonized.* The game tests the players' understanding of the meanings of homonyms as they might be significantly combined with other words.

Here, for example, are some typical cards from one such deck: PALETTE and PAINTER'S, PALATE and SENSITIVE, PALLET and SOFT, LODE and STONE, LOAD and HEAVY, and LOWED and COW.

After the sets have been prepared with words chosen to suit the ability and maturity of the players, the cards should be thoroughly shuffled and then dealt to the players. The rules of rummy are followed, as in SYNONYM RUMMY and ANTONYM RUMMY, above, but this time the players must find pairs of words that go together meaningfully. No credit will be given for a combination like *laps* and *lapse* unless the player can also lay down the cards with the words that go with them—let us say, *milk* and *time*. Naturally, the correct word order should be indicated when the cards are laid on the table.

The game can be made as easy or as difficult as the abilities and needs of the players may determine. Thus, an easy form of the game might be developed by having the matching card represent the meaning of the homonym rather than the word that can be combined with it. For example, *in* could be matched with *within* and *inn* with *tavern*. Among the words that offer interesting possibilities at the elementary level are *plain, ate, ball, foul, heard, hall, heel, hear, pain, made,* and *past.* A group of intermediate difficulty might include words like *hose, night, lesson, dying, earn, choose,* and *cereal.* More advanced players should be challenged with the homonyms of *stationary, cue, freeze, dam, council, cord, hair,* and *need.* For a really bright and mature group, try building combinations with homonyms of *idol, profit, current, leech, indict, hide, coin, liar, handsome, pole, step, vial, rough,* and *rack.*

Can you mention five common compounds or two-word phrases each of which contains a word denoting something botanical?
Grass widow, straw vote, haywire, poppycock, and mossback.

What's a synonym?
It's a word you use when you can't spell the other one.

Write a number over each of the blanks and produce nine common words: cocka———, ———tune, ———der, in———, any———, sed———, ———or, k———, or ———der.
Cocka2, 4tune, 10der, in2, any1, sed8, 10or, k9, 1der.

HOMONYM MATCH

INTERMEDIATE-ADVANCED   *Clock or timer*
2 *only*

In this game the players learn to distinguish among homonyms by matching them in complete sentences in which they are used correctly.

The first player forms a sentence in which he uses a word that he knows has a homonym. For example, he may begin by saying, "She will sew a dress."

The second player has to decide, within a given time, which word in that sentence has a homonym and then use the homonym correctly in a matching sentence of his own. He would be wrong, for example, if he said, "Is she still at the same address?" But he would be right and score a point if he said, "So what?" If he cannot think of a homonym to match his opponent's, he may challenge the latter to supply a sentence with its appropriate matching homonym. Since there is a penalty of two points for failure to do so, the formation of sentences with words that have no homonyms is discouraged.

Let us follow this particular dialogue for a while:

PLAYER 1: I know it.
PLAYER 2: No, you don't. Didn't you see it?
PLAYER 1: Yes, it's floating on the sea. It's a flea.
PLAYER 2: Perhaps it's trying to flee. I'll see you later.
PLAYER 1: On a desert isle I suppose.

Players may begin with the easy and obvious combinations like *so*, *sew*, and *sow*; *rain*, *reign*, and *rein*; *rode*, *road*, and *rowed*; *meat*, *meet*, and *mete*; and proceed to more difficult ones like *necklace* and *neckless*, *patience* and *patients*, *plum* and *plumb*; *praise*, *prays*, and *preys*; *feign*, *fain*, and *fane*; *gate* and *gait*, *gorilla* and *guerrilla*, *ewes* and *yews*, and *sight*, *cite*, and *site*.

Other words with homonyms that some players may have difficulty in spelling or using are *sink*, *combing*, *carrot*, *symbol*, *core*, *nice*, *new*, *grieves*, *pair*, and *mean*, not to speak of *gambol*, *yolk*, and *straight*.

In order to emphasize correct spelling and to familiarize the players with homonyms, the list appended at the back of this book may be used, with the players referring to it for words and pointing out the matching homonym on the list as they propose a matching sentence in which the homonym is correctly used. This procedure not only makes the game easier in some respects but it introduces the players to a wide variety of homonyms they might not have thought of and ensures that they know how to spell and use the homonyms properly.

CONCENTRATION

ALL LEVELS   *Blank cards (playing-card*
2 *only*   *size)*

This versatile game can be used to teach synonyms, antonyms, homonyms, common phrases, or any desired combination of them. As its name indicates, it promotes concentration and requires a good memory.

A deck of cards, arranged in matched pairs, is prepared by the parent or teacher. The pairs of words selected for the cards will depend on what is to be taught and the level of difficulty desired. Thus, if antonyms are to be matched, cards may include, at the elementary level, pairs like *fat* and *skinny*, *stop* and *go*, *night* and *day*, and *short* and *tall*, and correspondingly more difficult pairs at a more advanced grade. If common phrases are to be matched, the cards may include *spick* and *span*, *ham* and *eggs*, *willy* and *nilly*, *touch* and *go*, *to* and *fro*, *etc.* If homonyms are to be matched, pairs can be selected, as desired, from the list appended at the back of this book.

The number of cards in the deck will depend on the players' powers of concentration. A great strain is placed on their memory if more than forty cards—i.e., twenty pairs—are used at one time, but extra sets, with different pairs of words, can be kept in reserve for successive rounds.

All the cards, after being thoroughly shuffled, are spread out, helter-skelter, face down on the table. The first player then picks up two cards at random and shows them to his opponent. If the cards match—i.e., if they make an appropriate pair (synonyms, antonyms, homonyms, etc.)—the first player places them face up on his side of the table and scores one point. He may then have another try at finding a matching pair. If he cannot do so, he must return one of them, after showing both to his opponent, face down, to its former place.

The second player now picks one card at random from those lying face down on the table. He tries to remember the position and the wording of the card that was put down by his opponent in order to determine whether it will match the card in his hand. If, either through luck in picking up his second card or through correctly remembering the location of the card he needs, he succeeds in getting a matched pair, he lays both cards down, face up, on his side of the table, scores one point, and draws again. If, at this point, the second player has used the first player's discard, the second player now draws two cards. At all times, a card that is picked up from the table must be shown to one's opponent in order to give him a chance to memorize its location in case it is put down again.

The game proceeds in this way until the last card has been picked up from the table. The winner is the player with the highest score.

Complications can be added by gradually raising the level of difficulty in matching words in successive rounds and increasing, a pair at a time, the number of cards in the deck with each round. But in that case the back of each card should have written on it a number (1, 2, 3, etc.) as an aid to the players in associating it with the word on its face.

SYNONYM WAR

INTERMEDIATE-ADVANCED   *Blank cards (playing-card*
2 *only*   *size)*

This game teaches children to recognize synonyms and
enables the parent or teacher to select the ones he would like
to have the players learn.

The deck is prepared as in SYNONYM RUMMY with sets
of synonyms (preferably three or four in each set, like *easy,
simple, effortless, uncomplicated,* etc.) of varying difficulty,
selected with the aid of a thesaurus to meet the particular
needs of the players. The greater the number of sets of synonyms, the better; but a deck of at least fifty-two cards—i.e.,
thirteen sets of four synonyms—should be used, and the extra sets of cards can then be reserved to "escalate" the difficulty in successive rounds after the players have become familiar with the more elementary synonyms used at first.

The cards are thoroughly shuffled, and the deck is divided equally between the two players. Each places his
stack of cards in front of him, face down. This is his pile of
"ammunition."

Now the first player turns up the top card on his pile and
lays it face up on the table near him. Then the second player
does the same thing. If the card he turns up is a synonym of
the other, he takes his opponent's card, starts a separate pile
of paired synonyms, face down, and turns up another card.
If the card he draws does not match his opponent's, the latter
exposes another card from his pile. They continue taking
turns turning up one card at a time. Each time a player exposes a synonym of the card at the top of his opponent's
turned-up pile, he takes the whole pile, placing it on top of
his own pack. When all the cards in the stack are face up,
they are turned face down again, and the game continues
until one player has won all his opponent's ammunition.

The supply can then be replenished with fresh cards, and a new battle may begin. There can be many variations.

ANTONYM WAR   VAR. 1

INTERMEDIATE-ADVANCED   *Blank cards (playing-card*
2 *only*   *size)*

This is essentially the same game as SYNONYM WAR, except that the deck of cards is prepared with sets of antonyms of increasing difficulty, likewise selected from a thesaurus.

The game can be further complicated by preparing cards with synonyms of the antonyms, thereby adding to the players' vocabulary. In fact, the deck of antonyms may be sifted into the deck used in SYNONYM WAR. In that case, a matched pair of cards could consist of either synonyms or antonyms.

HOMONYM WAR   VAR. 2

INTERMEDIATE-ADVANCED   *Blank cards (playing-card*
2 *only*   *size)*

This variation is played in the same way, but the deck is prepared as in HOMONYM RUMMY, with sets of homonyms (preferably three to a set, like *for*, *fore*, and *four*) selected from the list appended at the back of this book, according to the abilities and maturity of the players. Two possible ways of matching cards in this game may be chosen. Homonyms may be matched with one another; or, in case some homonyms come in pairs only, like *night* and *knight*, each should be complemented by at least two cards, either of which could be matched with it (like *good* and *dark* with *night* and *errant* and *gallant* with *knight*), to make certain that players can select the appropriate word in each case.

What is the opposite of "not in"?
Did you say "Out"? Well, you're wrong. It's "in"!

WORD WAR   VAR. 3

INTERMEDIATE-ADVANCED   *Blank cards (playing-card*
2 *only*   *size)*

This is the supreme war game with cards and can serve as a
kind of "review" of synonyms, antonyms, and homonyms,
for it combines all three types of words.

In preparing the deck, the parent or teacher can include
some sets of words already familiar to the children from previous games of SYNONYM WAR, ANTONYM WAR, and
HOMONYM WAR, as well as new sets of words of greater
difficulty.

In this variation, any kind of match will entitle a player
to take his opponent's entire pile of turned-up cards: a synonym, an antonym, a homonym, or a word that combines
appropriately with one of a set of homonyms, synonyms, or
antonyms.

VIII. Group Games

Though some of the games in this chapter can be played by
only two, others can have three or more participants. In large
families, or where friends of the children join in, word games
involving a group, with teams of players, can add to the fun.
Here are a few that are best suited to parties or gatherings.

TEAKETTLE

INTERMEDIATE-ADVANCED
Large families or groups

This old favorite is an excellent game for teaching the difference in meaning between homonyms.

One player, the victim, goes out of the room, while the rest agree on a pair of homonyms. When the victim returns, he asks each player a question in an effort to determine what the homonyms are. The responses must be so phrased as to require the use of either one of the homonyms, but the word "teakettle" must be substituted for them. From these clues the victim must discover the words that "teakettle"stands for.

For example, suppose the homonyms chosen are KNOWS and NOSE. The dialogue between the victim and his tormentors might proceed as follows:

VICTIM: Is it something you buy?

PLAYER 1: You can buy a false teakettle, but not the real teakettle.

VICTIM: Is it something you wear?

PLAYER 2: Everyone teakettles he has a teakettle, but you can't wear a real teakettle.

VICTIM: Is it something you do?

PLAYER 3: It's something you *can* do. Everyone here now teakettles but you!

VICTIM: Is it something in this room?

PLAYER 4: It's as plain as the teakettle on your face.

After that clue, let us hope the victim knows his nose!

Good sets of homonyms for this game are *pries* and *prize*, *pore* and *pour*, *would* and *wood*, *sail* and *sale*, *read* and *red*, *steal* and *steel*, *tail* and *tale*, *hour* and *our*, and *flour* and *flower*.

The game can be complicated by using the word "teakettle" to represent three words that are homonyms, like *cent*, *scent*, and *sent*, or *seer*, *sear*, and *sere*, or *rode*, *road*, and *rowed*.

A variation of this game can be played by using "teakettle" to represent two entirely different meanings of the same word, such as *hind* (a deer and rear), *left*, *beam*, *part*, *fare*, *game*, *rose*, *safe*, *soil*, *stole*, etc.

For a grammatical variation of the same game, see COF-FEEPOT (page 294).

MYSTERY WORD

ADVANCED

Large families or groups

This game teaches the players the different meanings that the same word can have in different contexts.

Two of the players secretly agree on some word, preferably one that has a number of different meanings, like *free*. They then engage in a conversation with each other, a sentence at a time, in which clues to the word, as used in various senses, are given without any mention of the word itself. Meanwhile, the other players take turns trying to guess the word from the clues.

One point is scored by each of the two conversationalists every time any other player guesses wrong.

For example, with the word FREE, the conversation might begin like this:

PLAYER 1: I'd like that kind of pass to the ball game.

PLAYER 2: I like that kind of verse.

PLAYER 1: You don't feel that way in prison.

PLAYER 2: But that's the way little children ride on trains.

PLAYER 1: I wouldn't want a translation to be too much like that.

PLAYER 2: Some people are like that with their money.

When the word has been guessed, two other players take their turn as the conversationalists. The object is to see which two players can keep their word a mystery for the longest time.

A passenger asked a porter how long a train would be in the station. The porter answered, "Four minutes, sir. From ——— ——— ——— ——— ——— ———." The six dashes represent the same word or its homonym. What are the words?

" . . . *two to two to two two.*"

What word is the favorite of women?
The last word.

Why is it that I cannot spell "Cupid"?
Because when I get to C U, I forget everything else.

What should you do if you catch your dog eating up your dictionary?
Take the words right out of his mouth!

What single word would you put down to indicate that forty dollars had been borrowed from you?
EXCELLENT (XL-LENT).

What word do you associate with an icicle?
EAVESDROPPER.

How would you describe musicians who failed to arrive on time for their performance?
Disconcerted.

How would you describe wine merchants who found that their wine presses had broken down during the vintage?
Depressed.

What would you say of a superlative ocean liner that had nowhere to dock?
It had no peer (pier).

What would you say of a man who had lost his way in the woods and ate a poisonous tuber?
He obviously didn't know the right route (root) to take.

What fruit should a lover send his girl friend as a secret message that he cannot keep his tryst with her?
Cantaloupe.

PUTTING ON THE DOG

ALL LEVELS   *Clock or timer*
Large families or groups

This game capitalizes on children's love of big words and
fancy language. It adds to their vocabulary by acquainting
them with the "high-brow" synonyms of common words they
already know.

Essentially, this is a variation of SYNONYM MATCH
(page 146), but adapted to a large group that can be divided
into two teams of more or less equal maturity and ability.

The leader calls out a simple word, generally of one syllable, and, within a given time limit, the first player on Team 1
must match it with a "highfalutin" synonym. The matching
word need not be longer than one syllable, but it must definitely be high-brow.

If the player fails to match the word before the whistle is
blown, his opposite number on the second team gets a chance
to score. One point is gained for each correct synonym.

Here are a few examples of "upgraded" language:

eat	dine	give	donate
think	cogitate	pants	trousers
job	position	glasses	spectacles
wash	launder	stockings	hosiery
sweat	perspiration	city	metropolis

What is the difference between a cat *and a* comma?
A cat *has its claws at the end of its paws; a* comma *has its pause
at the end of a clause.*

When is it easy to read in the woods?
When autumn turns the leaves.

HIGH-BROW PROVERBS   VAR. 1

INTERMEDIATE-ADVANCED   *Paper and pencil*
Large families or groups   *Small slips of paper*
                                    Clock or timer

This variation, which makes use of polysyllabic humor, is
best suited to more mature groups that would like to learn
"big words" and to show off their knowledge of them. Children at this stage have to learn that words, like clothes, must
be chosen to suit the occasion. They need help in developing
a sense of the appropriateness of different levels of usage and
in appreciating the incongruities of tone in their choice of
language.

An excellent vocabulary-builder, this game introduces
new words in their context, teaches the correct use of synonyms, and provides practice in "shifting gears" from the colloquial to the formal level and back again to the colloquial.

Write a proverb on each of several slips of paper, and give
one to every player.

Within a given time, each player has to rewrite the proverb he has on his paper in the most elegant and elaborate
language possible. He then reads aloud his "translation" of
the proverb, and the other players must state what proverb
he started with.

For example, the proverb might be: "People who live in
glass houses shouldn't throw stones." The elegant version
might read as follows: "Denizens of vitreous abodes constructed from the transparent, brittle, and fragile substance
produced by the fusion of silica should abstain from impart-
ing momentum to missiles of petrified, lapidary, or mineral
material."

Conversely, what proverb is the colloquial way of saying,
"An imprudent emphasis on celerity in the performance of
a given task frequently has as its consequence an undesirable

retardation in the rapidity with which the completion of the task is achieved and a reduction in total productivity"? Why, "Haste makes waste," of course! Naturally, the same proverb admits of other high-brow versions, like "Accelerated execution is counterproductive."

Here is another proverb in the same vein: "Don't lament audibly about the inadvertent overturn of a vessel containing lacteal fluid." The translation into its common form should be easy.

The rich possibilities of this game may be seen from the following examples of proverbs that need to be brought back to earth:

"A canine that gives vent to its sentiments by a series of vocal effects seldom finds use for its bicuspids."

"The customary symbol of regal power does not necessarily indicate a condition of tranquility."

"Persons of exiguous intellectual power project themselves precipitately into situations in which the winged, ethereal likenesses of men hesitate to perambulate."

"Unwonted egotism precedes the effect of the force of gravity."

"Avoid calculating the possible number of your juvenile poultry before the usual period of incubation has been completed."

"Refrain from traversing a structure erected to afford passage over a waterway prior to the time of your arrival at its location."

"Each mass of vaporous substance suspended in the firmament has an exterior decoration of metallic hue."

These, of course, are just polysyllabic ways of expressing the ideas of such common proverbs as "A barking dog never bites," "Uneasy lies the head that wears a crown," "Fools rush in where angels fear to tread," "Pride goeth before a fall," "Don't count your chickens before they are hatched," "Don't cross a bridge before you get to it," and "Every cloud has a silver lining."

HIGH-BROW SLANG   VAR. 2

INTERMEDIATE-ADVANCED   *Paper and pencil*
Large families or groups

This variation makes its educational point by similar means.
It, too, contrasts the ordinary way of saying things with
"highfalutin" language and aims at teaching children that
good English is appropriate to the occasion.

Each player is to write down a slang expression. Then he
has to express the same thought in formal, dignified language. The players next take turns in reading aloud the elegant versions, while the rest try to translate them back into
their original form.

For example, "I put one over on him" might become "By
craft and cunning, I succeeded in achieving the object of my
stratagem, at his expense."

Conversely, "Refrain from assuming an overweening arro-
gance, haughty ostentation, or pretentious pomp" is a fancy
way of saying "Don't put on the dog!"

HIGH-BROW DEFINITIONS   VAR. 3

ADVANCED   *Paper and pencil*
Large families or groups

In this variation the players are called upon to display a considerable amount of verbal knowledge and skill. It adds to
their vocabulary and gives them practice in framing definitions. Incidentally, the game is also a good way of sharpening their ability to do crossword puzzles.

Each player is to write down a common word and then
define it in the fanciest and most elaborate language he can
think of. The players then take turns reading their definitions aloud, while the rest try to determine what words are
being defined.

For example, a *cranial habiliment* is nothing more nor less than a hat. Conversely, breakfast can become a *matutinal refection*, a clock a *horological mechanism*, blood, *sanguinary corporeal fluid*, and a native an *autochthonous denizen*. A *capsulized derivative of salicyclic acid* is aspirin, and a *fortuitous concatenation of eventualities* is an accident.

WHISTLE STOP

ALL LEVELS   *Whistle*
Large families or groups   *Clock or timer*

This game places a premium on alertness and mental celerity. Like CATEGORIES and its variations (page 108), it teaches children to group ideas logically. It can be used to build vocabulary in any field or subject—history, geography, science, music, etc.

Instruct the children to listen carefully as you call out a series of four words. Before you blow your whistle, they must say which word does *not* fit in with the other three. Of course, a correct answer must be explained by the player who gives it if he is to score a point for it.

If there is a tie among the children, or if there is doubt about who spoke up first, runoffs can be held to see who is the quickest in finding the incongruity.

The game can be made increasingly difficult, as the following sequence of combinations shows:

HARP, VIOLIN, ORCHESTRA, DRUM
BAT, FLAGPOLE, GOLF CLUB, TENNIS RACKET
MONKEY, FROG, GIRAFFE, DOG
ATLANTIC, PACIFIC, ARCTIC, TEMPERATE
HAT, HANDKERCHIEF, GLOVES, TROUSERS
SIT, TABLE, WALK, BEND
SUN, CLOUDS, RAIN, FOG
FATHER, MOTHER, BROTHER, UNCLE
VIXEN, DOE, DRAKE, COW

SHOES, FLOOR, FINGERNAILS, FURNITURE

(Yes, you polish all four of the last, but only three of them begin with F!)

Other ways of complicating the game are to make sets with synonyms, antonyms, homonyms, and different parts of speech, or to add to the number of items in each series.

BLOW THE WHISTLE!

ELEMENTARY-INTERMEDIATE   *Whistle*
Large families or groups   *Clock or timer*

Like WHISTLE STOP, this game demands a speedy response. It is essentially a game of word association designed to familiarize children with common groups of three words each.

Instruct the children to listen carefully as you call out a series of two words. Before you blow your whistle, they must add the third word that completes the group.

In case of a tie or doubt about who answered first, a runoff should be held.

Here, for example, are some sets that can be used in this game.

Red, white, and ———.
Sun, moon, and ———.
Ready, set, ———.
Tom, Dick, and ———.
Hook, line, and ———.
Man, woman, and ———.
Stop, look, and ———.
Lock, stock, and ———.
Healthy, wealthy, and ———.
Deaf, dumb, and ———.
Hop, skip, and ———.
Reading, writing, and ———.
Faith, hope, and ———.
Morning, noon, and ———.

Wine, women, and ————.
Knife, fork, and ————.
Ear, nose, and ————.
Ready, willing, and ————.
Fair, fat, and ————.
Give, devise, and ————.

The game can also be played with sets of two, like *nip* and *tuck*, *time* and *tide*, *fame* and *fortune*, *fair* and *foul*, etc.

PUNNY FUNNY

INTERMEDIATE-ADVANCED   *Paper and pencil*
Large families or groups   *Clock or timer*

This game appeals to children's love of jokes, especially puns or plays on words, and encourages creativity in inventing them. At the same time, it familiarizes the players with the spelling and meaning of common homonyms.

To establish the mood and to show what is wanted, begin with a little "spice" in the form of puns like those in this book. Then provide the players with a list of frequently confused homonyms taken from those in the list appended at the back of this book.

The players are given a reasonable amount of time to think up original jokes or amusing riddles in which these homonyms figure. When time is up, each player reads what he has produced. The one with the best or the greatest number of witty puns on the given homonyms wins the game.

Another way of playing the game is to let the players put their "teasers" to one another in the form of questions and see whether their opponents can then work out the rest of the joke for themselves. For example, given such homonyms as PLANE and PLAIN, NAVEL and NAVAL, NECKLACE and NECKLESS, PATIENCE and PATIENTS, PEAR and PAIR, GUILT and GILT, SEA and SEE, here is how one group, after a suitable time for cogitation, proceeded:

PLAYER 1 : When is a goldsmith likely to be embarrassed?

PLAYER 2 : When his gilt [guilt] is all over his face.

PLAYER 3 : When is a doctor most likely to complain?

PLAYER 4 : When he has lost all his patients [patience].

PLAYER 5 : How would you describe a double-chinned jewelry salesman?

PLAYER 6 : As a neckless [necklace] vendor.

PLAYER 7 : What's the difference between a nonfat diet and an international disarmament treaty?

PLAYER 8 : One is aimed at navel reduction; the other, at naval reduction.

PLAYER 1 : When is a person likely to have a broad, unencumbered field of vision in all directions?

PLAYER 2 : When he's on a plane [plain].

PLAYER 3 : When is a fruit like a couple?

PLAYER 4 : When it's a pair [pear].

PLAYER 5 : What's the difference between a blind man and a confused sailor?

PLAYER 6 : One can't see at all, and the other is all at sea.

Naturally, extra credit goes to the player who can come up with a double pun, like this:

Q. What's the difference between the principal part of a meal and thick hair on a horse?

A. One is the *main course*, and the other is a *coarse mane*.

In such a case, the extra credit is shared equally between the inventor of the double pun and anyone who can answer his question; if no one can, he gets all the credit himself.

The game can be complicated by giving the players only one of the pair of homonyms and by insisting on their spelling correctly each homonym they use.

What is a word of fifteen letters from which you can subtract twelve and leave ten?
PRETENTIOUSNESS.

Why can't a bicycle stand by itself?
It's too (two) tired.

What word is always pronounced wrong?
WRONG.

Why is a baggage car like a forest?
Because it is full of trunks.

When is a piece of wood like a queen?
When it is made into a ruler.

What appropriate phrase could be made by using all the letters of
"French Revolution"?
Violence run forth.

What musical instrument is bound to make misleading noises?
A lyre, of course.

How do you distinguish among the following: (1) a man who pur-
chases a masquerade costume, (2) several timely and economical
purchases, and (3) a group of clever fellows?
The first buys guise; the second are wise buys; and the last are
wise guys.

What common word means all of these things: (1) typical, (2)
prevalent, (3) miscellaneous, (4) approximate, and (5) an Army
officer?
GENERAL.

What is the difference between here *and* there?
The letter t.

A busy executive put the following sign outside his door: IM2BZ-
2CU. What was he trying to say?
I am too busy to see you.

WORD-Y

INTERMEDIATE-ADVANCED
Large families or groups

Blank cards (bingo or lotto size)
Small strips of paper
Small colored cardboard squares

Played like bingo, this game is a good way to review synonyms and antonyms.

Each player receives a card like the one shown below.

W	O	R	D	Y
OBESE	GOOD	IGNITE	ACKNOWLEDGE	VETO
BIG	UP	UNITE	LONG	PROMOTE
SELL	HATE	CAUTIOUS	FOE	ESTEEM
DEVIL	KIND	WORSE	PLEASURE	FREE
CLEAN	HEALTH	BROAD	PROVE	SOUR

Of course, aside from the top line, all the cards are different in that other words are used or the same words are placed in other boxes. Words can be selected according to the abilities of the players and should exemplify various parts of speech (nouns: FOE; verbs: IGNITE; adjectives: BIG; adverbs: UP; etc.). A few words like CLEAN should be of the type that can be used as more than one part of speech so that they can be matched with a number of different synonyms and antonyms—e.g., *dirty, scrub, pure*, and so on.

In addition, the players receive a number of small colored squares of cardboard that can be placed over the boxes on the card.

Slips of paper are prepared, each containing a letter of WORD-Y followed by either the synonym or the antonym of a word shown on a box in one of the cards—e.g., W-FAT, O-BRIGHT, R-HEAVY, D-SUFFER, etc.

From a box into which these slips have been placed, the

leader selects one and reads it to the players. Suppose he picks up O-LOVE. All the players now check their cards to see whether they have a box in the row under the letter O with a word that is the synonym or the antonym of LOVE. (In the particular card shown here, it is the third box down in the second column, with the word HATE.) Whoever has such a box writes the word *love* on one of his colored cardboard squares and places it over the box on his card.

The game proceeds in this way until one of the players has covered a whole row, horizontally, vertically, or diagonally. He then calls out "WORD-Y" and hands his card to the leader to have it checked. Of course, he gets no credit if he has improperly matched the word on his card with the word written on his cardboard square. Thus, although success in WORD-Y, as in most card games, does depend to some extent on luck, it also calls for a good vocabulary.

If this game is played according to the rules of lotto rather than bingo, a player would have to cover *all* the boxes on his card in order to win.

I DOUBT IT

ADVANCED
Large families or groups

Paper and pencil
Blank cards (playing-card size)

This is a dictionary game. It can be played just for fun, although it does build vocabulary.

Select a number of words from the dictionary that are not likely to be known to the players, like *moucharaby, passement, sciamachy, ultracrepidarian, stochastic, clone, terete, inconcinnity, misocapnic, sialagogue, oneirotic, staurolatry,* or *catachthonian.* (There are plenty more like them where these came from!)

Write each word on a card and under it its correct definition.

Now divide the players into two equal teams. Give a blank card to each member of Team A. Then pronounce and spell the first word on your list. Everyone on Team A must write the word on his card and under it a definition of it that he believes to be correct. If he does not know the meaning of the word, he is to write a definition that looks plausible and scientific. On the back of the card he is to write his name.

Next collect the cards and examine them to see whether anyone has the correct definition. If so, Team A receives two points. Shuffle the cards and return the pack to any member of Team A. If no player has correctly defined the word, insert your own card into the pack before shuffling it and returning it to a member of Team A.

When the first definition is read aloud from the card on which it has been written, the first player on Team B must decide whether or not it is correct. If he does not accept the definition as correct, he says, "I doubt it." The next definition is presented in the same way to the next player, and the same procedure is followed until all the definitions have been read and judged.

For every incorrect definition that is rejected, Team B receives one point. If the correct definition is accepted, Team B wins two points. No points are scored if a faulty definition is accepted or the correct definition is rejected. Of course, no information about the correctness of a definition or scoring is given until all the proposed definitions have been read and judged.

Then a new word is tried, with Team B this time writing the definitions, and Team A determining whether or not they are correct.

For example, for the word TERETE, the following definitions might be proposed:

1. Ruler of Sumerian city-state who combined religious and secular functions.
2. Saucerlike vessel of earthenware or metal used by South African tribes.

3. Upright timber on the bilge ways fore and aft to support a vessel in launching.

4. A species of Indian corn with exceptionally short tassels.

5. Having the shape of a cylinder, but with a taper.

6. A wild plum of the western United States.

In this case, the answer is No. 5.

~~~~~~

Read this three times, each time faster than before:

I twice priced iced ox tripe.
Price white-striped sox.
Write: "Right type of sliced tripe's price's right."
Typewrite: "Swipe tripe and white-striped sox."

Read this three times, each time faster than before:

I'm back to back a tobacco tax.
It takes tact to tax backs. It takes tact to back a tax. Back attacked taxes! Tax tacks! It takes tact to attack a tack tax. Attach back taxes. Tacks attach tax to back. Attach back tobacco tax to back and tack back tack tax back-to-back.

Read this three times, each time faster than before:

Wicked witches switch wishes.
Which wicked witches swish wicket switches?
Which witch swishes?
Which witches wish wicked wishes?
Which witch wishes?
Wish a witch; switch a witch;
Swish a witch; switch witches.
A witch's a witch; a swish's a swish; a wish's a wish.
Which witch switched a witch?
Which witch's which?

Say this three times, each time faster than before:

This snail's stale. His tail's stale. This snail's tail's stale. This snail's tail's still stale. This snail tale's stale.

Read this three times, each time faster than before:

Why try wine? Try tying twine. Tying twine tires? Try twisting twine or tying twists. Wrists tire? Try twice twisting twine. Twill's twine twice twisted; untwisted, 'twill untwine. Twist twill; 'twill twist. Untwist twill; 'twill untwist. Twist wrist; untwist wrist; rest wrist.

Read this three times, each time faster than before:

She's so selfish.
She should sell shellfish,
But shellfish shells
Seldom sell.

A broker canceled a customer's order when a telegram from him arrived with the one word CANCEL. *But the message that the customer really wanted sent was* CAN SELL.

A parent was much surprised to be told by her child that no reading was allowed in the school library.
But when she went to school to investigate, everything was cleared up. The sign in the library read:
NO READING ALOUD IN THE LIBRARY!

Can you use all the letters in the word LOWEST to make a sentence that is appropriate to its meaning?
We lost.

Using the letters of the word TRAIN, what sentence can you compose that would be appropriate for the meaning of the word?
It ran.

6

ALPHABET AND SPELLING
GAMES

A MAN named Turner registered at a hotel as Mr. Phtholognyrrh. He explained to the bewildered desk clerk that Phtholognyrrh is pronounced Turner because *phth* in *phthisic* is pronounced "t," *olo* is sounded as "ur" in *colonel*, *gn* has the sound of "n" in *gnaw*, and *yrrh* is pronounced "er" in *myrrh*.

This story well illustrates the absurdity of English spelling and the problem it presents to the child—and, for that matter, to the adult as well. There seems to be little consistency between spelling and pronunciation; there are exceptions to virtually all the spelling rules; and, to make matters worse, some of the most commonly used words are among the ones that are the hardest to spell. Yet spelling errors, precisely because they are the easiest to find and demonstrate, are widely taken as the most obvious signs of illiteracy or inadequate training.

Nevertheless, in spite of what may look at first like formidable difficulties, learning to spell can be a stimulating and challenging experience, full of fascination and excitement, if it is turned into a game or a series of games. Many of the games listed in the preceding chapter on vocabulary-building are, in fact, spelling games as well, and they could have been included here. By the same token, some of the games listed in this chapter could also have appeared with the grammar and sentence games. For it is practically impossible—and certainly not sound pedagogically—to separate spelling from vocabulary-building, grammar, and sentence structure.

I. Initial Letters

All these games use the alphabet, not as a series of isolated letters memorized in a fixed sequence, but as a means of representing sounds in the spelling of common words.

Several games can be played with *initial letters*.

ALPHABETICAL ADJECTIVES

ELEMENTARY   *Clock or timer*
3 *or more*

This game introduces a child to one of the parts of speech— a word that describes. Besides teaching spelling and the sequence of letters in the alphabet, it helps him to form coherent sentences.

Each player must try to describe himself or someone else in a series of adjectives whose initial letters follow an alphabetical sequence, like this:

"Jane is *a*musing, *b*eautiful, *c*harming, *d*elightful, *ea*ger ⁓ . ."

Or each player may be called upon in turn to add an adjective to this list within a given period of time. (See Variation 2, below.)

In what sort of syllables should a parrot speak?
In polysyllables, of course.

ALPHABETICAL NOUNS   VAR. 1

ELEMENTARY   *Clock or timer*

3 or more

In this variation the child is introduced, by a natural extension of the game, to another part of speech—the noun.

Make up any statement that needs to be completed with the addition of a noun—e.g., "I gave my girl some _____."

Now ask each player, in turn, to mention an appropriate noun, making up a series whose first letters follow an alphabetical sequence. A reasonable time limit should be set for each response.

Given the statement above, the players might proceed as follows:

PLAYER 1: *A*nts.

PLAYER 2: *B*ikinis.

PLAYER 3: *C*aramels.

PLAYER 4: *D*rums.

A point is gained for each correct addition, and two points are forfeited for each error.

ALPHABETICAL ADD-A-WORD   VAR. 2

ELEMENTARY   *Clock or timer*

3 or more

This is simply another form of the preceding variation, but with the complication that the list of items to be mentioned must be restricted to a particular *category*—fruits, food, toys, things made of wood, things you might purchase in a clothing store, things an astronaut might need on his trip to the moon, etc.

For example, if fruits are chosen, the answers might be *a*pples, *b*ananas, *c*oconuts, *d*ates, etc.

The child thus learns to group things logically, to use his imagination, and to add to his vocabulary. (See also page 108, CATEGORIES.)

In this way, a child can also be taught grammar if the category chosen is a particular part of speech—verbs, for example.

Here is the way a verb story might begin:

"On his trip to the country, Tom ————"

PLAYER 1: *A*rrived.

PLAYER 2: *B*athed.

PLAYER 3: *C*anoed.

PLAYER 4: *D*ressed.

PLAYER 1: *E*xplored.

PLAYER 2: *F*ished.

A reasonable time limit should be set on answers.

ALPHABETICAL ADVERBS WITH CHARADES   VAR. 3

ELEMENTARY-INTERMEDIATE

3 or more

This game has many educational values. Not only does it introduce the child to adverbs, but it fosters creativity and inventiveness and builds vocabulary.

It is basically a variation of the preceding game.

Begin with a sentence containing an active verb that can be modified by a series of adverbs. These must be added by each player in turn, in alphabetical order, but in a way that makes sense.

Here is one possible start:

"The pilot flew the plane ————."

PLAYER 1: *A*crobatically.

PLAYER 2: *B*umpily.

PLAYER 3: *C*arelessly.

PLAYER 1: *D*angerously.

PLAYER 2: *E*nthusiastically.
PLAYER 3: *F*rantically.

Before revealing his word, each player, with gestures or pantomime, acts it out, and the other players try to guess what it is, using as their clue the initial letter and the charade.

ALLITERATIVE ADD-A-WORD   VAR. 4

ELEMENTARY-INTERMEDIATE   *Paper and pencil*
3 or more   *Clock or timer*

This variation of ALPHABETICAL ADD-A-WORD increases the difficulty by requiring that all words on the list begin with the *same* letter of the alphabet. It helps children to appreciate the many ways in which the same initial letter can combine with others to form different sounds and words.

Thus, if adjectives are being added in a sentence, the description might look something like this:

"Jane is ———"

PLAYER 1: *A*rtful.
PLAYER 2: *A*ble.
PLAYER 3: *A*lert.
PLAYER 1: *A*ttentive.
PLAYER 2: *A*ctive.
PLAYER 3: *A*miable.

Each player is given only a limited amount of time to think of another word to add to this list. When no one can do so, a new list is begun with the next letter of the alphabet.

It is remarkable how many new words can be learned in this way, and if they are written on a sheet of paper, the children can learn their spelling as well.

ADD-A-WORD, whether in its strictly alphabetical or in its alliterative form, can also become an excellent device for training the memory and teaching a child to concentrate if each player is required, before adding his own word, to recite the entire list from the beginning. In that case, the person who keeps score also keeps the list in writing for reference.

ALLITERATIVE SENTENCES   VAR. 5

ELEMENTARY-INTERMEDIATE   *Clock or timer*
3 or more

This variation gives the child practice in building sentences.

Every word of the sentence is to have the *same* initial letter. Here are two examples:

"*A*be *a*lways *a*te *a*pples."

"*B*en *b*lew *b*lue *b*ubbles *b*ut *b*ecame *b*ored *b*y ———."

Each player can be called upon to add a word, within a given period of time, to the sentence being built up; or each player can try to make the longest sensible sentence, starting with a given letter.

ALLITERATIVE CATEGORIES   VAR. 6

ELEMENTARY-INTERMEDIATE   *Blank cards (playing-card*
3 or more   *size)*
                                       Clock or timer

This variation teaches children to group things logically and to find quickly the exact words they want. It is best played with a set of alphabet cards.

First, a category is announced or agreed upon. It may be anything familiar to the players—food, drinks, flowers, trees, countries, authors, people in the news, automobiles, presidents, etc.—and can be made as extensive or as restrictive as desired. For example, the category might be confined to things seen at the circus, on a trip to the country, a visit to the museum, etc.

The cards are first shuffled. Then a player draws one from the top of the deck at the same moment that a stop watch is started by the timekeeper. Within thirty seconds, the player must call out a word that begins with the given letter and is in the given category.

Suppose, for example, that food is the category. If the letter B is drawn, the player scores a point if he calls out in time a word like *bread, butter, baked beans,* or *beets.* Other players, having a little more time to think than the first player, receive credit for only half a point for each word they can add to his. Of course, if the first player is very quick, he may be able to call out more than one correct answer before time is up.

The game proceeds in this fashion, with the players taking turns in drawing cards from the pack.

If the game is played while the children are on an automobile trip, a card may be drawn as the car passes a given point—a particular telephone pole, house, or other landmark—and the player must call out his word before the car reaches some other agreed-upon point along the way. (Needless to say, the driver of the car should not be a participant in this game!)

What do you add to a road *to make it broad?*
The letter b, *of course!*

What word is more than a mile from one end to the other?
SMILES.

A man, on leaving a restaurant, wrote these numbers on a piece of paper: 102004180. What was he trying to say?
I ought to owe nothing, for I ate nothing.

What are ten ways of spelling the sound of o?
O *as in* go. Ow *as in* snow. Ough *as in* dough. Ew *as in* sew. Eau *as in* beau. Oe *as in* toe. Ot *as in* jabot. Oh *as in* oh. Oa *as in* boat. Owe *as in* owe.

II. From Letters to Words

As the title of this section indicates, these games give the child practice in building words either by adding letter to letter or by successively subtracting one letter from another to reveal words within words.

THE KING'S ENGLISH

ELEMENTARY-INTERMEDIATE   *Paper and pencil*
2 or more   *Clock or timer*

This is a way of building vocabulary and teaching spelling.

A box consisting of any number of squares is drawn to serve as a "chessboard." The greater the number of squares, the more complicated the game becomes.

For example, we may begin with twenty-five squares, arranged thus:

I	C	A	F	H
D	T	N	G	B
X	E	G	I	Z
Q	L	R	W	J
U	K	O	Y	D

Starting a word at any square, the first player moves his pencil, like a king in chess, to any adjacent square, up or down, to either side, or diagonally. The object is to spell a word of at least four letters. Thus, starting at W on the board illustrated above, the player can move successively, as shown by the arrows, to I, N, and E, to spell WINE; or, starting from G, to R, O, and W, to spell GROW.

Words made by adding S to a three-letter word are not allowed, and only one form of a word may be counted—not, for example, both *fate* and *fated*.

All kinds of complications can be added to THE KING'S ENGLISH—more squares, different letter arrangements on the board, a time limit on each move, or more restrictive rules. For example, a player may be forbidden to enter the same square twice in the same word.

In setting up the board, be sure to include all the vowels, as well as Y. In fact, about thirty per cent of the letters on the board should be vowels. The vowel most often used is E, followed by A, I, O, and U. All the letters are placed on the board arbitrarily.

Of course, a dictionary should be kept on hand when this game or any of its variations is played, and the children should be shown how to use it to settle disputed points.

A number of different forms of this game are possible.

THE KNIGHT'S ENGLISH VAR. 1

INTERMEDIATE-ADVANCED · · · *Paper and pencil*
2 *or more* · · · *Checkerboard*
· · · *Clock or timer*

This is basically the same game, but the words must be formed, within a given time, by moving a pencil from square to square as a knight does in chess—i.e., by moving two squares in either a vertical or horizontal direction, and then moving one square perpendicular to the direction of movement, alighting on a square of a different color from that on which it started. Therefore, the whole board should be used.

Which is easier to spell, "tweedledum" or "tweedledee"?
"Tweedledee."
Why?
Because it is spelled with more e's.

Why is the man whose home has the finest basement like the purchaser of a book that is in great demand?
Both own best cellars (sellers).

What word precisely describes an eight-sided cat?
OCTOPUS.

What occurs once in a minute, *twice in a* moment, *and not once in a* thousand years.
The letter m.

What letters are invisible and at the same time never out of sight.
I and S are in visible *and never out of* sight.

What six-letter word contains four E's?
TEEPEE.

What six-letter word has four S's?
ASSESS.

Why is the letter f like Paris?
Because it is the capital of France.

What nine-letter word contains only one vowel?
STRENGTHS.

How can you remember that "dessert" has a double s?
Just think of it as "sweet stuff."

THE QUEEN'S ENGLISH   VAR. 2

INTERMEDIATE-ADVANCED   *Paper and pencil*
2 *or more*   *Checkerboard*
                             Clock or timer

In this variation, the player moves his pencil from square to square with the freedom of the queen in chess—i.e., in a straight line in any direction, up, down, to either side, or diagonally, any number of squares. Once again, this calls for the use of the complete board and a time limit on each move.

Other variations along the same lines can be used to teach a child the moves of the various pieces in chess while he learns to spell and form words.

SPELLING HOPSCOTCH   VAR. 3

ELEMENTARY   *Ball*
2 *or more*   *Clock or timer*

This is an outdoor version of the game. It dispenses with pencil and paper and allows the children to be active while learning.

The "checkerboard" is chalked on the pavement, and the players form their words by jumping, as in hopscotch, from square to square, within a given time.

Boys playing this game can "call their shots" in advance and then try to hit the desired sequence of squares with a ball from a given distance.

Why are e *and* i *the happiest of the vowels?*
Because they are in paradise, *while the rest are in* purgatory.

COINING WORDS   VAR. 4

ELEMENTARY-INTERMEDIATE   *Paper and pencil*
2 *only*   *Coins*

This variation, for two players only, teaches both spelling and vocabulary.

Using a dime as a kind of ruler to guide your pencil around its circumference, draw twenty-five dime-sized circles in the form of a square, with five horizontal and five vertical columns. In each circle write a different letter of the alphabet, omitting only Q, in haphazard order—e.g., as shown below. (Of course, many other arrangements of the letters can be used, some of which may make it possible to "coin" more words than others.)

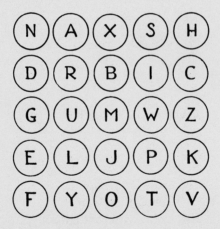

The first player places a dime over any circle he chooses. He must then "coin" as many words as he can by moving the dime from the letter selected in any direction—vertically, horizontally, or diagonally—one circle at a time. He receives one point for each letter in every word he can coin. The words need not begin with the letter he has covered with the dime; as long as that letter is used in a word, he can claim credit for it. In fact, the rules can be extended to include ab-breviations as well as words.

The players take turns placing the coin wherever they think they can get the greatest yield in coined words.

WORD MAZE   VAR. 5

INTERMEDIATE-ADVANCED   *Paper and pencil*
2 or more   *Clock or timer*

This variation builds vocabulary as it teaches spelling. It may also be considered a variant form of CATEGORIES (page 108).

There are two ways of playing this game. In its simplest form, it is played just like THE KING'S ENGLISH, above. The only difference is that the letters in the boxes (twenty-five arranged in a square, to begin with) are to be used to form words belonging to a specified category—e.g., toys, tools, musical instruments, fruits, types of automobiles, etc.

Each player is given a square of letters like the one shown here. This one was constructed with letters from the names of different kinds of birds. Starting at any letter and moving from it as a king does in chess, one box at a time in any di-

S	P	H	R	O
W	A	E	T	N
R	R	L	A	I
O	L	G	E	K
T	W	U	H	R

rection, horizontally, vertically, or diagonally, each player must spell out as many of these names as he can within a given period of time—say, ten or fifteen minutes. The player with the longest list wins the game.

In this particular word maze one can find the following birds: SPARROW, SWALLOW, PARROT, PETREL, OWL, TERN, EAGLE (and EAGLET), EGRET, GULL, HERON, KITE, TIT, and RHEA.

A maze like this can be easily constructed for any category, according to the interests and abilities of the players. First, decide on the category. Then, with the aid of a thesaurus, construct a list of people or things that fall under the category. Select a few common and well-known names and one or two that are less familiar. Finally, spell out the names in adjacent boxes, horizontally, vertically, and diagonally, until every box is filled.

For example, a similar maze can be prepared with the letters of the names of eleven containers of liquids (*cask, tun, tub, bottle, butt, can, keg, salver, carafe, flask, flagon*); another with the names of twelve animals (*cow, sow, sheep, ram, pig, cat, dog, horse, hog, mare, lamb, mule*); another with the names of eleven articles of men's clothing (*vest, socks, belt, ties, slacks, braces, coat, hat, shoe, shirt, ascot*); another with the names of sixteen states (*Texas, Georgia, Alaska, Oregon, Ohio, Utah, Indiana, Idaho, Alabama, Iowa, Nebraska, Maryland, Nevada, Maine, Kansas, Montana*); another with the names of fourteen presidents of the United States (*Truman, Roosevelt, Washington, Lincoln, Hoover, Coolidge, Hayes, Madison, Adams, Arthur, Grant, Taylor, Tyler, Wilson*); and another with the names of ten land vehicles (*auto, tram, car, cab, bus, taxi, train, coupe, cart, hansom*).

Thus, the game can be adapted to review the vocabulary of any subject: history, music, geography, etc.

Another way of playing this game is to reverse the order by giving the players ten or fifteen minutes to make their own twenty-five box squares with letters that could be used to form the names of people or things falling under a given category. The winner would be the player who produced a maze with the greatest number of names within the category.

After the time is up, the players can exchange mazes and work out the solutions. Thus, points can be scored either way —in constructing a maze and in threading one's way through another player's maze.

As the players gain proficiency, the game can be made more challenging by adding to the number of boxes in the maze.

STRINGING ALONG

ELEMENTARY-INTERMEDIATE   *Clock or timer*
2 *or more*

This game teaches spelling and vocabulary and trains the child's visual memory.

The first player starts by naming any letter of the alphabet. Each player in turn must "string along" by adding one letter, either before or after those already called out, to form a word. The ever-growing necklace of words, formed by adding one letter at a time at either end, constitutes a challenge to keep building longer words by the same process.

Thus, a game might proceed from *i* to *it* to *pit* to *spit* and *spite*, or *rip*, *trip*, and *tripe*. Another might begin with *o* and go on to *on*, *one*, *tone*, and *stone*. Still another might start with *a* and string along from *at* to *ate* to *rate* to *irate* and *pirate*.

The game can be made more difficult by permitting a letter to be inserted, as well, anywhere in the middle of a word to form a new word. Thus, *pit* might be transformed into *pint*, then to *print*, and finally to *sprint*. Since this places a greater strain on the memory, more time should be allowed for each answer.

CUTTING THE STRING

ELEMENTARY-INTERMEDIATE   *Clock or timer*
2 *or more*

This is the opposite of STRINGING ALONG, but it serves the same educational purpose.

Beginning with a word like *pirate*, each player in turn must slice off one letter at either end or internally to make some smaller word.

Good words to start with are *honesty*, *spinet*, *trash*, *flown*, *hasty*, *spore*, *party*, *sinewy*, *panty*, *spare*, *twine*, *stint*, *swinger*, *whist*, *tramp*, *snowy*, and *marshy*.

STRIP TEASE

ELEMENTARY   *Strips of paper*
2 *or more*   *Clock or timer*

This is a delightful way of getting children interested in spelling and in learning new words.

With a razor, a sharp knife, or a pair of scissors, cut two parallel slits, about half an inch apart, on a piece of cardboard. Now prepare several thin strips of paper or ribbon with different letters of the alphabet arranged vertically, one letter to a line.

Starting with three such strips, insert them as shown below into the slits in the cardboard.

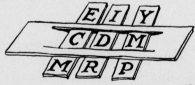

Each player, when he is given the cardboard with the strips, must try to make as many words as he can, within a given time, by sliding the strips up and down. The player who makes the most words wins the game.

After the players have gained facility in forming three-letter words, a fourth and fifth strip may be added, as desired. Or the three strips may be rearranged, with a different slip at the left or in the middle; or different slips may be used with other letters. The longer the strips, the greater the number of possible words that can be made.

III. Little Words and Big Words

In the games in this section, whole words as well as individual letters are used as building blocks in the construction of other, big words, or big words are dismantled into other, little words.

SPELLING GOLF

ELEMENTARY-INTERMEDIATE   *Paper and pencil*
2 or more   *Clock or timer*

The object of this game is to make words with the *fewest* number of letters. Therefore, it is particularly helpful in teaching spelling and vocabulary to children in the primary grades.

Begin by opening your child's favorite book to any page at random. Place a sheet of paper over the page so that it conceals all but the first three letters of the words that appear next to the left-hand margin.

Now write down the three-letter groups beginning the first six or seven lines, and give each player a copy of them.

As in golf, the object of the game is to keep the score *low*.

One point is the penalty for each letter needed by a player to add to the three-letter groups to form a word. The player using the fewest additional letters wins the game. If the three-letter group already forms a word, then more letters must be added to form another word. A reasonable time limit should be set, according to the abilities of the players.

Here, for example, is the way one player's sheet might look in comparison with another's:

	PLAYER 1	PLAYER 2
SOM	SOM*E* (1 point)	SOM*BER* (3 points)
THE	THE*M* (1 point)	THE*Y* (1 point)
LIF	LIF*E* (1 point)	LIF*T* (1 point)
SPE	SPE*ND* (2 points)	SPE*D* (1 point)
EXA	EXA*CT* (2 points)	EXA*LT* (2 points)

Players who find that they are evenly matched after five or six words can continue down the page, line by line, a group at a time, until one of them wins.

SPELLING HIGH JUMP   VAR. 1

INTERMEDIATE-ADVANCED   *Paper and pencil*
2 *or more*   *Clock or timer*

The object of this game is just the opposite of that of SPELL-ING GOLF, to make words with the *greatest* number of letters. Hence, it can be used to improve the spelling and build the vocabulary of players of intermediate or advanced grades.

The game begins like SPELLING GOLF, but its object, as in high jump, is to score *high* by adding, within a given time, as many letters as possible to the three-letter groups to form a word. The player using the most additional letters wins the game.

Here is the way the same letter groups used in SPELLING

GOLF might have been built up into long words by several different players of unequal ability:

PLAYER 1:	SOME*RSAULT*	(7 points)
	THE*REFORE*	(6 points)
	LIF*EGUARD*	(6 points)
	SPEC*IALIST*	(7 points)
	EXA*MPLE*	(4 points)
		30 points
PLAYER 2:	SOME*WHERE*	(6 points)
	THE*RMOMETER*	(8 points)
	LIFE*TIME*	(5 points)
	SPECT*ACULAR*	(8 points)
	EXA*MINATION*	(8 points)
		35 points
PLAYER 3:	SOM*NAMBULISM*	(9 points)
	THE*RAPEUTIC*	(8 points)
	LIF*ESAVING*	(7 points)
	SPEE*DOMETER*	(8 points)
	EXA*CTITUDE*	(7 points)
		39 points

In fact, even longer words than these can be made from these groups of letters: *somnolescence*, *theologically*, *lifelessness*, *specialization*, and *exasperation*.

As can be seen, the "high jumper" in this game has to have a good vocabulary and be good in spelling too.

~~~~~~

Take a vowel and a consonant, triple each, and arrange the letters to make a six-letter word.
EEE and DDD make DEEDED.

What flower does $\dfrac{M}{E}$ *represent?*
Anemone.

What common word could you get by pronouncing the letters SSWORPS?
SURE. SS as in mission, *WO as in* two, *and RPS as in* corps.

What common word could you get by pronouncing the letters PSOLOCCHOUSC?
CIRCUS. PS as in psychology, *OLO as in* colonel, *CCH as in* Bacchus, *OU as in* famous, *and SC as in* science.

"SUGAR is the only English word beginning with SU sounded as SHOO."
"Are you sure?"

Where does Thursday come before Wednesday?
In the dictionary.

What common word could you get by pronouncing the letters GHOTI?
FISH. GH as in rough, *O as in* women, *and TI as in* fiction.

A lady who had bought an unabridged dictionary returned it after a week. "I like what I've read of it so far," she said, "but I do find that the subject changes a little too often. Don't you have something less wordy and with more of a plot?"

What six-letter word has in it, without transposing any letters, seven other words?
HEREIN. The words are, in order: he, her, here, ere, rein, I, *and* in.

In what six-letter word can you find six other words without rearranging the letters?
BRANDY. The words are: brand, bran, ran, an, and, *and* a.

What letter is a plural verb of being?
R.

What two letters refer to a man's name?
AB.

WORD SUPERMARKET   VAR. 2

INTERMEDIATE-ADVANCED   *Paper and pencil*
2 *or more*   *Clock or timer*

This is a more difficult variation of SPELLING GOLF.

Taking any printed page, combine the first letter of the first line with the first in the second line, and write the two letters in the column headed WORDS on a sheet of paper with two columns. Head the second column PRICE.

Proceed in similar fashion with the third and fourth lines of the page, the fifth and sixth lines, and so on, until you have about ten two-letter random combinations listed vertically in the column headed WORDS. These letter combinations should be placed in the center of the column, with some space to their left and right, as indicated below:

WORDS	PRICE
IT	
OF	
AC	
SB	
ID	

Each player copies this chart on his paper. This is the "supermarket" in which the players are to go "shopping" for words at the lowest possible "price." The object of the game is to get a word for a "bargain"—i.e., to add as *few* letters as possible before or after each pair to make a word. Thus, SIT in the first line and OFF in the second would "cost" only one point each, whereas HUSBAND in the fourth line would "cost" five points for the five letters added to SB.

If a player cannot, within a given time, think of any word that can be formed by adding letters before or after the two-letter combination, the penalty or "cost" for that line is eight points.

No proper names, foreign words, or abbreviations may be

used, nor may any letters be inserted between the two that are given in the chart.

The best "word shopper" is the player with the lowest total score.

WORD AUCTION   VAR. 3

INTERMEDIATE-ADVANCED   *Paper and pencil*
2 *or more*   *Clock or timer*

This is a variation on WORD SUPERMARKET, but its object is the reverse, namely, to make words with the *greatest* number of letters. It is therefore suited to teaching spelling and vocabulary to children who have played SPELLING HIGH JUMP successfully.

As in WORD SUPERMARKET, each player is given a list of about ten combinations of two or three letters each. These are to be "auctioned off" to the highest "bidder,"—i.e., the one who can form the *longest* word incorporating each combination of letters. One point is scored for each letter added to the original group to form a word. The player with the highest total score wins the game.

When only two or three play this game, the players can take turns being "auctioneer." He calls out, for example, "What am I bid for NC?" Each player suggests the longest word he can think of in which this combination of letters is used. Thus, the player who formed the word INCH from these two letters would score two points, while a player who formed the word ENCYCLOPEDIA from the same combination would score ten points. The players should be given a reasonable time to form their words.

Any group of letters may be used, but it is best to work with those that are not commonly found at the beginnings or ends of words. A few good combinations are *bn, utu, ino, gg,* and *ndl.* Naturally, beginning with three-letter combinations makes the game that much harder.

WORD GOLF

INTERMEDIATE   *Paper and pencil*
1 or more   *Clock or timer*

This game develops skill in forming words and visualizing their spelling.

Each player is directed to set up a nine-hole "golf course" by numbering down the page from 1 to 9, skipping about five lines between each number and the next.

Now, opposite the number of each "hole," the players write a given set of scrambled letters (seven, eight, or nine) which you have previously made up from words like *composite* (*mtcieoops*) or *solitaire* (*eltrisioa*) or any others that you would like the children to learn to spell.

The object of the game is to achieve as low a score as possible by using *all* the letters in each set to form a word or words.

A "hole in one" is scored if a player can unscramble all the letters to form a single word (*composite*, *solitaire*, etc.).

A player's card might look like this:

1. MOSPIITT   OPTIMIST
2. HUGRELAT   LAUGHTER
3. NICPGMAA   CAMPAIGN
4. TISTEEHA   HESITATE
5. RLECAMKE   MACKEREL
6. RAMONPAA   PANORAMA
7. DIECNNTI   INCIDENT
8. LROBECFI   FORCIBLE
9. SCOEREVN   CONVERSE

Two points are scored if he can use all the letters to form two words. For example, from *composite* a player might form the words *compose* and *it* or *time* and *scoop* or *mice* and *stop;* and from *solitaire* he might form the words *sailor* and *tie* or *sortie* and *ail* or *arise* and *toil.*

A "hole in three" is scored if the player can use all the letters to form three words, and so on. Thus, from *composite* one might form the words *so*, *mop*, and *cite* or *it*, *sop*, and *come* or *is*, *come*, and *top*, or *mice*, *pot*, and *so*; and from *solitaire* he might form *is*, *rail*, and *toe* or *roe*, *is*, and *tail* or *it*, *roe*, and *sail* or *toe*, *is*, and *lair* or *liar*, *toe*, and *is* or *tire*, *a*, and *soil* or *as*, *rite*, and *oil* or *sire*, *at*, and *oil* or *ire*, *as*, and *toil*. Similar combinations can be made with the letters of the nine words listed above, or, in fact, with most words of eight or nine letters.

Each player works independently. A time limit can be set to add a little tension to the game. Of course, no letters should be left over. If they are, a penalty of one point for each letter should be subtracted from the points gained by making words.

As the players gain facility, words of greater length may be selected for scrambling.

HIDDEN WORDS   VAR. 1

INTERMEDIATE-ADVANCED   *Paper and pencil*
1 or more   *Clock or timer*

This variation of WORD GOLF is a lesson in correct spelling.

Each player must, within the time limit, form as many words as possible, consisting of four or more letters, from the letters of a given long word.

Scoring may be done in one of two ways. Either a point may be credited for each word formed; or, to encourage the forming of longer words, a point may be given for each *letter* of each word formed. Thus, if the given word were TELESCOPE, six points would be earned for the word *closet* or *select*, five for *scope*, *close*, *elect*, and *stole*, and four for *cope*, *lope*, *pole*, *lest*, *lost*, *lose*, *cost*, *tope*, *pose*, *pest*, *lees*, and *pelt*.

The game can be made more difficult and challenging if,

after the long word is given, the first player states the definition of some word that can be formed from it—e.g., *choose* for *select*, above. The players then compete to see who can be the first to discover the hidden word that has been defined. To get away from the use of paper and pencil, and to make the game more of a contest and less of a test, the problem can be tossed from one player to the next, with a scorekeeper tallying the points. Of course, in that case each player will have to spell his word orally as well as name it in order to get full credit for it. After the players have had some practice, a really big word—say, *gesticulate*—may be selected, and the game may be played at a considerably higher level of difficulty.

Here, for example, is how advanced and experienced players might respond to one another's definitions of words that can be formed from GESTICULATE:

PLAYER 1: Tardy.

PLAYER 2: Late. L-A-T-E. Frame for holding canvas.

PLAYER 3: Easel. E-A-S-E-L. Silent

PLAYER 4: Tacit. T-A-C-I-T. Deceitful cunning.

PLAYER 1: Guile. G-U-I-L-E.

The game could proceed in the same way with definitions of *elegist* (seven points), *gestate* (seven points), *elastic* (seven points), *tactile* (seven points), such six-point words as *select*, *estate*, and *eaglet*, five-point words like *guilt*, *agile*, *liege*, *tease*, and *siege*, and many others formed from GESTICULATE. Naturally, no credit is given if a player cannot form the word defined or if he proposes a word that cannot be formed with the letters from the given word. The same is true if a player cannot define some word not already formed. This way of playing the game can be used to teach children to say exactly what they mean when framing definitions.

If the game is played in this fashion, allow some time at the beginning for all players first to make up their own lists of words formed from the given word. Then, as words are defined and formed, each player can cross them off his list.

What does this mean: S
              N
                O
                  W?

Snow is falling.

What are the only words in the English language that contain all six vowels in the proper sequence: A, E, I, O, U, and Y?
FACETIOUSLY *and* ABSTEMIOUSLY.

What do the following sentences have in common?
"Whom could zany ex-peanut-vendors' jokes quite befog?"
" 'Why X-ray more injured pavement?' she asked quizzically. 'Baffling!' "
Both sentences contain all the letters of the alphabet, like the famous sentence: "This quick brown fox jumped over the lazy dog."

What is the difference between a king's son, a monkey's mother, a bald head, and an orphan?
The first is heir apparent; the second, a hairy parent; the third has no hair apparent; and the fourth, nary a parent.

Can you name some five-letter words from which, if you take two letters, one remains?
STONE, BONES, HONEY, MONEY, ATONE, *etc.*

What word of five letters has six left after you take two away?
SIXTY.

What word has five consecutive vowels?
QUEUEING.

What six-letter word has four O's?
VOODOO.

What word has five E's and no other vowel?
EFFERVESCENCE.

SCRAMBLED LETTERS   VAR. 2

ELEMENTARY-INTERMEDIATE   *Paper and pencil*
2 *or more*   *Clock or timer*

With this variation, children can be given training in logical classification, practice in spelling, and a knowledge of the precise vocabulary of any particular subject.

Begin by having the players decide on categories of interest to them (sports, cars, toys, colors, countries, authors, flowers, fruits, musical instruments, etc.).

Next, each player makes a list, in a given period of time, of all the words he can think of that are connected with any one of these categories.

Now the players scramble the letters of each of the words they have listed.

The first player then announces the category he has chosen and gives the scrambled letters of one of the words on his list. With these clues, the next player must unscramble the letters and form the correct word.

For example, suppose a player chooses the category of sports. His list of scrambled letters might look something like this:

SUSAHQ—SQUASH
TONABNIMD—BADMINTON
YERCARH—ARCHERY
TOAFLOLB—FOOTBALL
NALDHLAB—HANDBALL
RSCOEC—SOCCER
FLOG—GOLF
TOCQUER—CROQUET
BOTLSAFL—SOFTBALL
CINFNEG—FENCING
GIXNOB—BOXING
GONTONIGBAG—TOBOGGANING

KNITAGS—SKATING
SLABELBA—BASEBALL
CEOYHK—HOCKEY
KAEBSTLBLA—BASKETBALL
RSAECOLS—LACROSSE
ISQTUO—QUOITS
EBDULHFAFSRO—SHUFFLEBOARD
DLRABLSII—BILLIARDS
EBVYLAOLLL—VOLLEYBALL
SGWTNIERL—WRESTLING
IENTNS—TENNIS
LOOP—POLO
NLWBIOG—BOWLING

Since a player is likely to select first his longest and most difficult set of scrambled letters to present to his neighbor for unscrambling, the number of letters in the word can be used as a basis for crediting points. Thus, a player who successfully unscrambles the word EBDULHFAFSRO would get twelve points, while the player who unscrambles LOOP would get only four points. If a player misses, he earns no points, but he remains in the game.

To add to the interest, a time limit should be set for unscrambling the letters.

WORD POKER   VAR. 3

INTERMEDIATE-ADVANCED   *Paper and pencil*
1 or more   *Clock or timer*

This variation is essentially like HIDDEN WORDS in that the players strive to form as many words as they can from the letters of a given long word. But the scoring approximates the rules of poker in depending on the kind of "hand" a player can put together.

Suppose, for example, that the given word is TOREADORS.

For every "pair" a player can form—i.e., a word consisting of two letters of the given word, like *to*, *do*, *or*, *at*, *as*, etc.—he scores one point.

For every "three of a kind" he puts together—i.e., a word consisting of three letters of the given word, like *ear*, *eat*, *are*, *rot*, *rod*, *dot*, *sod*, *sot*, etc.—he scores two points.

For every "four of a kind" he forms—i.e., a word consisting of four letters of the given word, like *read*, *dear*, *road*, *door*, *dare*, *date*, *rote*, *tore*, *sore*, *rose*, etc.—he scores three points.

For every "straight" hand he assembles,—i.e., a word consisting of five letters of the given word, like *store*, *tread*, *reads*, *roads*, *roars*, *dears*, *dates*, *stare*, etc.—he scores four points.

A "flush" is a word pyramid (for ways of constructing one, see WORD PYRAMIDS, page 206), starting with one letter and building up to five or more, as shown below, with letters from the given word. A pyramid with five words counts five points. One point is added for every word above five.

O
OR
OAR
ROAR
ROARS

A "straight flush" is any sentence in which only the letters of the given word are used as many times as they are needed. It counts ten points. For example, with the letters of TOREADORS we might make sentences like *To do or read so!* or *Dear sot, do read!*

A "royal flush" is a sentence using only the letters of the given word as many times as they are used in the word, without having any letters left over. It counts fifteen points. An example formed from the letters of TOREADORS would be: *Read "roots."*

It is best to begin with a big word having many vowels, like *transmigration*, and to give the players plenty of time to work out their "hands."

IV. One Word Leads to Another

These games train the child to scrutinize closely the spelling of words and to notice their distinctive characteristics.

WORD LADDERS

ALL LEVELS   *Paper and pencil*
1 or more

Children often fail to see the difference in spelling between words that look alike except for a single letter. This is an excellent game for sharpening their powers of observation and helping them to notice the effect of small differences between the spelling of one word and that of another.

A child can play the game by himself, taking all the time he needs to climb to the top of the word ladder; or, if he has a companion, the two of them might compete to see who can reach the top in the fewest steps. In fact, a whole group could play the game at the same time.

The top and bottom rungs of the word ladder are two words of equal length that are related to each other in some way, either as antonyms (*love-hate*, *rich-poor*, *wet-dry*, *black-white*, *lose-find*, etc.) or as complements (*boy-man*, *seek-find*). The problem is to pass from the lowest rung of the ladder to the highest in the fewest number of steps by changing only one letter at a time to make a new word.

Thus, to pass from BOY to MAN with very few intermediate steps, we might proceed as follows:

MAN
BAN
BAY
BOY

To change from DRY to WET, we could follow this sequence:

WET
MET
MAT
MAY
DAY
DRY

The player passing from the lowest rung to the highest with the fewest number of changes wins the game.

It should be easy to pass from HIM to HER and from POT to PAN in a single intermediate step, from WOOD to COAL, FAIR to FOUL, FROCK to CLOAK, LOVE to HATE, and FOAL to COLT in two intermediate steps, and from SEEK to FIND, FIND to LOSE, and WARM to COLD in three intermediate steps.

Generally, in a three-letter word, the changes are not hard to make; but with words of four or five letters, it may be necessary to make as many as a dozen or more changes to climb to the top of the ladder. Thus, the game can be made progressively difficult by adding to the number of letters in the original words.

A point worth noting is that in going from a word like *fish* to a word like *clam*, one must find a way of shifting the sequence of the two inner letters from vowel-consonant to consonant-vowel. A good way of effecting this change is to form one or more intermediate words with a double vowel, or two vowels, in the middle.

This, for example, is the way we might make the transition from FISH to CLAM in ten steps:

CLAM
CLAD
CLOD
CLOT
COOT

COLT

COST

CAST

FAST

FIST

FISH

Here are some good sets of words to begin and end word ladders: RICH-POOR (in eight steps), BLACK-GREEN (eight steps), LEAD-GOLD (in just *three* easy steps!), SOUP-NUTS (five steps), SLOW-FAST (seven steps), SICK-WELL (four steps), HEAT-COLD (four steps), and EYE-EAR (three steps). It is even possible to go from EASY to HARD in five steps, to pass from LESS to MORE in four steps, to change RAIN to SNOW in seven steps, and to make FLOUR into BREAD in six steps. After a while the players might like to try changing FAIL to PASS or WATER to BOOZE!

What you can't do with words!

WORD MASQUERADE   VAR. 1

INTERMEDIATE-ADVANCED   *Paper and pencil*
2 or more   *Clock or timer*

This variation teaches the spelling of new words, the meanings of words, and the art of defining words.

Like WORD LADDERS, this game calls for converting one word into another by changing a single letter. But instead of using each newly formed word as a step to another, the players always make their changes only in the original word they started from. It appears disguised, as in a masquerade.

The first player, having chosen his word, defines it without revealing what it is, saying, "My word means ———." Then he defines some word that can be formed from it when its first letter is changed, but again without naming the word, saying, "Change my first, and I (definition)." Next he defines a new word formed from the original word when its second letter is

changed; and he proceeds in this fashion, changing successively, one at a time, each of the letters of the original word,
to form new words which he defines.

Given these clues, the second player must, within a given
time, state what the original word was and name the new
words formed from it. He is credited with one point for each
word he gets right.

Suppose, for example, that the first player says:

"My word means a type of insect. Change my first, and I
pant. Change my second, and I am a slender, twisted piece of
something. Change my third, and I twist out of shape. Change
my fourth, and I perform ablutions."

Here it appears that the original word consists of four letters meaning "a type of insect." The second player may not
be able at first to think of a four-letter word meaning "a type
of insect," but he may know that WASH means to "perform
ablutions." Since three of the letters in WASH are in the original word, he is easily led to conclude that it is WASP. Change
the first, and GASP means "pant." Change the A to I, and
the word WISP means a "slender, twisted piece of something." Change the S to R, and WARP means to "twist out of
shape."

If the second player misses any of these, he gets credit for
whatever words he does discover. If he misses all of them, he
is passed by, and the third player gets a chance. On the other
hand, if the second player finds all the words, it becomes his
turn to make a metagram.

His might go like this:

"My word means excavate. Change my first, and I am a
beverage. Change my second, and I am part of a lion. Change
my third, and I am a measure of distance. Change my fourth,
and I am a herb."

The answers here are MINE, WINE, MANE, MILE, and
MINT.

The game becomes much more difficult to play if more
than four letters are in the original word.

WORD PYRAMIDS   VAR. 2

ELEMENTARY-INTERMEDIATE   *Paper and pencil*
2 *or more*   *Clock or timer*

This variation teaches spelling, word-building, and vocabulary. It can be played as a race against time by several participants competing to see who can build the highest pyramid.

Verbal pyramids are built from the top down. They start with the apex, which consists of a single letter—the same for all players.

Each player then adds one letter at a time to make new words, rearranging previously used letters if necessary. These new words are listed below the original letter to form a pyramid. The player with the highest pyramid in the given time wins the game, provided that he has formed all his words correctly.

Here, for example, is how three different players might form pyramids starting with the letter A:

A	A	A
AT	AM	AY
EAT	MAT	SAY
MEAT	TEAM	STAY
STEAM	MATES	STRAY
STREAM	MASTER	ASTRAY
		ASHTRAY
		ASHTRAYS

The game can be made more difficult if the players are not allowed to change the order of the letters in the previous word.

To show how many small words are contained in a large word, the whole procedure may be reversed by starting at the foot of the pyramid with a word like *ashtrays* and working upward by dropping a letter at a time.

WHAT'S MY WORD?

INTERMEDIATE-ADVANCED *Paper and pencil*
2 *only*

This game teaches spelling and builds vocabulary.

Both players think of a word consisting of an agreed-upon number of letters. Each then writes on his paper as many dashes as there are letters in his word.

The first player, naming a letter of the alphabet, inquires whether the letter is in his opponent's word. If it is, the second player must write the letter over the dash that represents it and show this to the first player. If the letter is used more than once in the word—as the *s* is, for example, in the word *delicatessen*—it must be written wherever it is represented by a dash. The first player, seeing the letter written in one or more spaces on his opponent's paper, continues asking about other letters until the letter he calls out is not in the word.

Now it is the second player's turn to ask about the letters in the first player's word. The game continues in this way until one of the players successfully guesses the word of the other from seeing its letters gradually filled in.

Of course, each player should keep his own record of missed letters, so that he does not repeat them.

The number of letters in the words will depend on the size of the players' vocabularies, but it is best to start with no more than five or six letters and to work up to nine- and ten-letter words.

WORD MAP VAR. 1

INTERMEDIATE-ADVANCED *Paper and pencil*
2 *only*

This variation of the game is an excellent way of teaching common place names and their spelling. It is essentially the same game as WHAT'S MY WORD? except that the words are all taken from the field of geography: the names of continents, oceans, countries, states, cities, mountains, lakes, etc.

The problem at the outset is for each player to think of a word of this kind with the particular number of letters agreed upon. This can be gradually increased. The progression might proceed thus:

Four letters: *Asia, Etna, Cuba, Nile, Utah, Ohio*

Five letters: *India, China, Chile, Spain, Tibet, Samoa*

Six letters: *Canada, Africa, Mexico, Naples, France, Arctic*

Seven letters: *Vietnam, Uruguay, Chicago, Alabama, Indiana, Pacific*

Eight letters: *Honduras, Thailand, Colombia, Virginia, Labrador, Portugal*

Nine letters: *Australia, Venezuela, Louisiana, Wisconsin, Minnesota, Nicaragua*

Ten letters: *Antarctica, California, Yugoslavia, Washington, Valparaiso*

Eleven letters: *Switzerland, Afghanistan, Mississippi, Connecticut*

Another way of making the game more difficult is to restrict the choice of place names to particular areas (the Western Hemisphere, North America, etc.) or types (capitals of countries, rivers, etc.).

Can you compose a sentence of just seven words using all the letters of the alphabet?

"Challenging lawyer's freak quiz vexes bad-tempered juror."

Why should a farmer avoid the letter n?

Because it will make a sty nasty.

Why should men avoid the letter a?

Because it makes men mean.

HISTORY MYSTERY   VAR. 2

INTERMEDIATE-ADVANCED   *Paper and pencil*
2 *only*

As can easily be seen, the game of WHAT'S MY WORD? is
ideally suited to teaching the vocabulary of any specialized
subject, including history. In this variation, the words selected
are the names of famous historical personages: generals, presidents, statesmen, etc.

The game is played in the same way and can be made increasingly difficult by adding to the number of letters in the
word. A typical series might progress from names with four
letters (like *Tito*, *Taft*, and *Marx*) through five-letter names
(like *Nehru*, *Lenin*, and *Grant*), six-letter names (like *Hitler*,
Stalin, *Wilson*, and *Caesar*), seven-letter names (like *Ken-
nedy*, *Lincoln*, and *Madison*), eight-letter names (like *Na-
poleon*, *Columbus*, and *Hannibal*), and nine-letter names
(like *Roosevelt*, *Cleopatra*, and *Jefferson*) to ten-letter names
(like *Washington*).

The difficulty can also be increased if the choice of words
is narrowed down to a particular era (antiquity, the Renais-
sance, the Middle Ages, the twentieth century).

WORDS AND MUSIC   VAR. 3

INTERMEDIATE-ADVANCED   *Paper and pencil*
2 *only*

Besides being adaptable to such school-oriented subjects as
geography and history, the game of WHAT'S MY WORD?
can be used to familiarize the players with the terminology of
any field, such as music, and with the spelling of terms like
rhythm, *melody*, *sonata*, *piano*, etc.

It is best to begin with four-letter words like *oboe*, *tuba*,
aria, *bass*, *coda*, and *lute*. Then you may proceed to five-letter

words like *viola*, *octet*, *fugue*, *opera*, *flute*, *suite*, *étude*, and *motet*. With some practice, players may then advance to six-letter words like *treble*, *minuet*, *septet*, and *presto*. Venturesome players might wish to try seven-letter words like *prelude*, *harmony*, *trumpet*, *bassoon*, *mazurka*, and *soprano*. If your partner insists on eight-letter words, you can always use *concerto*, *clarinet*, *trombone*, *symphony*, *oratorio*, *overture*, and *sonatina*.

If all this is not difficult enough, you may restrict the choice of words to musical instruments, composers, names of operas, or types of musical forms.

THE CASE OF THE MISSING VOWEL   VAR. 4

INTERMEDIATE-ADVANCED   *Paper and pencil*
2, 4, *or any even number*

In this variation, which likewise teaches spelling and vocabulary, the players are given a clue from the context of each word in a sentence.

Each player writes a sentence with the vowels omitted. Suppose, for example, that it is agreed that the sentence should be a proverb. Two particular proverbs would look like this:

HNST S TH BST PLC.
BRDS F FTHR FLCK TGTHR.

The players exchange papers, and each tries to determine the missing vowels in his opponent's sentence as well as their correct placement. The first to complete the sentence wins.

The sentences given above are the familiar proverbs, HONESTY IS THE BEST POLICY and BIRDS OF A FEATHER FLOCK TOGETHER.

One way of complicating the game is to run all the letters together to conceal the breaks between words, thus:

HNSTSTHBSTPLC.

In that case, each player should be told how many words are in the sentence.

Here is another easy example, this time in verse form:

PRSVRYPRFCTMN;
VRKPTHSPRCPTSTN.

Putting the vowel E in the right places yields this piece of Biblical wisdom:

P*E*RS*E*V*E*R*E* Y*E* P*E*RF*E*CT M*E*N;
*E*V*E*R K*E*EP TH*E*S*E* PR*E*C*E*PTS T*E*N.

Of course, the sentences do not have to be restricted to proverbs or moralistic verse. One can begin with a less pedagogic approach. Just for fun, try this:

VNNORMOUSLPHANTSNDXTRMLYXPNSIVDIBLS.

Once again, all that is needed is the introduction of the vowel E in the right places in order to unlock the secret:

*E*V*E*N *E*NORMOUS *E*L*E*PHANTS N*E*ED *E*XTR*E*M*E*LY
*E*XP*E*NSIV*E* *E*DIBL*E*S.

In this case, the sentence contained more than one vowel. But it is easy and amusing to make up silly sentences using one vowel only, like the following:

TLSTJCKSPRTCNCTCHLLBDGRYCTSLNKYRTSBLCKBTS-
NDRTYNTSTHRRYSRNCH.

This looks much more difficult than it is. Once you realize that only the vowel A is needed to make "sense" (if that's what you can call it) of this group of letters, all you need to do is find the right places to insert the missing letter:

*A*T L*A*ST J*A*CK SPR*A*T C*A*N C*A*TCH *A*LL B*A*D GR*A*Y
C*A*TS, L*A*NKY R*A*TS, BL*A*CK B*A*TS, *A*ND *A*RTY *A*NTS
*A*T H*A*RRY'S R*A*NCH.

The players might agree to choose, at first, well-known advertising slogans, lines from popular songs, nursery rhymes, personal remarks (compliments or insults), movie titles, etc.

On the other hand, at a more advanced stage, this variation lends itself to teaching the vocabulary and even the basic concepts of any subject (geography, history, science, music, etc.).

CONCEALED CONSONANTS   VAR. 5

INTERMEDIATE-ADVANCED   *Paper and pencil*
2, 4, or any even number

This variation calls for concentration on the part of the players. It teaches spelling, vocabulary, and sentence sense—i.e., the feeling for the beginning and the ending of a sentence.

Instead of omitting the vowels, as in the preceding variation, each player must write a sentence in which the *same* consonant is omitted throughout. Papers are then exchanged, and the players try to determine what consonant is needed and where it should be inserted to complete the sentence. The first player to do so wins the game.

Here is a typical problem, taken from the field of baseball.

Make a sentence by inserting the same letter (a consonant) eleven times among the letters of the following sequence:

IEMEFAEDIIEIIGS.

Here the letter is N and is inserted to make the sentence:

NINE MEN FANNED IN NINE INNINGS.

Once again, the sentences may be restricted to a particular field (games, space travel, history, etc.) or type (proverbs, slogans, etc.), or the players may be invited to use their imaginations to make up amusing or fanciful sentences like the following.

By inserting the letter G thirteen times, make the following sequence of letters into a sentence:

ARIMACINAROYLEISLESSARAVATINTHANAILINIOLO.

This problem could be offered to a group of players by any one of them to see which player could solve it first. Plenty of time should be given.

The answer is:

A *GRIMACING GARGOYLE* IS LESS *AGGRAVATING* THAN A *GIGGLING GIGOLO.*

As an aid to concentration, the players may be told the

number of words in the sentence. For example, the problem might be put thus:

By inserting the same letter as often as you like, make the following sequence of letters into a sentence consisting of six words:

LEEPLENEIAMOTDITREINGDIEAE.

In this case, the players must not only discover for themselves the letter to be inserted, but must decide how many times it is to be used, where it is to be placed, and where the words end.

The resulting sentence, formed by inserting the letter S twelve times, is:

SLEEPLESSNESS IS A MOST DISTRESSING DISEASE.

This game can be played at any level of difficulty, depending on the knowledge and ability of the players. The successive complications may be graded in this fashion:

1. First limit the number of words in the sentence to four or five; then gradually increase its length.
2. At first indicate the breaks between the words, but then run all the letters together.
3. With the letters run together, state how many words there are in the sentence, but later let the players determine this for themselves.
4. Begin by letting the players know what consonant is to be inserted, but afterward leave it to them to discover the right one.
5. First let the players know how many times the consonant is to be used, but then keep them in ignorance of this fact too.

TEACHER: *What ten-letter word starts with gas?*
STUDENT: *Automobile.*

What letter is most useful to a deaf woman?
The letter a, *because it makes* her hear.

SECRET WORD   VAR. 6

ADVANCED   *Paper and pencil*
2 *only*

This game, like WHAT'S MY WORD?, of which it is a more
complicated variation, develops vocabulary and teaches spelling.

Each of the two players chooses a secret word and writes it
on his paper. At the outset, it might be well for them to agree
to select words of no more than four letters and to build up to
longer ones as they gain in skill and experience.

Let us suppose that Player 1 chooses the word GAME, and
Player 2 chooses TRAP.

Now Player 1 chooses another word of four letters—say,
MILK—and, after writing it in the space below his secret
word, asks his opponent, "How many letters in MILK are in
your secret word?"

"None," answers Player 2.

At least Player 1 now knows that his opponent's word does
not contain the letters M, I, L, or K, and he can avoid these
letters in making up later test words. As a reminder to himself, he therefore crosses these letters off the alphabet he has
written on his sheet.

Now Player 2 gets his chance to try a test word. Suppose
he tries SLIM. He learns that one of its letters is in his opponent's secret word. But which one? Since he does not yet know,
he circles these letters on his alphabet as a reminder to use
them in later rounds. Note, though, that if he later tries the
word SEAT, as a test of the S in SLIM, he will be told that
two of the letters in SEAT are in his opponent's secret word,
but he will still be in the dark about which ones they are.

But now suppose Player 1 hits upon the test word PART.
All four letters are in his opponent's secret word, but Player 1
still has not guessed what it is. He has to think of other words

that could be made with the letters P, A, R, and T. The next time around he might guess RAPT, but he still would not be right.

Obviously, then, Player 2, whose secret word consisted of four letters that could make two other words, had an advantage over Player 1, whose secret word contained letters that could form only that word and no other. For even after Player 1 had guessed all the letters of his opponent's secret word, he still had to use additional questions to hit on the right combination.

The winner is the player who first guesses his opponent's secret word.

ALPHABETICAL DICE

| ELEMENTARY-INTERMEDIATE | *Dice* |
| 2 *or more* | *Clock or timer* |

This game teaches both spelling and vocabulary.

First, prepare four or five sets of "dice" by marking each of the six sides of a number of cubes with a different letter of the alphabet. Be sure that each cube has a mixture of vowels and consonants.

Begin with any pair of dice, and let the first player have two throws, turning up two letters with each throw, or four letters in all. He scores one point for each letter of any word of three or four letters that he can form, within a given time limit, with the letters he turns up. Each player then takes his turn with the dice. The second time around, each player is allowed three throws, and he scores one point for each letter of any word of five or six letters that he can form, before time is up, with the letters he throws. The game keeps "escalating" in this fashion.

When the limited possibilities of a single pair of dice seem to have been exhausted, another pair may be substituted, or one die of the original pair may be matched with a new one.

SYLLABLE DICE

ELEMENTARY-INTERMEDIATE   *Dice*
2 *or more*   *Clock or timer*

In this variation, the cubes are prepared in the same way, but this time with a different three-letter syllable on each of the six sides. Typical syllables might be: *bel, rad, cat, dem, ere, act, ide, dic, loc, ear, not, ens, pul, rar, eve, fri, hap, min, gre, ham, gin, sil, ins, pet, kno, ost, lac, pan, pou, ros, spi, ucc, sus, tin, vas, wis, wee.*

Each player takes his turn throwing a die. He scores one point for each letter of any word he can form that contains the syllable he has turned up. The syllable may appear at the beginning or the end or in the middle of the word and need not even be pronounced as a syllable in the word. Of course, a time limit is placed on each player.

Thus, a player who turns up UCC might form the words *buccal, succotash, stucco, succulent, buccaneer, succumb, succinct, success,* etc.

~~~~~~~~~~~~~~~~~~~~~~~~~~~~~~~

Why did Noah object to the letter d?
Because it made the ark dark.

What do bees do with their honey?
They cell it!

Why is o *the noisiest vowel?*
Because all the others are in audible.

What letter of the alphabet is needed to make a shoe?
The last.

Why is a teacher of girls like the letter c?
Because she makes lasses *into* classes.

V. Spelling "Demons"

Studies of the spelling errors most commonly made show that a relatively small number of words—called "spelling 'demons' "—account for most of the mistakes. The games in this section help the child to master the spelling of these particularly troublesome words.

SPELLING CONCENTRATION

INTERMEDIATE-ADVANCED   *Blank cards (playing-card*
2 *only*   *size)*

One of the problems of spelling that causes a great deal of confusion is the choice between two differently spelled but similarly pronounced endings—e.g., *able* or *ible*, *ance* or *ence*,—and sometimes even among three alternatives—e.g., *al*, *el*, and *le*, *ous*, *eous*, and *ious*, or *cede*, *ceed*, and *sede*. This card game helps to clear up such confusions and to fix the right spelling in mind. It is best played by no more than two.

First decide on the troublesome words you wish to have the players learn to spell. If the problem is with ABLE and IBLE, the words may be chosen from the following list according to the maturity of the players.

ABLE: acceptable, advisable, applicable, believable, changeable, comfortable, comparable, dependable, desirable, excitable, excusable, favorable, imaginable, movable, perishable, presentable, profitable, recognizable, regrettable, suitable, valuable.

IBLE: forcible, admissible, permissible, collapsible, convertible, defensible, divisible.

(For more advanced players, the words *formidable*, *probable*, *eligible*, *legible*, *possible*, *plausible*, *credible*, *audible*, and *responsible* may be added.)

If the problem is with AL, EL, and LE, words may be selected from the following list.

AL: acquittal, refusal, dismissal, appraisal, recital, carousal.

EL: angel, apparel, enamel, gavel, gravel, hovel, label, level, navel, nickel, novel, parcel, satchel, carrousel.

LE: angle, article, axle, candle, cradle, eagle, pickle.

(For more advanced players, the words *dial*, *equal*, *marshal*, *naval*, *metal*, *mettle*, *medal*, *meddle*, *moral*, *morale*, *rival*, *vial*, *principal*, *principle*, *fondle*, and *manacle* may be added.)

If the problem is with OUS, EOUS, and IOUS, the following list may prove helpful as a source of words.

OUS:　callous, credulous, famous, jealous, poisonous, ridiculous, anonymous, desirous, grievous.

EOUS: courteous, gorgeous, hideous, righteous, erroneous, advantageous, simultaneous, spontaneous, nauseous.

IOUS: ambitious, cautious, anxious, conscious, delicious, delirious, envious, fictitious, ingenious, religious.

(For more advanced players, the words *analogous*, *solicitous*, *generous*, *gaseous*, *miscellaneous*, *homogeneous*, *sacrilegious*, *conscientious*, *malicious*, and *facetious* may be added.)

If the problem is with ANCE and ENCE, the selection may be made from the following list.

ANCE: acquaintance, admittance, appearance, attendance, guidance, hindrance, maintenance, performance, perseverance, balance, tolerance.

ENCE: competence, conference, confidence, excellence, existence, experience, independence, intelligence, occurrence, preference, reference.

(For more advanced players, the words *variance*, *vigilance*, *correspondence*, *persistence*, *assistance*, and *decadence* may be added.)

As for confusions among words ending in CEED, CEDE, and SEDE, the following list should be used.

CEED: proceed, succeed, exceed.

CEDE: accede, concede, intercede, precede, recede, secede, cede.

SEDE: supersede.

Having chosen the words you want, write the ending of each on one card and the rest of the word on another card. For example, one card might have *able* and the other *desir*. Prepare forty such cards, or twenty pairs, in all. Extra sets, with different words, can be kept in reserve for successive rounds. Of course, a pack should contain examples of each type of ending.

After being thoroughly shuffled, the cards are spread out, face down, on the table. The first player then picks up two cards at random and shows them to his opponent. If the cards make a properly spelled word when put together, the first player places them face up on his side of the table, scoring one point. He may then have another try at finding a matching pair. If he cannot do so, he must return one of the cards, after showing both to his opponent, face down, to its former place.

The second player now picks one card at random from those lying face down on the table. He tries to remember the position and the letters on the card that was put down by his opponent in order to determine whether it will make a word when matched with the card in his hand. If he succeeds in getting a pair that will spell a word, he lays both cards down, face up, on his side of the table, scores one point, and draws two cards at random. If he remembers that the discard will not make a pair with his first card, he may draw one more card at random. At all times, a card that is picked up from the table must be shown to one's opponent in order to give him a chance to memorize its location in case it is put down again.

The players proceed in this fashion until the last card has been picked up from the table. The winner is the player with the highest score.

The game can be made gradually more difficult by introducing harder words in successive rounds and increasing, a pair at a time, the number of cards in the deck with each round. In that case you can aid the players in associating a card with the word on its face by writing a different number (1, 2, 3, etc.) on the back of each.

SPELLING RUMMY

INTERMEDIATE-ADVANCED   *Blank cards (playing-card*
2 *or more*   *size)*

This is another card game designed to end confusions about the spelling of words with similarly sounded endings, like the ones in SPELLING CONCENTRATION. In addition to those already listed for that game, there are words ending in *or* (e.g., *actor, creditor, debtor, donor, victor, captor, sailor, pastor,* etc.) and those ending in *er* (like *carpenter, lawyer, painter, seller,* etc.), to say nothing of those that end in *ar* (like *cellar, liar, calendar,* etc.).

The words chosen should suit the ability and maturity of the players. Prepared by parent or teacher, the cards should consist of sets, as in the preceding game. In each set one card should contain the ending—e.g., *or*—and the other the rest of the word—e.g., *tail*. About sixty cards, or thirty sets, should be prepared for two, three, or four players; sixty-six, or thirty-three sets, for five players; and around seventy, or thirty-five sets, for six players.

Now shuffle, cut, and deal. If two play, ten cards are dealt to each player; if three, seven cards; and if there are four or more players, six cards. The next card is then placed face up, beside the rest of the deck, which is laid face down.

Each player in turn must either draw a card from the top of the deck without showing it, or take the card that is lying face up beside the deck. After adding the new card to his hand, he must discard one from it, laying it face up either on top of the one already face up or in its place. Only the top card may be drawn from either of the two piles.

The object of the game is to collect sets of cards that will form properly spelled words when placed side by side. Whenever a player gets such a set, he lays it face up on the table.

The first to get rid of all the cards in his hand wins the game. If several rounds are played, a point is scored for every word a player forms by laying down sets of cards; and at the end of a number of rounds, the points are totaled to determine the winner.

How can the letter w *be used to bring music up to date?*
It changes SING to SWING.

Make just one word from the following letters: DEJNOORSTUW.
Just one word.

What common word has the vowels OEI together in that order?
CANOEIST.

What three words each have five consecutive consonants?
BORSCHT, LENGTHS, and STRENGTHS.

Write the letter o *six times in succession, like this:* o o o o o o
Now, inserting one consonant six times over, make a sentence that reads the same backward and forward.
"Toot, Otto, toot."

In the following code the same consonant must be inserted fourteen times: A L H O U G H H E W O O S I E R E D H E Y O L D H E O F O L D A L E. What sentence will be made?
Although the two tots tittered, they told the oft-told tale.

> *A word there is,*
> *Five syllables contains;*
> *Take one away—*
> *Not one of them remains!*

The word is MONOSYLLABLE. Take away MO and you leave NO SYLLABLE.

SPELL-O

INTERMEDIATE-ADVANCED	*Paper and pencil*
3 *or more*	*Blank cards (bingo or lotto size)*
	Small slips of paper
	Small colored cardboard squares

This game, which is very similar to bingo, is a good way to review the spelling of words, like the ones in SPELLING CONCENTRATION and SPELLING RUMMY, whose endings are confused. To the lists included with those games may be added words about which there is often doubt whether they end simply in *ly* or in *ally*. Here are a few examples of each type that may be included in this game along with the words previously listed.

ALLY: comically, tragically, accidentally, practically, fantastically, incidentally, physically, rhythmically.

LY: apparently, persistently, advantageously, consciously, independently, innocently.

The number of players is limited only by the materials available.

Each player receives a card like the one shown opposite.

Of course, aside from the top line, all the cards are different.

In addition, the players receive a number of small colored squares of cardboard that can be placed over the boxes on the card.

Slips of paper are prepared, each containing a letter of the word SPELL-O followed by a word or part of a word that needs to be completed by one of the endings shown on the card above—e.g., L-METALLIC, P-ANG, S-SAIL, O-APPEAR, etc.

From a box into which these slips have been placed, the

S	P	E	L	L	O
OR	EL	ABLE	LY	LE	IBLE
AR	OUS	ANCE	ALLY	AR	ABLE
ER	IOUS	ENCE	OR	OUS	ANCE
AL	EOUS	ANT	ER	IOUS	ENCE
LE	IBLE	ENT	AL	EOUS	OR

leader picks one and reads it to the players. Let us say he selects L-GAS. All the players now check their cards to see whether they have a box in the row under the letter L with letters that will correctly spell a word beginning with GAS. (In the particular card shown here, it is the lowest box in the row, with the letters EOUS.) Whoever has such a box writes the beginning of the word GASEOUS on one of his colored cardboard squares and places it over the box on his card.

The game proceeds in this way until one of the players has covered a whole row horizontally, vertically, or diagonally. He then calls out "SPELL-O" and hands his card to the leader to have it checked. Of course, he gets no credit if he spells a word incorrectly—e.g., if he places GAS over the box marked IOUS. Thus, SPELL-O is more than just a game of chance; it calls for a knowledge of spelling as well as a certain amount of good luck.

This game can also be played in accordance with the rules of lotto rather than bingo. In that case, in order to win, a player would have to cover *all* the boxes on his card.

SPELLING DOMINOES

INTERMEDIATE-ADVANCED   *Blank cards (playing-card*
3 *or more*   *size)*

This is an excellent game for reviewing the spelling of all
the words listed in SPELLING CONCENTRATION, SPELL-
ING RUMMY, and SPELL-O, with endings that are often
confused.

Thirty-six cards are prepared with a double square on the
face of each. Suppose the six endings to be learned in this
game are ABLE, IBLE, OR, ER, ANCE, and ENCE. For each
of these endings, six cards are prepared with the ending in
one of the two squares. In the other square of the first card in
each of the six sets write the beginning of a word that ends
with the letters in the first square. Thus, you might have the
following six combinations: ABLE and PROB, IBLE and
POSS, OR and ACT, ER and CAMP, ANCE and GUID, and
ENCE and COMPET. In the other square of each of the other
five cards in each set write, successively, the beginning of a
word that could be made with each of the other five endings.
The results might look like these:

Cards with ABLE on one square would have, in the other
square, PROB, POSS, DON, SELL, TOLER, and EXIST.
(Note that TOLER can be matched with ANCE as well as
ABLE, and PROB can be matched with both ABLE and ER.)

Cards with IBLE on one square would have, in the other
square, DIVIS, SUIT, SAIL, BEAR, VARI, PREFER. (Note
that SUIT might be matched with either ABLE or OR; BEAR
could be matched with either ABLE or ER; VARI can be
matched with either ABLE or ANCE; and PREFER could be
matched with either ABLE or ENCE. The more of these
double-duty beginnings that you have, the better.)

Cards with OR on one square would have, in the other
square, ACT, TEST, SENS, MIN, HINDR, EXPERI. (Note

that SENS might be matched with IBLE or OR, and that MIN could be matched with either OR or ER.)

Cards with ER in one square would have, in the other square, SLEEP, REDOUBT, PERMISS, PAST, BAL, and CONFER. (Note that PAST could be matched with either ER or OR.)

Cards with ANCE in one square would have, in the other square, GUID, COMFORT, CONVERT, VISIT, SING, and PREFER. (Note that PREFER could be matched with either ENCE or ABLE, and SING could be matched with either ABLE or ER.)

Cards with ENCE in one square would have, in the other square, COMPET, EXCUS, RESPONS, CANT, CARPENT, and TEMPER. (Note that CANT could be matched with either OR or ER.)

Of course, with these six endings many other words can be formed; and with such endings as *ar*, *al*, *el*, *le*, *ally*, and *ly*, still more words could be added. Thus, the possibilities are by no means restricted to the thirty-six words used in this sample. The particular words chosen would depend on the abilities and maturity of the players.

The cards are shuffled and laid face down in a pack on the table. Each player in turn then draws one card until he has six. If a player finds that he has in his hand cards that contain squares which, when laid side by side, will form a word, he puts them down, when his turn comes, face up on the table. The next player may lay down one or more cards from his hand, either independently or to complete a word with the aid of the letters at either end of a set that has already been laid down by another player. If a player cannot form a word, he has to draw a card from the top of the deck and keep on doing so until he finds a suitable match. The object of the game is to be the first to get rid of all the cards in one's hand.

The game can be complicated by choosing more difficult words than the ones listed here or by adding to the number of endings and cards.

SPELLING GRAB BAG

ELEMENTARY-INTERMEDIATE   *Blank cards (playing-card*
2 *or more*   *size)*

The words most frequently misspelled are common ones like
*divide, among, believe, forty, separate, truly, until, similar,
woman, writing, library, ninety, occasion, piece, grammar,
disappoint, describe, coming,* etc. This game can be used to
help children to learn the spelling of these and many other
everyday words.

Prepare a set of cards on each of which is written a pho-
netic respelling of some ordinary word which you would like
the players to learn how to spell. For example, your cards
might look like this: RUF, KWIK, VU, KOF, KAJI, AJASENT,
AWKID, SKWOSH, ORENJ, MUSKITO, DUZ, FAWTH,
SED, KONSHENS, CONKER, etc. The number of cards will
depend on the number of players.

Shuffle the cards and throw them into a box or bag. Each
player then draws a card blindly from the bag when his turn
comes, pronounces the word, and spells it. If he misses, the
next player gets a chance to spell the same word. When only
two or three play this game, a point is scored for each letter
of a correctly spelled word. If a larger group plays, those who
misspell a word are eliminated, as in a spelling bee, and the
one who finally "survives" wins the game.

Words for the game can be taken from those misspelled by
the players in previous games, from the spelling lists given
to children by their teachers, or from the lists in the spelling
books included in the bibliography at the back of this book.

Why is the letter e *like death?*
Because it is the end *of* life.

What word has three consecutive sets of double letters?
BOOKKEEPER.

SPELLING WAR

INTERMEDIATE-ADVANCED   *Blank cards (playing-card*
2 *only*   *size)*

A good way to avoid confusing words with similarly pronounced but differently spelled endings is to group together
all those that end in the same way. In addition to the endings
listed for such games as SPELLING CONCENTRATION,
SPELLING RUMMY, and SPELL-O, above, there are several
others that are equally troublesome—e.g., *ary, ery, and ory*
(to say nothing of *orie* in *calorie* and *erie* in *coterie*), *ury,*
acy, asy (as in *apostasy*), *isy* (as in *hypocrisy*), *esy* (as in
heresy), and *ecy* (as in *secrecy*).

First decide on the words you wish the players to learn to
spell. If the problem is with ARY, ERY, ORY, and URY, the
words may be chosen from the following lists according to
the abilities of the players.

ARY: bestiary, customary, commentary, salivary, calvary,
     ordinary, janizary, arbitrary, parliamentary, con-
     trary, numerary, momentary, luminary, unitary,
     beneficiary, monetary, secretary, apothecary, dic-
     tionary, apiary, aviary, capillary, mortuary, culi-
     nary, dromedary, solitary, actuary, sanitary, corol-
     lary, sumptuary, proprietary, notary, votary, ca-
     nary, February, voluntary, tributary, estuary, honor-
     ary, tutelary, salutary, secondary, mercenary, statu-
     ary, legendary, imaginary, sanctuary, stationary,
     eleemosynary, intermediary, military, necessary,
     obituary, ordinary, sanguinary, planetary, tempo-
     rary, vocabulary, reactionary, visionary, elementary.

ORY: tory, story, history, offertory, accessory, savory, chic-
     ory, hickory, dory, pillory, allegory, migratory, ob-
     ligatory, propitiatory, interrogatory, emory, depila-
     tory, amatory, declamatory, category, territory,

compensatory, signatory, repertory, auditory, repository, dilatory, prefatory, oratory, nugatory, observatory, commendatory, contributory, exclamatory, confiscatory, inflammatory, glory, derogatory, defamatory, circulatory, dormitory, crematory, conservatory, desultory, depository, transitory.

ERY: hosiery, fiery, fishery, bakery, haberdashery, napery, drapery, nunnery, cemetery, battery, flattery, artillery, raillery, forgery, lottery, pottery, mystery, thievery, embroidery, millinery, stationery, monastery.

URY: penury, jury, injury, perjury.

As for the sound of the ending in words like *argosy*, *jealousy*, *secrecy*, *apostasy*, *fantasy*, *heresy*, and *hypocrisy*, the words ending in ACY can be added.

ACY: accuracy, advocacy, celibacy, plutocracy, democracy, bureaucracy, contumacy, papacy, efficacy, fallacy, legacy, aristocracy, plutocracy.

Once the words have been selected, sets of cards are prepared consisting of one card with an ending written on it— say, ORY—and six or seven cards on which are written the beginnings of words that could be formed with that ending— say, INVENT, MANDAT, DEROGAT, CATEG, T, D, etc. (In the case of some endings, the number of possible words that can be formed with them may be fewer.) Enough sets should be prepared so that the deck has at least thirty-five cards, and several easily confused endings should be represented. Extra sets of cards with additional endings or with additional words to be formed with the given endings can be set aside for raising the level of difficulty in successive rounds when the deck can be expanded after the players have become familiar with the spelling of the easier words.

The cards are thoroughly shuffled, and the deck is divided equally between the two players. Each places his stack of cards face down in front of him.

Now the first player turns up the top card on his pile and

lays it face up on the table near him. Then the second player does the same. If the card he turns up can form a word when juxtaposed with the other, he takes his opponent's card, starts a separate pack with the pair, and draws again. If the card he draws cannot make a word when placed alongside his opponent's, the latter exposes a card from his pile. The players continue taking turns drawing one card at a time. Each time one of them can use the card he has drawn to make a word with the card at the top of his opponent's turned-up pile, he takes the whole pile, placing it on top of his matched pack. When all the cards in the stacks are face up, they are turned face down again, and the game continues until one player has won all his opponent's ammunition. The supply can then be replenished with fresh cards, and a new battle may begin.

SPELLING DUEL

ALL LEVELS   *Clock or timer*
2 *only*

This is really a spelling bee carried on between two players. Each is given a list of ten words of approximately equal difficulty. Alternately each player "flings" some word from his list at his dueling antagonist. Three seconds is the time limit for each word. The referee must not only keep time but check to see that words are properly pronounced and spelled.

One point is given for each correct spelling. When all twenty words have been completed, the duelists exchange "swords"—i.e., their lists of words. This time half a point is given for each correct spelling. The players keep exchanging the same list until both spell every word correctly within the allotted time. Then a new list is given to each.

The game can be complicated by making the lists longer—say, twenty words—and by including ever more difficult words.

The player who accumulates the greatest number of points wins the game.

MY WORD!

ELEMENTARY-INTERMEDIATE   *Blank cards (playing-card*
2 *or more*   *size)*

This game teaches both vocabulary and spelling.

Write on each of fifty-two cards a different letter of the alphabet. Half the deck should consist of all twenty-six letters; the other half should contain three E's, two each of A, O, U, R, and S, and one each of N, F, W, Y, T, H, C, P, B, D, M, G, and L.

Shuffle the cards thoroughly and lay them face down on the table. Let each player draw one card. The one drawing the card with the letter nearest the beginning of the alphabet plays first; the one drawing the card with the letter next nearest plays second; and so on.

After the cards so drawn have been replaced and the deck has once again been shuffled, the first player draws a card and places it face up on the table. The next player does the same. As soon as any player can combine one or more of his own letters, lying face up before him, with those exposed by any other player or players so as to make a word, whether by addition or insertion, he calls out "My word!" and takes their letters, spelling the word and placing it in front of him on the table. A word so made may be taken by another player with a letter that, when added or inserted, makes a new word.

After all the cards have been drawn, the score is calculated by giving each player two points for each letter of every word he has set down before him and subtracting one point for each letter he has left that does not form part of any complete word.

How do you remember whether to spell "friend" with the i *before the* e *or with the* e *before the* i?
Think of the end *of the word.*

VERBAL PING-PONG

ALL LEVELS   *Coins*

2 only

Like TIMED TONGUE-TIP TEASERS (page 137), this is a
fast game calling for nimble wits and rapid verbal responses.
An excellent way to review spelling, it is best played with a
third person keeping time and priming the players.

A good way of keeping time is to set a coin spinning while
the players take turns giving responses as fast as they can to
see how many they can complete before time is up.

The person calling the plays might begin by asking, "How
many words can we mention that have double letters? Ready?
Go!" The first player might call out, "Rubber!" and the second, "Scribble!" and the play might go back and forth at a
furious pace with such words as *newsstand, jazz, jigger*, etc.,
until the coin stopped spinning.

Now the game can be made a little more difficult. "Let's
try words with a double O. Ready? Go!" By this time the
players have warmed up, and they might toss back and forth
words like *spool, loom, look, book, took, tool, igloo, roost,
droop, boor, food, flood, troop*, etc.

The game may be varied further by specifying other letters
to be doubled: G's, as in *tagged, beggar*, etc.; T's, as in *better,
letter, battle, bottle, attend*, etc.; P's, as in *happy, zipper, dap-
per*, etc.; N's, as in *fanning, pennant, inning*, etc.; C's, as in
success, flaccid, access, etc.

Then after the possibilities of double letters appear to have
been exhausted, the game could be used to review various
prefixes—say, *dis, mis, re, pre, anti, ante*, etc.—and suffixes—
e.g., *ize* (*capitalize, terrorize, hospitalize*, and the like), *al,
eous, ious*, etc., or endings like *ology, able, ible, ism, itis*, and
so on.

A more difficult variety of this game involves naming

words with silent letters, like *plumber, debt, mortgage, know, lamb, comb, column, receipt, psychology, wrestle, answer, subtle, hymn, knob,* and *wrote.* This is an excellent way of reviewing troublesome spelling words.

At a still higher level of difficulty one can play this game with words that begin and end with the same letter, like *barb, bulb, area, tact, did, fief, hash, kick, maim, prop, rear, roar,* etc.

Really experienced and skillful players who would like to match wits in this game can try volleying palindromes—i.e., words that are the same whether spelled backward or forward, like *level, dad, pep, nun, eye, ewe, did, noon, bob, deed, tot, redder, eke, tenet, peep, madam, ere, rotator, deified, radar, refer,* and *bib.*

At its loftiest heights, this game can challenge the players to bounce back and forth a series of onomatopoeic words— i.e., words that sound like what they mean, such as *purr, whiz, buzz, bang, hoot, hum, murmur, whisper, sizzle, clang, fizz, hush,* etc.

How do you remember to spell "principal" with an a *when you mean the head of a school?*
Just recall that the principal is your *pal.*

How do you remember to spell "stationary" with an a *to distinguish it from "stationery"?*
Just remember that when something is stationary, it makes nary *a move.*

Pronounce POTHZWABYUCKELING.
There's nothing to pronounce! Every letter is silent: the p *as in* pneumonia, o *as in* leopard, t *as in* ballet, h *as in* catarrh, z *as in* rendezvous, w *as in* wrong, a *as in* dead, b *as in* dumb, y *as in* today, u *as in* four, c *as in* czar, k *as in* knock, e *as in* blue, l *as in* would, i *as in* cruise, n *as in* condemned, *and* g *as in* gnu.

VI. Spelling Rules

Some people say that spelling rules are hardly worth learning because there are so many exceptions to them. Yet there is no doubt that a mastery of these rules can help in the spelling of thousands of words. As for the exceptions, they are generally few in number in comparison with the multitude of words that follow the rules.

These games have been designed to teach the child to apply the rules and to familiarize him with the common exceptions.

DOUBLE QUICK

INTERMEDIATE
2 or more

Blank cards (playing-card size)
Clock or timer

A frequently troublesome point in spelling is whether or not to double a final consonant when adding a suffix. This game helps to teach the application of the spelling rule that in words of one syllable or words accented on the final syllable a final consonant is doubled only if preceded by a single vowel and followed by a suffix beginning with a vowel. Since this rule applies to more than three thousand words, it is extremely useful.

Prepare a number of cards by writing on each a common suffix—e.g., MENT, ING, ER, OR, ED, ENCE, ANCE, AL, Y, EE, EST, ABLE, and IBLE. Then prepare another set of cards with words that could precede one or more of these suffixes, like RED, SHIP, TIN, PLAN, OCCUR, REFER, BEGIN, DEAL, FARM, HAPPEN, OFFER, ACQUIT, BAR, BEG, BENEFIT, GRAB, STOP, WAR, DIFFER, LIMIT, ABHOR, ADMIT, PERMIT, COMMIT, etc.

Lay the first set of cards face up on the table so that each

card is clearly visible to all the players. Shuffle the other set
and lay the pack face down on the table.

The first player now draws a card from the top of the pack,
turns it up, and has three seconds to match it with one or
more of the endings shown on the cards lying face up and to
say whether or not the final consonant should be doubled.
He earns one point for each word he spells correctly. Thus,
with PLAN, he can form PLANABLE, PLANNABLE,
PLANNED, PLANNING, PLANED, PLANER, PLANING,
and PLANNER, making eight points in all. If a player misses,
he earns no credit. The players take turns until all the cards
have been used in the stack lying face down. The winner is
the player who accumulates the greatest number of points.

EYES AND EASE   VAR. 1

INTERMEDIATE   *Blank cards (playing-card*
2 *only*   *size)*
                             Bell or whistle
                             Clock or timer

Another bothersome problem in spelling is whether to write
ie or *ei* in hundreds of words like *receive, science, conscience,
siege, seize, weird, relieve, leisure, height, weight, ceiling, de-
ceit,* and *financier*. There does not seem to be much consistency in the spelling of even the few words listed here.

In fact, however, there is a rule, and the common exceptions to it are easily learned: *i* before *e*, except after *c*, or
when sounded as *a*, as in "neighbor" and "weigh." The sentence "Neither weird financier seized either species of leisure" takes care of the major exceptions. And this game will
help to fit the application of a rule to any number of words.

Prepare four cards, two with IE written on them and two
with EI. If two boys are playing, each should have an IE card
pinned on the outside of his left jacket pocket and an EI card
pinned on the outside of his right jacket pocket so that the

letters on each card can easily be seen. Of course, the jacket pockets should be larger than the cards being used. If girls play the game, each should be provided with a pair of boxes or baskets, and the cards should be pasted or taped to the outside of these so that the lettering is clearly visible.

Now prepare two duplicate sets of cards with words having *ei* or *ie* in them, writing on each card two dots to represent these letters, thus: REC . . VE, DEC . . VE, MISCH . . F, HANDKERCH . . F, FR . . ND, V . . W, INTERV . . W, FORF . . T, GR . . VE, W . . GHT, N . . GH, N . . GHBOR, H . . GHT, R . . GN, R . . N, Y . . LD, W . . LD, W . . RD, V . . N, FRONT . . R, RETR . . VE, L . . D, L . . SURE, S . . VE, SH . . K, SHR . . K, SH . . LD, M . . N, ACH . . VE, FOR . . GN, COUNTERF . . T, CHANDEL . . R, CASH . . R, N . . CE, V . . L, S . . ZE, PERC . . VE, P . . CE, BES . . GE, FR . . GHT, . . GHT, CONC . . T, CONSC . . NTIOUS, TH . . F, BR . . F, P . . R, TH . . R, F . . RCE, ANC . . NT, OMNISC . . NT, etc.

Start with about twenty-five cards in each set, leaving the others for later rounds. Shuffle the cards in each set, and lay the two sets face down on the table, one before each player.

At a given signal, each player picks up the top card from the deck before him, looks at it, and within three seconds, must put it into his left or his right pocket or into her left or right basket, according to the player's instantaneous judgment about its spelling. When the signal is given again—a bell or a whistle will do very well—the players proceed to the next card on their respective decks and follow the same procedure, until all the cards in each deck have disappeared into the players' pockets or baskets.

Now the players empty first the left and then the right pocket or basket and compare their results. If there are any discrepancies, one player or the other has made a mistake. One point is gained for each card correctly placed to form a properly spelled word.

The two cards bearing any word on which both players have scored are set aside, but the two cards bearing any word on which either player has made a mistake are included in the new set of decks, consisting of additional words, that are used in the second round. This is played and scored in the same way. In each succeeding round, holdovers from previous rounds will be included if any mistakes were made. In this way players have an incentive and an opportunity to learn from their mistakes and to fix the right spelling in their minds. The winner is the player earning the greatest number of points.

QUICKY   VAR. 2

INTERMEDIATE   Blank cards (playing-card
2 only   size)
                             Bell or whistle
                             Clock or timer

Similar difficulties arise about whether to keep or to drop the *e* in words like *truly, duly, lovely, hopeful, hoping, judgment, lovable, dosage, noticeable, outrageous, courageous, manageable,* etc. The rule in this case is that words ending in a silent *e* usually drop the *e* before a suffix beginning with a vowel but retain the *e* before a suffix beginning with a consonant. As can be seen from the examples given here, there are some exceptions to this rule too. But both the rule and the exceptions can easily be learned by playing this game.

The procedure is the same as in EYES AND EASE, except that the four basic cards consist of two cards with E and two with Ɇ. The duplicate sets of words should be written on the cards in this fashion: JUDGE+MENT, LATE+NESS, DESIRE+OUS, ADVANTAGE+OUS, EXCITE+ING, ICE+ING, PEACE+ABLE, TIE+ING, GUIDE+ANCE, NINE+TEEN, ARGUE+MENT, OWE+ING, WHOLE+LY, SINGE+ING, HOE+ING, ACKNOWLEDGE+MENT, SHOE+ING, IMMENSE+LY, PURSUE+ING, SINCERE+LY, VALUE+

ABLE, WRITE+ING, ARRANGE+MENT, FINE+LY, CA-NOE+ING, USE+AGE, MILE+AGE, IMAGINE+ARY, IMMEDIATE+LY, COMPLETE+LY, BECOME+ING, AR-RIVE+AL, REMOVE+AL, AMUSE+MENT, ENCOUR-AGE+MENT, HOPE+ING, etc.

Now proceed as in EYES AND EASE, giving the players three seconds for each card they turn up, until every card in each of two matched packs of twenty-five has been placed in one category or the other. Then compare the results, score the round, eliminate cards with words that both players spelled correctly, and add the remaining cards to the sets with new words, so that the difficult words are reviewed. The result should be mastery of this spelling rule and of its most common exceptions.

WORDS FOR THE WISE   VAR. 3

INTERMEDIATE-ADVANCED   *Blank cards (playing-card*
2 *only*   *size)*
                                           Bell or whistle
                                           Clock or timer

This variation is the most difficult. It helps the players to apply the rule that determines whether a final y is retained when a suffix is added or whether it is changed to some other letter or letters. In other words, the game is concerned with the spelling of words such as *countries, monkeys, tried, shyly, drier, flies, babyish, piteous, copying, follies, alleys,* and *allies.*

The rule in these cases is that a final y preceded by a consonant becomes *ie* before *s* and *i* before all other suffixes except those beginning with *i.* The exceptions are words derived from adjectives of one syllable, like *dryness* and *slyly,* and words in which the consonant preceding the final y is a *t* and the suffix is *ous,* in which case y changes to *e,* as in "bounteous."

Eight basic cards are prepared: two with Y, two with I, two with IE, and two with E. Each set of four is laid face up on the table before the player who is to work with it. Then duplicate sets of words are written on cards in this fashion: AT-TORNEY+S, HEAVY+LY, LONELY+NESS, CRAZY+EST, PLENTY+OUS, MEDLEY+S, LIBRARY+S, PULLEY+S, BUSY+LY, APPLY+ED, CARRY+S, KINDLY+NESS, READY+LY, ACCOMPANY+ING, IMPLY+S, MODIFY+ER, SPY+S, DEFY+ANT, TASTY+EST, BURY+ED, CEN-TURY+S, KIDNEY+S, FRIENDLY+NESS, FACILITY+S, STUDY+ING, CHIMNEY+S, FRY+ED, LIVELY+ER, NECESSARY+LY, LADY+S, TROLLEY+S, BUSY+NESS, CITY+S, DENY+ED, PITY+ED, PITY+OUS, TURKEY+S, LILY+S, VALLEY+S, BODY+S, DRY+LY, COZY+LY, DIZZY+NESS, FLURRY+S, HURRY+ED, etc.

Each set of duplicate cards is shuffled and laid face down in front of the player who is to use it. About twenty-five cards in each set are sufficient for the first round.

At a given signal, each player turns up his top card and, within four seconds, must lay it face down on the table behind the basic card that bears the letter that will correctly spell the complete word. Then, at a blast from the whistle, they proceed to the next card, and so on, until all the cards in the deck have been gone through in this way.

When the cards are turned face up, one point is scored for each correctly spelled word. All cards which both players put in the right pile are eliminated from the deck for the second round, and others are substituted for them. In each succeeding round the same procedure is followed. The high scorer is the winner.

How do you remember how to spell "across"?
Just think of a cross.

How do you remember the correct spelling of "piece"?
Just think of a piece of pie.

VII. Group Games

Some of the preceding games require but two players. In larger families, or where the children's friends are invited to join in the fun, games specifically suited to larger groups may serve the same educational purpose. Here are a few that are best played with more than just two or three.

SPELLING BEE WITHOUT THE STING

ALL LEVELS   *Clock or timer*
Large families or groups

This is the ideal way of teaching the spelling "demons"—the words that almost everyone has trouble with. The words used can be graduated in difficulty to suit the abilities of the group. Lists for this purpose can be found in a number of the spelling books mentioned in the bibliography.

The players are arranged in a semicircle around the moderator and take turns spelling each word as it is given to them. Ten seconds are allowed for each answer. If a player spells his word correctly, the next player is given another word; if he misspells the word, the next player is given the same word. This word is repeated until someone spells it correctly. Players who misspell words are eliminated, and the last "survivor" wins the round.

Another method of conducting a spelling bee is to give a player one point for each word he spells correctly and to let him proceed as far as he can down the list until he misses. His score is totaled, and then the next player picks up by trying to spell the word missed by the player before him. When the game is played in this way, the words in the list should be of relatively equal difficulty. At the end, the player with the greatest number of points wins the game.

Still another method of holding a spelling bee is to divide the players into two evenly matched teams, each sitting or standing in a line facing the other. Players alternate spelling words, with the first speller on Team A followed by the first speller on Team B, until everyone on each team has had a chance. Players who misspell a word are eliminated from their team, until one team has been entirely eliminated.

Finally, a spelling bee may be conducted in such a way as to require the player on the opposite team to call immediately "Right!" or "Wrong!" on hearing a word spelled by his adversary. If he calls a correctly spelled word wrong or an incorrectly spelled word right, he is eliminated just as if he himself had misspelled a word. Thus, either or both of the opponents may be eliminated on the same word.

WORD POLYGAMY

INTERMEDIATE-ADVANCED   *Paper and pencil*
Large families or groups   *Clock or timer*

This game adds to the vocabulary of the players at the same time that it teaches them to spell compound words.

The players are given a word like *heart* which they must "marry" to as many words as they can think of in order to form compatible "couples"—i.e., compound words. Each player takes about five minutes to write down his list of "mates," taking care to spell the compound words correctly.

The word *heart*, for example, might form part of such compounds as *heart-warming, heart-heavy, hardhearted, heart strain, heartache, lionhearted, heart-to-heart, heartstring, heartrending, heartsick, heartfelt, heartburn, heartbroken,* etc.

When the five minutes are up, the first player reads his list, indicating in each case whether the compound is spelled as two separate words, a hyphenated word, or a solid. Any word he reads that is duplicated on another player's list must be crossed off each list on which it appears, including his own. The players then take turns reading their lists and crossing off duplicates, until all the lists have been read. Five points are scored for any word not on another list. If all the words on all the lists are crossed off, or if there is a tie, another round is played, this time with a different starting word.

No credit is given for words improperly compounded. The dictionary, of course, is the final arbiter in case of dispute.

Other words well suited for this game are *self*, *weak*, *strong*, *water*, *thick*, *thunder*, *foot*, *hand*, *head*, *broad*, *double*, *soft*, and the names of colors (*black*, *blue*, *yellow*, etc.).

MAGIC TELEGRAMS

INTERMEDIATE   *Paper and pencil*
Large families or groups   *Clock or timer*

Here is an initial-letter game that teaches spelling, punctuation, and sentence structure.

The participants sit in a circle, each with a sheet of paper and a pencil.

As the leader reads ten letters of the alphabet, one by one, the players write them down, leaving a space after each. Thus, suppose that the letters N, D, C, T, L, F, S, A, P, and J are selected. The players would all write them down in this manner:

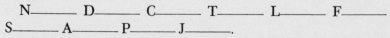

N_____ D_____ C_____ T_____ L_____ F_____
S_____ A_____ P_____ J_____.

The object of the game is to fill in a word after each letter to compose a message for a "magic telegram."

Any ten letters may be chosen, but it is best to avoid X, Z, or too many vowels.

After eight or ten minutes, each player is asked to read his

magic telegram. Many will be amusing, and others completely nonsensical.

Interest can be further heightened if a particular *subject*
is assigned or agreed upon, or if the telegram must be sent to
a particular *person*—a member of the group, for example.

ALPHABETICAL TELEGRAMS   VAR. 1

INTERMEDIATE   *Pencil and paper*
Large families or groups   *Clock or timer*

In this variation, the letters given are arranged alphabet-
ically. However, the telegrams need not begin with the first
letter of the alphabet. Players are free to use their ingenuity,
starting anywhere in the alphabet, in devising coherent telegrams of a given number of words—say, ten. For example,
one player might choose to build his telegram on the initial
sequence D, E, F, G, H, I, J, K, L, M, while another might try
his luck with I, J, K, L, M, N, O, P, Q, R.

ALLITERATIVE TELEGRAMS   VAR. 2

INTERMEDIATE-ADVANCED   *Pencil and paper*
Large families or groups   *Clock or timer*

This variation, which is for more advanced players, makes
the game more challenging by requiring that the same letter
be used to begin each word, as in ALLITERATIVE SEN-
TENCES (page 178). Here too, the players would be free to
choose any letter of the alphabet and use it to begin each of
the ten words in the telegram. Or some of the common letters
(not Z or X) might be assigned to individual players.

Why is the letter p *like a Roman emperor?*
Because it is Nero.

INITIAL LETTERS

INTERMEDIATE-ADVANCED   *Clock or timer*
Large families or groups

This game teaches both spelling and vocabulary. It calls for alertness and a good memory. The larger the group, the better.

An initial letter is agreed upon—say, B. The first player thinks of a word beginning with B, but consisting of only three letters, and defines it. The next player must tell what the word is. If he does so, he must think of a word beginning with B, but consisting of four letters, and must define it. Then the succeeding player must guess what the word is and, in turn, define a five-letter word beginning with B. As the words begin to grow longer, some players may be unable to guess them or to think of longer ones. These players drop out of the game. The last player to remain wins. For example:

PLAYER 1: B plus two letters is a receptacle.
PLAYER 2: Bag or bin. B plus three letters is a drink.
PLAYER 3: Beer. B plus four letters is an explosion.
PLAYER 4: Blast. B plus five letters is shiny.
PLAYER 5: Bright. B plus six letters floats in the air.
PLAYER 6: Balloon. B plus seven letters is worn as an ornament.
PLAYER 7: Bracelet. B plus eight letters is used for carrying papers.
PLAYER 8: Briefcase. B plus nine letters is . . .

In order to allow players to stay in the running for a longer time and to extend the game, it can be simplified by requiring that *all* the words consist of only three letters until someone drops out, then of four letters until the next player misses, and so on. A time limit should be set for answers.

When the possibilities of any one letter seem to have been exhausted, the group can go on to the next letter in the alphabet.

SILLY SYLLABLE

INTERMEDIATE-ADVANCED   *Clock or timer*
Large families or groups

This is essentially a variation of the preceding game. It too teaches spelling and builds vocabulary.

An initial syllable is agreed upon, preferably one that already consists of a word, like *cat*. The first player then thinks of a word beginning with the sound of *cat* and provides a clue to its meaning by asking, "What sort of cat _____?" The next player must guess what the word is. If he does so, he too must think of a word beginning with *cat* and provide the succeeding player with a similar clue to its meaning. The game proceeds in this way, with players dropping out as they are unable to guess the word or to think of new words beginning with the same syllable. The winner is the last player to survive this process of elimination.

Here is how the game might begin:

PLAYER 1: What sort of cat is made of water?

PLAYER 2: A cataract. What sort of cat is a plant?

PLAYER 3: Catnip. What sort of cat do you find in Sunday school?

PLAYER 4: A catechism. What sort of cat do you find in the library?

PLAYER 5: A catalogue. What sort of cat is a calamity?

PLAYER 6: A catastrophe. What sort of cat is an insect?

PLAYER 7: A caterpillar. What sort of cat is bad for the nose?

PLAYER 8: A catarrh. What sort of cat is underground?

PLAYER 9: A catacomb. What sort of cat is a type?

PLAYER 10: A category. What sort of cat is a chemical substance?

PLAYER 11: A catalyst.

When the possibilities of one initial syllable seem to have

been exhausted, another may be used. For example, *pen* will make *peninsula*, *pendulum*, *penance*, *pencil*, *penalty*, *pentagon*, *pensive*, *pennant*, *penthouse*, *pending*, etc.; *new* will make *neuralgia*, *neutral*, *pneumatic*, *numeral*, *numismatics*, *nuisance*, *nucleus*, *nutriment*, etc.; and *cur* will make any number of words (*currency*, *curriculum*, *curse*, *curd*, *curve*, *curb*, *curtain*, etc.), as will *man*, *miss* (see DON'T MISS A WORD! on page 90), *ox*, *pal*, *pan*, *pet*, and many others.

LETTER ALONE

ELEMENTARY   *Pencil and paper*
Large families or groups   *Clock or timer*

This is just a fun game with the alphabet.

Give the players about five minutes to make up as many questions as they can to which the answer, in each case, is a single letter of the alphabet. After time is up, the first player asks his first question. The second player has only five seconds to give the answer. If he had the same question on his own list, he crosses it off and proceeds to ask the next player a different question.

One point is scored for each correct answer. No points are scored for errors or for failure to supply a question or an answer or for repeating a question or for not meeting the time limit.

Here is how such a game might proceed:

PLAYER 1: What letter asks a question?

PLAYER 2: Y. What letter is a sheep?

PLAYER 3: U. What letter is a person having fun?

PLAYER 4: U. What letter is a vegetable?

PLAYER 5: P. What letter is a signal or a clue?

PLAYER 6: Q. What letter is a verb expressing debt?

PLAYER 1: O. What letter is an exclamation of surprise?

PLAYER 2: O. What letter is a large body of water?

PLAYER 3: C. What letter is a bird?

PLAYER 4: J. What letter is a long line?

PLAYER 5: Q. What letter is a slang expression?
PLAYER 6: G. What letter is an organ of the body?
PLAYER 1: I. What letter refers to yourself?
PLAYER 2: I. What letter is a beverage?
PLAYER 3: T. What letter is an insect?
PLAYER 4: B.

LETTER PAIR OFF   VAR. 1

ELEMENTARY-INTERMEDIATE   *Pencil and paper*
Large families or groups   *Clock or timer*

This variation is a little more difficult and may be played after the possibilities of LETTER ALONE seem to have been exhausted.

In this case the players must think up questions to which the answer, in each instance, consists of two letters of the alphabet.

Here is how one such game might proceed:

PLAYER 1: What two letters mean too much?
PLAYER 2: XS. What two letters can mean whatever you mean?
PLAYER 3: NE. What two letters mean a creeping vine?
PLAYER 4: IV. What two letters mean a message received by cable?
PLAYER 5: YR. What two letters mean cautious, crafty, cunning?
PLAYER 6: KG. What two letters refer to a county in England?
PLAYER 1: SX. What two letters mean shabby?
PLAYER 2: CD. What two letters refer to your vision?
PLAYER 3: IC. What two letters refer to my vision?
PLAYER 4: UC. What two letters are a man's name?
PLAYER 5: ON. What two letters are not difficult at all?
PLAYER 6: EZ. What two letters would you use when you have scraped the bottom of the barrel?

PLAYER 1: MT. What two letters refer to a doll?
PLAYER 2: QP. What two letters would you use as a term of endearment?
PLAYER 3: QT. What two letters are a number?
PLAYER 4: AT. What two letters are a kind of pepper?
PLAYER 5: KN. What two letters mean to surpass?
PLAYER 6: XL.

There are, of course, many other two-letter combinations, like *bd*, *pt*, *rt*, *ln*, *le*, *lc*, *kt*, *me*, *dk*, *tp*, *sa*, *nv*, etc., that can be used in this game, to say nothing of repeated letters like *t*'s and *e*'s and *y*'s and *u*'s.

LETTER TRIPLE UP   VAR. 2

ALL LEVELS   *Pencil and paper*
Large families or groups   *Clock or timer*

In this more difficult variation of the same game, the players, after having had their wits sharpened with LETTER ALONE and LETTER PAIR OFF, are given time to formulate questions that can be answered by a combination of three or more letters of the alphabet.

Here is a sample beginning:

PLAYER 1: What three letters do you say when you are playing hide and seek?
PLAYER 2: ICU. What three letters refer to a foe?
PLAYER 3: NME. What three letters name a flower?
PLAYER 4: PNE. What three letters spell a girl's name?
PLAYER 5: MLE.

The humorous possibilities of this game can be exploited by asking questions that have to be answered in complete sentences made up of letters of the alphabet, like *gonicurkg* or *cfufnemnx* or *omleyruic* or *ylcicuoabapne* or *bdirturacdkgnme* or *oinvuln* or *oicuuuatmttpp* or *ucittu* or *ucixlumle* or *iuunexsic* or *oiuutmnx* or *lnucimat* or *ixqqu.*

Can you translate YYURYYUBICURYY4ME?
Too wise you are; too wise you be; I see you are too wise for me.

What one letter of the alphabet will spell "potatoes"?
O. Keep putting it down until you have put eight o's.

How can you remember the spelling of "laboratory"?
Recall that we labor at *or* work on *a problem in a laboratory.*

How can you remember the spelling of "attendance"?
Think of an invitation soliciting your attendance for a dance at ten
o'clock at night: at ten, dance!

How do you remember the spelling of "cemetery"?
"Cemetery" is spelled with e's (ease). Just think of a cemetery in
which every tombstone has the letter e on it. And when you pass by
a cemetery at night, wouldn't you be tempted to cry "EEEE!"?

What does this combination of letters spell: GHOUGHPTEIGH-
BTEAU?
POTATO. GH as in hiccough, *OUGH as in* though, *PT as in* pto-
maine, *EIGH as in* neighbor, *BT as in* debt, *and EAU as in* bureau.

What is the most curious letter in the alphabet?
Y.

What number contains the five vowels a, e, i, o, and u?
FIVE THOUSAND.

What letter of the alphabet will set one of the heavenly bodies in
motion?
T, because it will make a *star* start.

Why is the letter d *like a wedding ring?*
Because we can't be *wed* without it.

CHOOSY

INTERMEDIATE-ADVANCED
Large families or groups

This is a game that encourages creativity and imagination, places a premium on a good memory, and teaches spelling, all at the same time.

The leader begins by announcing, "I am soliciting contributions for Choosy ——— [here inserting his or her own name—say, Jane], who detests *ease*. What will you give Choosy Jane?"

Each player must in turn name a gift for Choosy Jane that does not have the letter E in it. If he names a gift that has already been mentioned or that contains the letter E, he is eliminated.

Here is how the game might proceed:

LEADER: What will you give Choosy Jane?
PLAYER 1: A sword.
LEADER: And what will you give her?
PLAYER 2: A belt.
LEADER: You're out. There is an *e* in "belt." What will you give her?
PLAYER 3: A gun.
LEADER: And what will you give her?
PEAYER 4: A new red hat.
LEADER: You're out. There is an *e* in "new" and another in "red." What will you give her?
PLAYER 5: A gun.
LEADER: You're out. She already has a gun. What will you give her?

After one time around, contributions may be solicited for someone who does not like bees. Thereafter, gifts can be restricted to meet the special tastes of a Choosy who does not like seas, eyes, jays, ells, ems, ens, peas, cues, or teas.

Once the players have had a chance to develop their technique, they may try to please a particularly choosy Choosy who dislikes *both* ease and eyes. In this way, the game can be made increasingly difficult.

This game can also be used to teach the specialized vocabulary of any subject and the spelling of the words connected with it. For example, Choosy could be a musician who detests the wise and has no taste for peas or ease. It may then take some imagination and ingenuity to think of gifts that would be suitable for him. Similarly, whether Choosy is about to go on a trip to Europe, or is a sailor, a soldier, a baseball player, or an astronaut, his special needs will always have to be satisfied with gifts that take account of his peculiar likes and dislikes.

If the leader fails to spot a mistake made by one of the other players, he loses his position, and another player takes his place.

FORBIDDEN LETTER   VAR. 1

ALL LEVELS
Large families or groups

This variation likewise sharpens spelling skills and broadens vocabulary.

At the outset, everyone agrees to omit a certain letter in answering the questions put by the leader. However, the leader is free to use the letter in phrasing his questions. Anyone who answers in a sentence containing the forbidden letter is out.

The leader may ask any question he likes. Suppose, for example, that everyone has agreed to forbid the use of the letter I. The game may proceed like this:

LEADER: What do you use to keep things cold?
PLAYER 1: Ice.
LEADER: You're out. "Ice" begins with an *i*. What do you use?

PLAYER 2: I use a refrigerator.

LEADER: You're out too! You used an *i*. What do you use?

PLAYER 3: Cold storage.

The game continues in this fashion until only one player, the winner, is left.

After the first time around, a different letter may be forbidden.

When the players develop some skill in this game, they may make it harder by forbidding more than one letter or by forbidding doubled letters (*tt*, *ee*, *oo*, etc.) or other common combinations (words ending in *ion*, words with *ie* or *ei*, etc.). Moreover, the leader can use his questions to test the players' vocabulary in any subject—geography, history, music, games, etc.

If the leader fails to spot an error made by any one of the players, he is replaced by someone else.

LIKES AND DISLIKES   VAR. 2

ADVANCED

Large families or groups

Here is a variation that calls for close attention and keen wits. It develops the ability to visualize and remember the spelling of words, to note the respects in which words resemble one another in spelling, and to discriminate between words spelled according to different principles.

The leader begins by telling the players what he likes and what he dislikes: "I like ———, but I dislike ———." Everything that he names among his likes must be spelled according to the same principle—with or without some letter or combination of letters—and everything that he names among his dislikes must be spelled according to the opposite principle. The players then try to infer, from his likes and dislikes, the spelling that he likes and the spelling that he dislikes.

Thus, the game might proceed in this fashion:

LEADER: I like yellow, but I don't like blue.

PLAYER 1:   Then you would like orange, but not purple. (Here, Player 1 supposes that the leader likes colors or words with an o.)

LEADER: No, I would not like orange. I like bees, but I don't like moths. (Here he gives the players an additional clue to his likes and dislikes.)

PLAYER 2:   Then you would like apples, but not nuts.

LEADER: Right you are! What else would I like and dislike? (Player 2 has inferred that the leader likes double letters—as in YELLOW, BEES, and APPLES—but the secret is kept between them, and the other players are tested.)

PLAYER 3:   You would like blood, but not water.

One point is scored by every player who gives a correct response. After one round, the players are put to further, more difficult, tests by the leader, who may like words with e, words without i, words beginning with a vowel, words ending with a consonant, or any other spelling combination. Any player who thinks he understands what the leader likes must give an example of his own. The game can be made quite difficult if the leader can think of likes that start successively with the letters of the alphabet in their proper sequence (a, b, c, etc.) or end with these letters or involve other special arrangements. The player with the most points scored wins the game.

What seven-letter word, representing a woman, is turned into a word meaning a man when the last three letters are dropped, then again into a word denoting a woman when one more letter is dropped, and finally into a word representing a man when another letter is dropped?

HEROINE—hero, her, and he.

WORD RACE

ELEMENTARY-INTERMEDIATE   *Clock or timer*
Large families or groups

This is a wonderful game for developing verbal facility and readiness.

The first player, given the clock, names a letter of the alphabet—say, M. When he says "Go!" and starts the clock, the clock, the player at his right must, within a minute, name as many words as he can think of that begin with that letter. As the words pour out—ME, MY, MOO, MAN, MOUSE, MITT, MATE, MAT, MOTHER, etc.—the first player counts them and keeps time. Plurals, repetitions, or variations of the same word are not allowed.

At the end of a minute, time is up, and the second player is credited with one point for each word he named. Then it is his turn to hold the clock as he times the player at his right in thinking of words that begin with some other letter of the alphabet—say, B. The game proceeds in this way until all the players have taken a turn, each with a different letter. The one who gets the most words wins the game.

It should be agreed at the outset that letters like X and Z are not to be used.

The game can be made more difficult by requiring that all the words be of two syllables, of three syllables, or at least of three syllables.

~~~~~~

What is even more wonderful than a counting dog?
A spelling bee.

The two letters o o give good advice. Can you interpret them?
Owe nothing.

What common word could you get by pronouncing the letters EAKNRHEIDJ?

ENRAGE. *EA as in* jealous, *KN as in* knife, *RH as in* rheumatism, *EI as in* heir, *and DJ as in* adjudicate.

What common word could you get by pronouncing the letters TIYMNI?

SHIMMY. *TI as in* conscientious, *Y as in* lyric, *MN as in* column, *and I as in the last syllable of* limousine.

What common word could you get by pronouncing the letters UGNAGMEO?

ENEMY. *U as in* bury, *GN as in* gnat, *A as in* any, *GM as in* diaphragm, *and EO as in* people.

What common word could you get by pronouncing the letters IOLOKNYN?

YEARNING. *I as in* onion, *OLO as in* colonel, *KN as in* know, *Y as in* mystic, *and N as in* bronchial.

What common word could you get by pronouncing the letters LFOSWAY?

FUSSY. *LF as in* half, *O as in* brother, *SW as in* sword, *and AY as in* quay.

What common word could you get by pronouncing the letters OYTH?

WHITE. *O as in* choir, *Y as in* style, *and TH as in* thyme.

To appreciate the many different ways in which ough *is pronounced, look at the following old verse. It seems as if it should rhyme, but if you read it aloud, you will find that it does not.*

Wife, make me some dumplings of dough;
They're better than meat for my cough.
Please let them be boiled till hot through,
But not till they're heavy and tough.
Now I must be off to my plough,
And the boys, when they've had enough,
Must keep the flies off with a bough,
While the old mare drinks at the trough.

7

GRAMMAR AND SENTENCE
GAMES

Most of us associate grammar with memorizing a confusing mass of definitions and rules. The very word is enough to bring back unpleasant memories of hours spent in doing tedious drills and exercises.

Yet learning the parts of speech, syntax, and sentence structure can be a lark if you know how to make a game of mastering language skills.

With each of the following games you can teach your child something about the way words are put together to form phrases, clauses, and sentences. They promote fluency and readiness of expression and encourage articulateness and coherence.

How do you parse the word KISS?

"Kiss" is a noun, though often used as a conjunction. It is never declined; it is more common than proper; and it is used in the plural and agrees with all genders.

I. Parts of Speech

Words are distinguished grammatically, as parts of speech, according to the different ways in which they are used in a sentence. The games in this section introduce the child to the various parts of speech and acquaint him with the expressive functions and possibilities of each.

ADJECTIVE MATCH

ALL LEVELS   *Clock or timer*
3 or more

The best way to learn any part of speech is to play a game with it. This game not only familiarizes the players with the function of the adjective as a modifier of the noun but provides practice in using adjectives appropriately by "mating" them with nouns to make a good match.

The children should understand that adjectives are the artists among the parts of speech. They paint a picture of the noun for us. We are going to try to find nouns to "paint" with our adjectives.

The first player calls out an adjective—say, to begin with, something rather simple, like *good*. The next player must then, within a given time, supply a noun that would be appropriately used with *good*, like *boy*, *book*, etc. He scores a point if he does so. Then it is his turn to think of an adjective for the next player to match to a noun.

As long as the adjectives are relatively simple, like *broad*, *first*, *beautiful*, *smooth*, *long*, *ripe*, etc., there is usually no problem in finding a mate for them. If, however, a player cannot think of an appropriate noun or suggests one that does not fit the adjective—like *diffuse table*—he fails to score, and the player first proposing the adjective must supply a fitting noun for it.

Naturally, then, the players will seek to offer adjectives that are not quite so easy to match as the ones mentioned above. The game becomes more complicated if players try to find the right nouns for adjectives like *subtle, dubious, sagacious, excruciating, delectable, insatiable, conciliatory, prim,* and *tawdry.* In this way, a parent can gradually raise the level of difficulty by introducing the new adjectives which he would like the children to learn. By the repetition of the adjective in an appropriate context the child will also learn its use.

ADJECTIVE RUMMY VAR. 1

INTERMEDIATE-ADVANCED *Blank cards (playing-card*
2 *or more*   *size)*

This is a quieter variation of ADJECTIVE MATCH. Essentially, it consists of matching adjective cards with noun cards.

Fifty-two cards are prepared in advance. For each card with an adjective written on it there should be at least one other card on which a matching noun is written. A few simple and common adjectives and nouns should be included, so that the same adjective might be matched by a number of possible nouns. The person preparing the cards—parent or teacher—can adjust the grade of difficulty of the game according to the abilities of the players and can choose words from areas of experience familiar to them.

The two sets of cards, kept separate, are then shuffled, and the adjective cards are dealt out (between five and seven to a player, depending on the number participating in the game), while the noun cards are left in a pile, face down. Each player in turn picks up a noun card from the pack and then lays on the table, face up, forming another pack, one of the cards in his hand—either the noun card he has picked up or one of his adjective cards that he thinks may be hard to match—for possible use by another player. Players may draw from the top of either pack, the one consisting of cards lying face up or the pack of cards lying face down, but only when their turn comes.

Here, for example, is how a game might look in progress if we could peek over the players' shoulders:

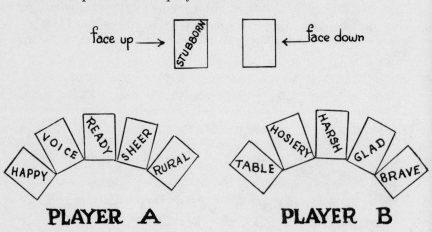

The object of the game is to build up a hand of good matches. The test of a good match is that it should be possible for the player to use the pair in a meaningful sentence—e.g., SHEER HOSIERY, or HARSH VOICE. As these matches are produced, the cards are laid, face up, in pairs on the table. The first player to put out his entire hand in this fashion wins the game.

The entire procedure can also be reversed by dealing out the noun cards and requiring the players to find cards with suitable matching adjectives.

Why is the word GIRL not a noun?
Because ALAS is an interjection.

WORD PAINTING   VAR. 2

ALL LEVELS   *Blank cards (playing-card*
3 *or more*   *size)*
                              Clock or timer

This is another variation which emphasizes the function of the adjective as a modifier of a noun. It trains the memory and builds vocabulary at the same time.

A deck of cards is prepared with a number of nouns selected by parent or teacher in accordance with the abilities and interests of the players—e.g., *monkey*, *name*, *magician*, *bicycle*, *mountain*, *intrusion*, *greeting*, *inquiry*, and *home*. The pack is then shuffled and laid face down on the table.

The first player, drawing the top card of the pack, holds it up for the other players to see. He must now suggest, within a given time, some adjective that will "paint" the noun. Thus, if he has drawn HOME, he may say "Happy home."

Now the next player must think of another adjective to paint the same noun—perhaps *unhappy* or *convalescent*. The game proceeds in this fashion until a player either repeats some adjective that has already been given, proposes an unsuitable adjective, or cannot think of another adjective within the time limit. It then becomes his turn to pick the next card from the top of the pack and to begin another round.

Players score one point for each correct adjective and lose two points for each miss or fumble.

One way of making the game more difficult as well as instructive is to require that each player give two appropriate adjectives to paint each noun—e.g., *polite*, *persistent inquiry*; *amusing*, *fictitious name*; *loud*, *hearty greeting*; etc. This is a good way of teaching the use of precise, vivid language.

The game can also be made more challenging by beginning with a deck that includes cards with nouns admitting of a relatively limited range of appropriate modifiers, like *nour-*

ishment, sickle, ownership, audition, breadth, compatriot, etc. Of course, the time limit would have to be adjusted with the increase in difficulty.

Finally, the procedure can be reversed: the words written on the cards may all be adjectives—in effect, different kinds of "paint"—and the players may be invited to use them to draw different pictures. In this case too, it is possible to pass from relatively easy types of adjectives, like *good, clean, smooth,* etc., to those offering a more limited range of possible nouns with which they might be appropriately matched— e.g., *perfunctory, lackadaisical, glib, sanctimonious,* or *derogatory.*

ADVERB MATCH   Var. 3

ALL LEVELS   *Clock or timer*
3 or more

A good way of learning the important difference between adjectives and adverbs is to play this variation after several rounds of ADJECTIVE MATCH. Here the problem is to match adverbs with verbs, adjectives, or other adverbs.

The procedure followed is basically the same as that in ADJECTIVE MATCH. To begin simply, the players might start by matching adverbs with verbs.

Since you are not trying to make the children grammarians, you need not go into the fine points of grammatical definition. Just tell the players that verbs are like motors and that some adverbs are like power adjusters. Thus, a word like *slowly* adjusts the power of a verb like *ran.* Other adverbs, like *soon, now, then, later, meanwhile,* etc., answer the question When? Still others, like *here, there, somewhere,* etc., answer the question Where? And others, like *carefully, slyly, dishonestly,* etc., answer the question How?

The first player might propose the adverb *quickly* and challenge the next player to supply an appropriate verb. The problem can be made increasingly difficult as players pass from such adverbs as *badly*, *slowly*, and *smoothly* to adverbs like *ingratiatingly*, *sullenly*, *impiously*, *zealously*, *gallantly*, and *ingenuously*.

The game can be complicated further by permitting players to suggest adverbs that might modify suitable adjectives—e.g., *intensely*, *exuberantly*, *triumphantly*, *dogmatically*, *suavely*, etc.

At a more advanced stage, players might be encouraged to propose some adverbs that could be matched with other adverbs—e.g., *unusually*, *almost*, *much*, *always*, *too*, etc., provided that pairs so made do not consist of two successive words ending in *ly*.

Finally, the reverse procedure may be followed. Beginning with verbs or adjectives, players can be required to find adverbs to match them meaningfully and to keep on doing so until their verbal resources have been exhausted. Here, too, there is much room for a gradual ascent to loftier realms of language, from verbs like *walk*, *eat*, *jump*, and *play* to *abstain*, *disapprove*, *relent*, *spurn*, and *despair*; and from adjectives like *happy*, *peaceful*, and *rich* to *dramatic*, *impressive*, *dolorous*, and *benevolent*. In fact, this game is an effective means of broadening the range of children's vocabulary, making their use of words more precise and pictorial, and discouraging the overuse of hackneyed expressions like *terribly*, *wonderfully*, *frightfully*, *nicely*, and *fantastically*.

Why is the letter d *like a squalling child?*
Because it makes Ma mad.

What twelve-letter word contains six S's?
DISPOSSESSES.

What two letters of the alphabet describe the conditions of a pavement in winter?
IC.

ADVERB RUMMY   VAR. 4

INTERMEDIATE-ADVANCED   *Blank cards (playing-card*
2 or more   *size)*

This is a variation of ADJECTIVE RUMMY, above. It is
played in the same way and admits of similar modifications,
except that the cards dealt out to the players have adverbs
written on them, while the cards left face down on the table
contain verbs, adjectives, and other adverbs that might be
matched with the other set.

MODIFIER RUMMY   VAR. 5

INTERMEDIATE-ADVANCED   *Blank cards (playing-card*
3 or more   *size)*

This variation takes the players the next step of the way toward sentence-building with the basic parts of speech: adjectives, nouns, verbs, and adverbs. It should be played only
after several rounds of ADJECTIVE RUMMY, WORD
PAINTING and ADVERB RUMMY, above.

The pack of cards used in ADJECTIVE RUMMY, the pack
used in WORD PAINTING, and the pack used in ADVERB
RUMMY are combined, and the enlarged deck is thoroughly shuffled. Then the cards are dealt out as they come
from the top of the pack. The number of cards dealt to a
"hand" may be varied from five to nine, depending on the
number of players.

As before, the players draw from the top of either the pile
of rejected cards lying face up or the pack of cards lying face
down. The object of the game is to find "good matches,"—
i.e., combinations that would make sense as parts of a meaningful sentence: adjectives with appropriate nouns, and adverbs with suitable verbs, adjectives, or other adverbs.

When such combinations are formed, they are laid face up

on the table, until one player has put out his entire hand in this way. He is the winner of the round, and all players score one point for each card laid on the table as part of a match. The game can be played for as many rounds as desired, with points totaled up at the end to see which player has the most.

EVERYDAY GRAMMAR

INTERMEDIATE

2 or more

In this variation your child's attention is focused on the vocabulary of everyday life, but with the object of learning the parts of speech and seeing how they function in ordinary language.

The players begin by agreeing on a particular area of everyday experience that they would like to talk about—e.g., baseball, school, home, etc. Then they agree on a particular part of speech to start with—say, verbs. Each player, in turn, must now say something, in a complete sentence, about the subject agreed upon, but using a verb specifically suited to it. Thus, if the first player had to use a verb in a sentence about boxing, he might say, "The champion *feinted* with his left." The story of the entire fight must then be told with a different verb in each successive sentence:

PLAYER 2: The challenger *countered* with a hard right to the jaw.

PLAYER 3: His opponent *jabbed* lightly with his left.

A verb, once used, may not be repeated.

After a game like this, the average youngster is not likely to forget that a verb can express *action*.

In the same way, sentences can be made up with adjectives or adverbs to tell a whole story—of a ball game, a day at school, or a trip to the dentist. Besides teaching grammar, this game stimulates imagination and develops the ability to shape complete sentences.

GRAMMAR RUMMY

INTERMEDIATE-ADVANCED

2 *or more*

Blank cards (playing-card size)

This game teaches the child to recognize the most important parts of speech and the essential elements of a sentence; to make verbs agree in number with their simple or compound subjects; to use the parts of speech to build sentences with subject, predicate, and modifiers; and to develop "sentence sense,"—i.e., the ability to distinguish between a whole sentence and a fragment (like a phrase, for example).

Fifty-two cards will be needed to make a complete deck. But instead of being ordinary playing cards, these will have words written on them.

On ten of them write nouns (*cat, dog,* etc.); on ten others, verbs (*run, walk,* etc.); on seven, phrases (*to the house, in the street,* etc.); on nine, articles (*a, an, the*—three of each); on six, conjunctions (*and, but, or,* etc.); and on ten, adjectives (*big, white,* etc.).

Now shuffle, cut, deal, and play, following the rules of rummy.

In a two-handed game, ten cards are dealt, one at a time, to each player; in a three-handed game, seven cards; and when four or more play, six cards. The next card is then placed, face up, beside the rest of the deck, which is laid face down.

Each player in turn must either draw a card from the top of the deck, without showing it, or take the card that is lying face up beside the deck. When adding the new card to his hand, he must discard one from it, laying it face up on top of the one already face up. Only the top card may be drawn from either of the two piles.

Whenever a player has put together a complete sentence, he lays on the table, face up, all the cards forming the sentence. After drawing and discarding, any player may get rid of a card from his hand by adding it meaningfully to some sentence already laid down by another player.

The object of the game is to be the first to get rid of all the cards in one's hand by laying them out in sentences. Or the rules can be modified to require the laying out of sets of nouns, verbs, adjectives, phrases, etc.

According to the maturity of the players, the game can be complicated in a number of interesting ways.

For example, the parts of speech may be selected to exemplify different *types* of each—common and proper nouns (*house, John*), abstract and concrete nouns (*bravery, button*), singular and plural nouns (*family, friends*), transitive, intransitive, and copulative verbs (*remember, live, is*), active and passive verbs (*move, was taken*), present, past, and future tenses of verbs (*likes, enjoyed, will come*), regular and irregular verbs (*walked, fought*), singular and plural verbs (*has, have*), coordinate and subordinate conjunctions (*or, because*), etc.

Then too, the pack of cards can be enlarged to include pronouns in various cases (*I, him, their, us*) and adverbs (*slowly, here*). Or the proportions of the different parts of speech in the total "mix" can be varied.

Finally, the words written on the cards can be selected from particular fields, like sports or the arts for nouns, or from categories, like colors, shapes, sizes, and numbers for adjectives.

GRAM-O

ELEMENTARY-INTERMEDIATE	*Blank cards (bingo size)*
3 or more	*Small slips of paper*
	Small colored cardboard squares

This game, which is very similar to bingo, is an excellent way of reviewing the parts of speech. The materials needed require some preparation; but once they have been produced, they can be used over and over again.

Each participant receives a card like the one shown below.

G	R	A	M	O
NOUN	ADVERB	PROPER NOUN	ADJ.	PRONOUN
ADJ.	PREP.	INFINITIVE	NOUN	VERB
ADJ.	PRONOUN	FREE SPACE	PARTICIPLE	NOUN
VERB	GERUND	VERB	PREP.	ADVERB
PREP.	NOUN	ADJ.	VERB	GERUND

Of course, aside from the top line, all the cards are different.

In addition, the players receive a number of small colored squares of cardboard that can be placed over the boxes on the card.

Slips of paper are prepared, each containing a letter of the word GRAM-O followed by a word representing a particular part of speech—e.g., A-LITTLE.

From a box into which these slips have been placed the leader picks one and reads it to the group. Let us say he selects A-LITTLE. All the players now check their cards to see whether they have a box labeled ADJECTIVE in the row under the letter A. (In the particular card shown here, it is the lowest box in the row.) Whoever has such a box writes the word on one of his colored cardboard squares and places it over the box on his card.

The game proceeds in this way until one of the players has

covered a whole row horizontally, vertically, or diagonally. He calls out "GRAM-O" and steps up to have his card checked. Of course, he gets no credit if he incorrectly identifies the part of speech of any of the words he has claimed credit for. Thus, GRAM-O is not simply a game of chance; it calls for a knowledge of grammar as well as a certain amount of good luck.

The game can be made more interesting if the words that are chosen are capable of being used as more than one part of speech. *Seeing*, for example, can be both a present participle and a gerund, depending upon how it is used in a sentence, and *well* can be a noun, an adjective, an interjection, or an adverb, depending upon its meaning.

To narrow down the possibilities in such cases, the word may be given in a sentence, so that the players must determine its part of speech from the way in which it is used.

GRAMMAR DOMINOES

INTERMEDIATE-ADVANCED   *Blank cards (playing-card*
2 *or more*   *size)*

It would be hard to imagine a pleasanter way of reviewing the parts of speech than by playing this game.

Twenty-eight cards are prepared, four for each of seven parts of speech: nouns, pronouns, verbs, adverbs, adjectives, prepositions, and conjunctions. The face of each card consists of a double square. Each square is marked as in dominoes, but instead of using numbers, words exemplifying the parts of speech are inserted, according to the following pattern.

For each part of speech there should be one "doublet,"— i.e., one card with the same word in each of the two squares. For example, you might use *book* (noun), *slice* (verb), *large* (adjective), *quickly* (adverb), *I* (pronoun), *but* (conjunction), and *under* (preposition).

Six more noun cards should now be made, with the other

square filled, in every case, by a different one of the other six parts of speech—e.g., *fork* and *or* (conjunction), *floor* and *after* (preposition), *chair* and *short* (adjective), *house* and *bite* (verb), *table* and *quietly* (adverb), *hat* and *them* (pronoun).

Five more adjective cards should next be prepared, with the other square filled, in every case, with a word exemplifying a different one of the remaining five parts of speech— e.g., *short* and *she* (pronoun), *tall* and *very* (adverb), *beautiful* and *slash* (verb), *big* and *between* (preposition), and *small* and *since* (conjunction).

The next four cards should contain adverbs in one square and, in every case, a word of a different one of the remaining four parts of speech—e.g., *sharply* and *because* (conjunction), *loudly* and *among* (preposition), *easily* and *chop* (verb), and *almost* and *him* (pronoun).

Three cards containing verbs in one square should have in the other, in every case, a word illustrative of one of the remaining three parts of speech—e.g., *carve* and *into* (preposition), *speak* and *nor* (conjunction), and *bend* and *you* (pronoun).

Two cards with pronouns in one square should have in the other a word, in each case, representing one of the other two parts of speech still remaining—e.g., *her* and *and* (conjunction) and *our* and *before* (preposition).

Finally, one card should be prepared with a preposition in one square and a conjunction in the other—e.g., *over* and *also*.

(A quick and easy method of preparing the entire deck is to match the parts of speech with the numbers on a set of dominoes: 0—nouns, 1—verbs, 2—adjectives, 3—pronouns, 4—prepositions, 5—adverbs, and 6—conjunctions. Thus, the 0-0 domino would correspond to the noun doublet, the 0-1 domino to the combination of noun and verb, etc.)

The cards are shuffled and laid face down, in a pack, on the table. Each player in turn draws a card until he has seven. If a player finds that he has in his hand cards that can be matched with one another—noun with noun, verb with verb, etc.—he puts them down, when his turn comes, face up on the table with the matching words adjacent to each other. The next player lays down one card from his hand to match any word at either end of a set already laid down. If a player cannot form such a match, he has to draw a card from the top of the deck and keep on doing so until he finds a suitable match. The object of the game is to be the first to get rid of all the cards in one's hand.

It will be noted that in the set described here, some of the words may be used as more than one part of speech. *After* may be a preposition (He came after me) or a conjunction (After I came, he left) as well as an adverb (Trouble followed after), and the same is true of *before*. Similarly, *bite* may be used as both a verb (Does that dog bite?) and a noun (Give me a bite of that apple), and the same may be said of *floor*, *chair*, *house*, *table*, *slash*, *chop*, and *bend*. The advantage of including some words of this type in the deck of cards is obvious. Players who understand the dual or triple function of a word can use it to match counterparts of more than one part of speech and thereby improve their chances of winning. Of course, if a player's judgment about a word's part of speech is challenged, he has to illustrate its use in that sense in a sentence. A dictionary may also be used to settle disputes of this kind.

The game can be complicated in a number of ways. The words chosen need not be as simple as the ones given here. Moreover, if the words are properly selected, the rules of the game may be modified to permit meaningful combinations— e.g., *beautiful girl*, *big house*, *run quickly*—and players can be encouraged to add to these to form complete sentences. Finally, nouns, verbs, adjectives, and adverbs can be chosen for their suitability in expressing ideas in any field of interest to the players—sports (or a particular sport), hobbies, history, geography, science, music, etc.

Three little words you often see
Are ARTICLES, a, an, and the.
A NOUN's the name of anything,
As school or garden, hoop or swing.
ADJECTIVES tell the kind of noun;
As great, small, pretty, white, or brown.
Instead of nouns the PRONOUNS stand:
Her head, his face, our arms, your hand.
VERBS tell of something being done:
To read, count, sing, laugh, jump, or run.
How things are done the ADVERBS tell:
As slowly, quickly, ill, or well.
CONJUNCTIONS join the words together,
As men and women, wind or weather.
The PREPOSITION stands before
A noun, as in or through a door.
The INTERJECTION shows surprise,
As oh! how pretty! ah! how wise!
The whole are called nine parts of speech,
Which reading, writing, speaking teach.

What is the objective of "he"?
She, of course!

What five-letter word contains four personal pronouns with the letters in the correct order?
USHER—us, she, he, *and her. (Other personal pronouns are I, me, we, him, they, them, and it.)*

Is it better to say, "The yolk of an egg is white" or "The yolk of an egg are white"?
Neither is right. The yolk of an egg is yellow.

Which is correct: "Nine and five are thirteen" or "Nine and five is thirteen"?
Neither. The sum of nine and five is fourteen.

GRAMMAR PYRAMID

INTERMEDIATE-ADVANCED   *Blank cards (playing-card*
1 only   *size)*

With this game a child can review the parts of speech all by himself.

Prepare a deck of forty-eight cards by attaching to them removable stickers on each of which is written a different word. There should be six different words exemplifying each of eight parts of speech: nouns, pronouns, verbs, adjectives, adverbs, prepositions, conjunctions, and interjections. In the easier form of the game, each word should have written under it the name of the part of speech it exemplifies; but after the child has gained some familiarity with grammar, this clue should be omitted.

For example, the nouns chosen could be: *wolves, Daniel, honesty, home, toy,* and *box;* the verbs: *look, works, played, is, was,* and *will be;* the pronouns: *which, he, this, those, that,* and *what;* the adjectives: *beautiful, best, worse, polite, softer,* and *comfortable;* the adverbs: *aback, more easily, down, graciously, most,* and *always;* the prepositions: *with, by, for, to, from,* and *in;* the conjunctions: *as, or, but, and, if,* and *that;* and the interjections: *ouch, well, hurrah, oh, alas,* and *bravo.*

Note that some of the words included here could be used as more than one part of speech—e.g., *box, toy, look, works, this, those, that, what, best, as, down, most,* and *well.* In the more difficult form of the game, when the part of speech is not indicated on the cards, the player is free to treat a word as any part of speech that it can be used as in a sentence. Moreover, as we see here, the words chosen for each part of speech can be used to exemplify a variety of possibilities—plurals of nouns and verbs; different tenses of the verb (past, present, and future); active and passive forms; different degrees of comparison in adjectives and adverbs; proper and common nouns; abstract and concrete nouns; interrogative, relative, personal, and demonstrative pronouns; and coordinate and subordinate conjunctions.

The player deals out twenty-eight cards face up in the form of a pyramid, the top row of which consists of seven cards, the next row of six, the next of five, and so on to the apex, which consists of one card. In each successive row the cards should be laid down so as to overlap the lower corners of adjacent cards in the row above. The remainder of the pack is held face down in the player's hand.

The object of the game is to remove all the cards in the pyramid by picking up combinations of two free cards that make a pair of words of the same part of speech (two nouns, two adverbs, etc.). Only a card that is fully uncovered, with no card partly overlapping it, is free to be picked up. So the player begins by removing either one of the cards in the row of two that can make a pair with the apex card, if this is possible. As cards are removed in this way and turned face down in pairs at the side, other cards are uncovered in the row above and may be likewise removed if they can be paired with each other or with the card turned up from the top of the pack in the player's hand. But if, for example, a card with a noun partly covers another card with a noun in the row above, this combination cannot be used, because both cards must be free to begin with.

If the apex card cannot be paired with either of the two cards freed when it is picked up, it is placed face up on the table, as the first card in the "boneyard" pile, and the player turns up the top card in the pack in his hand. He may use this to make a pair with any uncovered card in the pyramid; if he cannot do so, he adds it, face up, to the boneyard pile and proceeds to turn up the next card from the top in the reserve pack in his hand.

He proceeds in this way, combining uncovered cards with each other, with the top card in the boneyard pile, or, as a last resort, with the top card turned up from the reserve pack, and adding to the boneyard pile all turned-up cards that he cannot pair with cards in the pyramid. If, after going through the entire reserve pack, the player has not yet removed all the cards in the pyramid, he may turn the boneyard pile over and go through it again, turning up one card at a time from the top of the deck and building up a new boneyard pile if necessary. This may be turned over and used just once more, but it must not be shuffled. If, after the third time around, the player still has not removed all the cards in the pyramid, he has lost the game.

This is not just a game of chance. Skill is needed not only in detecting pairs but in choosing which two cards to pair when three or more cards are uncovered containing words of the same part of speech. This choice should be determined by a study of the cards in the row above to see which ones, if any, when uncovered, will allow further pairing.

SUITE WORDS

INTERMEDIATE

1 only

Blank cards (playing-card size)

This game for reviewing the parts of speech is a very easy form of solitaire that a player can expect to win three out of four times. It can be gradually made more difficult.

Prepare a deck of forty-eight cards by attaching to them removable stickers on each of which is written one word. Each of eight parts of speech denoted by the mnemonic NACPAPAV —noun, adjective, conjunction, pronoun, adverb, preposition, article, and verb—should be represented by six words, selected according to the level of maturity of the player. A typical set might include the following:

Nouns: *health, hand, expense, arm, telephone, brain.*

Adjectives: *those, positive, best, daily, sick, conscientious.*

Conjunctions: *because, and, as, but, or, if.*

Pronouns: *which, each, that, he, any, whom.*

Adverbs: *hardly, very, doubtless, aback, down, easily*.

Prepositions: *by, for, in, to, with, from*.

Articles: *the, the, a, a, an, an*. (As there are only three articles, each should be duplicated.)

Verbs: *grow, be, expand, drown, possess, see*.

At first, the name of the part of speech of each word should be written underneath it as an aid to its identification; but later, as the child develops proficiency, the cards can be prepared without this information. In that case, the game can be made more interesting if words are selected that can be used as more than one part of speech—e.g., *this* (adjective and pronoun) and *growl* (noun and verb). Such words should, of course, be matched with others like them—e.g., *each* (adjective and pronoun) and *strike* (noun and verb), so that there will always be six examples of each part of speech.

After the deck is shuffled thoroughly, the cards are dealt out from the top, one at a time, and laid face up on a "carpet" consisting of four rows of five cards each, as shown below.

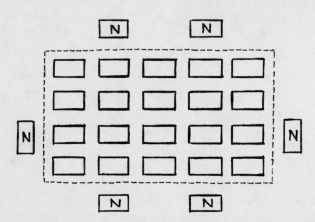

As soon as a noun is turned up, it should be laid outside the carpet at any one of the six places shown on the diagram with an *N*.

Once this has been done, the player must be alert for the next part of speech in the suite—the adjective. If he turns up an adjective, he places it on the noun and watches next for a conjunction. Should another noun be turned up in the meantime, this too is placed outside the carpet, and any adjective already laid down is picked up and placed on top of this noun. The player proceeds in this way, building up each suite outside the carpet with words turned up from the deck or already laid down on the carpet, in an effort to complete a suite of eight parts of speech arranged in the order indicated in the mnemonic. The object of the game is to complete six such suites.

If the carpet is filled, additional cards that are turned up and not used to build a suite are placed in a scrap pile. Of course, the cards already laid down on the carpet should be used first to build suites before any more cards are drawn from the deck. Spaces in the carpet resulting from the transfer of cards to suites are filled with the next word turned up from the original deck. Suites can also be built up by drawing the top card from the scrap pile. If all the cards in the original deck are used up, the scrap pile may be turned over, and the game continued. At first, this may be done three times. But the game can be made more difficult if the player is forbidden to turn the scrap pile over more than twice or even just once.

GRAMMAR SOLITAIRE

| INTERMEDIATE-ADVANCED | *Blank cards (playing-card* |
| *1 only* | *size)* |

A pleasant way of reviewing the parts of speech, this game can be made increasingly difficult with each replay.

Prepare a deck of fifty-six cards by attaching to them removable stickers on each of which is written a different word. There should be seven different words exemplifying each of eight parts of speech: nouns, pronouns, verbs, adverbs, adjectives, conjunctions, prepositions, and interjections. At first,

each word should have written under it the name of the part
of speech it exemplifies; but as the child becomes more familiar with grammar, this aid should be omitted. If, to make the
game more challenging, any word is chosen that can be used
as more than one part of speech, care should be taken to
match it with another word that can also be used in the same
ways, so that there will always be seven words to exemplify
each of the parts of speech.

Dealing from the top of the deck, the player follows the
rules of solitaire, laying one card face up on the table and six
more face down in a horizontal row alongside it. He then lays
a card face up on top of the second card from the left and
adds to each of the remaining five face-down cards in the row
one card likewise face down. Next he lays a card face up on
top of the third card from the left and completes the rest of
the row by laying a card face down on top of each of the remaining four piles. He proceeds in this way until each of the
piles has a card at the top face up. The first pile should then
consist of one card, face up; the second, of two cards, of which
only the top card should be face up; the third, of three, with
two face down; and so on to the seventh, which should contain six cards face down and one card on top face up.

The object of the game is to arrange the cards in each of
the seven piles in the following order, beginning from the top
and proceeding downward in a row: interjection, noun, pronoun, verb, adverb, adjective, conjunction, and preposition.

First, the player tries to move the cards that are already
face up—e.g., by placing a preposition from one pile so that
it slightly overlaps the bottom of a card with a conjunction on
another pile. This move makes it possible to turn up the top
card of the pile from which the card with the preposition was
removed. The player continues to move cards from one pile
to another, sometimes one card at a time, sometimes a whole
sequence of cards, to complete a set of eight parts of speech in
the correct order.

If he cannot move cards that are already face up, he may

turn up the top card of the reserve pack in his hand to see whether it will fit anywhere. If it does, he places it in its appropriate row and proceeds with any further moves that then become possible. If he cannot use the card he turns up, he places it face up in a "boneyard" pile. The top card in this pile is also available for use in adding to any row if the card turned up from the reserve pack is used first.

When all the cards in a pile have been turned face up and moved to another row, the space is free and may be filled with any card, whether from the top of the reserve deck or from the top of the boneyard pile. Naturally, the player should try to move cards from one pile to another so that all cards lying face down are eventually turned up.

The game is won when all seven sequences have been completed. If the player cannot complete all seven sequences after going through his reserve deck and turning over his boneyard pile, without shuffling it, five times, he loses the game. Later the number of rounds permitted may be limited to three and finally to just two.

How would you describe a moneylender in grammatical terms?

A moneylender serves you in the present tense, lends to you in the conditional mood, keeps you in the subjunctive, and ruins you in the future.

What is the superlative of temper?
Tempest.

From the eight letters of what common noun can sixteen different pronouns be formed?

SMITHERY. The pronouns are: he, her, hers, him, his, I, it, its, me, she, their, them, theirs, they, thy, *and* ye.

Can you read this sentence?

STAND	TAKE	TO	TAKING
I	YOU	THROW	MY

I understand you undertake to overthrow my undertaking.

SIMILARITY WAR

INTERMEDIATE-ADVANCED   *Blank cards (playing-card*
2 *only*   *size)*

This is an excellent game that can serve as a comprehensive review not only of the parts of speech but of synonyms, homonyms, and rhymes. In short, it sharpens the players' perception of the many different ways in which words can be similar: grammatical function, pronunciation, meaning, etc.

Prepare a deck of fifty-two cards by attaching to the center of the face of each card a removable sticker small enough not to obscure the numbers. On each sticker write a different word. The words should be so selected as to exhibit the maximum number of similarities in sound, meaning, and parts of speech. Especially desirable are words that can be used as more than one part of speech, homonyms, synonyms, and rhymes.

A sample list might consist of: *bread, bred, lead, led, red, read, wed, thread, tread, pale, pail, sale, sail, hale, hail, tail, tale, rale, rail, mail, male, stare, stair, wear, ware, hair, hare, bear, bare, fair, fare, roll, role, sole, soul, bowl, goal, fowl, foul, stole, howl, growl, wan, gone, walk, talk, end, bend, look, book, carry,* and *marry.* Note that, aside from the obvious rhymes and homonyms included in this set, there are many words that could be used as more than one part of speech; some words, like *lead* and *read,* may be pronounced in two different ways; and other words, like *wed* and *marry, tread* and *walk, goal* and *end, pale* and *wan,* and *stare* and *look,* are synonyms.

Each player receives twenty-six cards. The first player turns up the top card of his deck, and his opponent does likewise. If the first player realizes that there is some similarity between the two cards turned up, he identifies it—rhyme, synonym, two verbs, homonyms, etc. For each similarity correctly identified he receives two points. If the same two words form a pair in more than one respect—e.g., if they are both nouns and rhyme, like *lead* and *thread*—a player who identifies both likenesses receives four points. Sometimes the player whose turn it is first may be able to identify only one similarity; when he is finished, his opponent may then score two points plus one (i.e., three points) if he can identify an additional likeness between the words.

When no similarities can be identified, or when the possibilities offered by any two words appear to have been exhausted, each player turns up an additional card. The one whose card shows the higher number scores one point and gets all the cards on the table. He then goes first in turning up the next card. The game continues in this way until all the cards in the deck have been turned up. The player with the most cards scores five points, and the winner is the one with the most points.

Can you think of a sentence in which the same word is used as five different parts of speech: interjection, adjective, noun, verb, and adverb?

"Well, *it's* well *that the water in the* well *does* well *up so* well."

How can you convert any word that is not a noun into a noun?

Just put quotation marks around it and use it in a sentence to name itself. For example, in the sentence "'To' is a preposition," the word enclosed by the pair of single quotation marks is a noun *(the name of a word) used as the subject of the sentence.*

THE LATE MR. EARLY

"You've been coming early lately, Early."

"Yes, I've been early of late after being behind before."

Write and punctuate a meaningful sentence with nine that's *in succession.*

"Teacher said, when we asked her concerning that 'that,' that that 'that'—that 'that' that that discussion was about—was a conjunction.

II. Sentences

Here are some games to give children practice in putting words together to make sentences of varying length, construction, and arrangement.

SENTENCE-FORMING FUN

INTERMEDIATE-ADVANCED   *Paper and pencil*
2 *or more*   *Clock or timer*

This game encourages creativity and imagination in sentence construction, gives practice in "cementing" the parts of a sentence together into a meaningful whole, and teaches punctuation in context.

From a dictionary or a spelling book, select at random ten or twelve words, preferably as unrelated as possible. In fact, the less connection there is among the words, the better.

The players write these words in a vertical list, one at a time. Here, for example, is the way one such list might look:

IMPRESSED
ASTRONAUT
STRIKING
RUSHED
STREAMLINED
WHERE
NUTS
NOWHERE
SMOOTHNESS
HOT

Now, each player tries, within a given time, to compose a sentence using all the words in the order in which they are listed. To this end, he may write a few words either before or after each given word in such a way as to connect it to the rest of the words in his sentence.

When time is up, the sentences are read aloud and compared. The person writing the best sentence wins.

Thus, using the words in the list above, one might compose the following sentence:

IMPRESSED by the ASTRONAUT, whose appearance was STRIKING, the mob RUSHED toward the STREAMLINED spacecraft, WHERE NUTS and bolts were NOWHERE to be seen, to feel the SMOOTHNESS of its HOT surface.

SENTENCE GHOST

INTERMEDIATE-ADVANCED   *Clock or timer*
2 *or more*

Children playing this game should be familiar with the classic game of GHOST (page 112), of which it is a variation.

SENTENCE GHOST develops the ability to recognize a sentence, to determine when a sentence ends, and to expand and develop a sentence with phrases and clauses. In fact, this game can be used to teach the whole art of constructing sentences of different types:

Declarative—one which makes a statement, like "John is a good sport."

Interrogative—one which asks a question, like "Is John a good sport?"

Imperative—one which expresses a command, like "John, be a good sport."

Exclamatory—one which exclaims, like "What a good sport John is!"

The game also lends itself to teaching the players how to construct sentences of different forms:

Simple—with one main clause and no subordinate clauses, like "John is a good sport" or the interrogative, imperative, and exclamatory types of this sentence.

Complex—with one main clause and one or more subordinate clauses, like "As we all know, John is a good sport."

Compound—with two or more main clauses but no subordinate clauses, like "John is a good sport, but Bill is not."

Compound-complex—with two or more main clauses and
one or more subordinate clauses, like "As we all know,
John is a good sport, but Bill is not."

The first player, thinking of a sentence of more than two
words, calls out just its first word. Then the second player,
thinking perhaps of the same sentence or of some other sentence of at least three words, adds a second word. Each succeeding player must think of a sentence that begins with the
words already called out and must add one word, but *he must
avoid completing any sentence.*

Generally, only one minute is allowed for a player either
to add a word or to challenge the preceding player to say
what sentence he had in mind. If the preceding player cannot
meet this challenge, either because he really had no sentence
in mind or because what he had in mind did not constitute a
sentence, he is penalized by becoming "a fifth of a ghost." If
he does meet the challenge, then it is his challenger who is so
penalized, as in GHOST. A player suffers the same penalty if
he completes a sentence of three or more words and someone
else points this out.

A second penalty makes a player two-fifths of a ghost, etc.
The other rules of GHOST apply to this game as well.

The tendency of the game, of course, is to encourage the
players to lengthen sentences by adding adjectives, adverbs,
phrases, and clauses.

Here, for instance, is how a game might proceed:

PLAYER 1: Trust.

PLAYER 2: A.

PLAYER 3: (avoiding a noun that would end the sentence):
Small.

PLAYER 1: Or.

PLAYER 2: Perhaps.

PLAYER 3: Not.

PLAYER 1: I challenge you to say what sentence you had in mind.

PLAYER 3: Trust a small or perhaps not so small a man.

BACKWARD SENTENCE GHOST   VAR. 1

ADVANCED   *Clock or timer*

2 *or more*

This is an excellent variation for training the visual memory. It also gives practice in sentence construction.

Basically, it is the same game as SENTENCE GHOST, above, except that a player must compose his sentence by inserting a word *in front of* the ones already called out. In effect, the sentence is to be constructed *backward*.

Here is one possible beginning:

PLAYER 1 (perhaps thinking of "How do you feel?"): Feel.

PLAYER 2: The.

PLAYER 3: By.

PLAYER 1: Or.

PLAYER 2: Smell.

PLAYER 3: The.

(Note that each player must mentally "play back" the words he has heard and imagine them as ending some sentence: ". . . the smell or by the feel.")

The possibilities for developing this particular ending may be left to any players who might like to continue from here.

What is the difference between a pretty young woman and a pretty, young woman?

In the first phrase, "pretty" is used as an adverb, and the woman is pretty young; in the second, "pretty" is used as an adjective, and the woman is pretty as well as young.

SENTENCE SUPERGHOST   VAR. 2

ADVANCED   *Clock or timer*
2 *or more*

This more complicated variation is best played by those who
have had some practice in SUPERGHOST (page 114). It is
an excellent way of teaching children sentence structure and
style.

The rules are the same, except that a player must add a
word *either before or after* the ones already called out. In
short, one can form a sentence backward or forward from any
word occurring at either the beginning or the end of the
given group. Again, only sentences of three or more words
count.

Naturally, in order to help other players understand what
is happening, each player must indicate the placement of his
additional word by repeating the entire phrase. If the game
proves to be too great a strain on the players' memory, they
may be permitted to use paper and pencil to keep a record of
what has been called out.

Here, for example, is a simple beginning:

PLAYER 1: Dollars.
PLAYER 2: Dollars and.
PLAYER 3: In dollars and.
PLAYER 1: In dollars and cents.
PLAYER 2: Happiness in dollars and cents.

Even at this point, this particular game offers many possibilities of further development at either end of the given
phrase.

---

*Can you think of a sentence in which the same word is used as
three different parts of speech: adverb, adjective, and noun, in that
order?*

"No, no one said 'no.' "

SENTENCE SUPERDUPERGHOST   Var. 3

Advanced   *Paper and pencil*
2 *or more*   *Clock or timer*

This variation calls for the greatest powers of concentration and a thorough mastery of sentence structure, as well as a good vocabulary. It should be played only by those advanced enough to have gone successfully through several rounds of SUPERDUPERGHOST (page 115) and the variations above. A time limit should be placed on each answer.

What makes this variation different is that a player may compose his sentence by inserting a word before, after, or *between* the words already called out, in order to avoid completing a sentence, as long as he can still make some other sentence. Only sentences of four words or more count.

Here is how one such game began:

Player 1 (thinking of "It is a beautiful day"): Beautiful.
Player 2: Beautiful girl.
Player 3: Beautiful but girl.
Player 1: Beautiful but not girl.
Player 2: Beautiful perhaps but not girl.
Player 3: Beautiful perhaps but not girl as.

Whoever wants to know more about this girl (or perhaps not a girl after all) will have to play out the rest of this particular game with an advanced group of alert youngsters.

A newspaper, reporting the speech of an eminent psychologist, quoted him as having said, "Woman without her man would be a savage."

Immediately a storm of protest from women readers broke over the poor man's head. Calm was restored only after he wrote a letter to the newspaper charging that he had been misquoted. What he had really said was: "Woman! Without her, man would be a savage."

GRAMMAR GHOST

INTERMEDIATE-ADVANCED   *Clock or timer*

2 *or more*

This is a good game for reviewing the parts of speech, adding to the players' vocabulary, and improving their spelling.

The rules are the same as those for GHOST (page 112), except that the words must all belong to the same part of speech.

For example, suppose it is agreed that all the words are to be adjectives. The first player, thinking of some adjective—say, SHORT—consisting of more than three letters, calls out the first letter, in this case S. Then the second player, thinking of some other adjective or perhaps of the same one, adds a second letter, say H, which might also help to spell SHARP. Now each succeeding player must think of an adjective that begins with the same letters that have already been called out and must add one letter, but he must avoid completing any word.

As in GHOST, a minute is allowed for a player either to add a letter without completing a word or to challenge the preceding player to say what word he had in mind. The penalties are the same as in GHOST.

Of course, the game can be varied so that all the parts of speech except articles—nouns, verbs, pronouns, interjections, adverbs, prepositions, and conjunctions—can be covered as well as adjectives.

For more difficult variations, see BACKWARD GHOST, SUPERGHOST, and SUPERDUPERGHOST (pages 113–115).

Can you think of a declarative sentence that can have two entirely different meanings?

"He likes his father better than his mother."

This could mean that he likes his father better than he likes his mother, or that he likes his father better than his mother likes his father.

SCRAMBLED SENTENCE

ELEMENTARY-INTERMEDIATE   *Blank cards (playing-card*
1 or more   *size)*

This is a very simple game that teaches the players how to put words together to form sentences, to punctuate correctly, and to connect ideas intelligibly.

According to the age and maturity of the players, select some saying, quotation, or proverb, or make up a sentence on any subject like history or geography. For example, with small children, one might take a Mother Goose nursery rhyme; with somewhat older players, the sentence might describe a person, an animal, a place, or a thing, or it might be a familiar advertising slogan or a statement of some well-known fact of history or common experience.

Break the sentence up into a succession of words, and write these on cards. Make a duplicate set of cards for each player.

Now shuffle each set so that the sentence is thoroughly scrambled in every case.

The first player to put the sentence together wins the game.

WORD TRADING

INTERMEDIATE   *Blank cards (playing-card*
2 or more   *size)*

This is a more complicated variation of the preceding game and has the same educational value.

Make up a deck of cards consisting of the words of several related sentences of equal length, one for each player. Suppose, for example, that there are two players and that the sentences are: "Travel to outer space will soon become as easy as an automobile trip across the country by superhighway. At any rate, that is what a good many writers of science fiction would like us to believe." Write every one of these thirty-six words, eighteen in each sentence, on a separate card.

Now shuffle the cards thoroughly and divide the deck equally between the players. Each player examines his hand, rearranges the cards, and tries to construct a sentence with them, without showing them to the other player.

Next, the players begin to trade cards. Player 1 may decide that the word THAT does not fit into the sentence he is trying to construct with his cards. Since it is the word he can find the least use for, he lays it down on the table. Player 2 may not see how the word THAT can help him with his problem, but he is obliged to pick it up and add it to his hand at this point. Perhaps Player 1 will later discover that he made a mistake in discarding the word THAT. In that case, he will have to wait until his opponent is ready to give it up. Meanwhile, Player 2 now has to discard a word from his hand. And so the players keep trading words, one at a time, as they try various rearrangements of their cards, until one or the other sees exactly what he needs to win. Since by this time a player may remember having given up to his opponent a word he now feels he needs, he may ask for the word. His opponent is not obliged to give it up, but may in turn ask for some word he now knows the other player has. The dialogue may proceed as follows:

PLAYER 1: I gave you THAT at the beginning. I'd like it back. I'll give you AS in exchange.

PLAYER 2: I gave you AT before. I'll take it back in exchange for THAT.

It might seem as if, when one player has finally got his sentence all lined up and lays it down, the other, having all the words in his sentence, would also put it together at once. In fact, however, it sometimes happens that a player has all the words he needs but still cannot see how they hang together. In any case, the first player to put down a complete sentence wins the round.

If three play, there must be three sentences, and each player should receive a third of the cards. In that case, the sentences should be somewhat shorter—not more than twelve words each. If there are four players, four sentences of no more than eight words each should be used, and each player should be dealt exactly eight cards. With more than two players, trading may become quite spirited, and the same card may pass from hand to hand several times before finding its right place. Tension rises as players come near to completing their sentences.

SENTENCE DICE

ELEMENTARY-INTERMEDIATE   *Dice*
2 or more

This is an excellent way to review the parts of speech as they are used in sentences.

First prepare your "dice." Use a different cube for each of the major parts of speech: noun, subject pronoun, possessive pronoun, and active verb. Adjective and adverb dice can be added in later rounds.

For example, the subject pronoun cube might have one of the following on each of its six sides: *i, we, he, she, they, you.* The verb cube could have *wanted, stole, enjoyed, got, held, kept.* The noun cube might have *car, dice, cards, money, candy, ball.* The possessive pronoun cube would have *my, our, his, her, their, your.*

Each player is given a chance to throw the four dice simultaneously. He must then try to make a sentence of the scrambled words he turns up. One point is scored for each sentence. A player who forms one sentence gets another chance to throw the dice. If he cannot form a sentence, he loses his turn.

Additional sets of dice should be held in reserve with other words for each part of speech and with additional parts of speech—articles, adjectives, and adverbs.

SENTENCE BRIDGEBUILDING

INTERMEDIATE-ADVANCED   *Newspaper or magazine*
1 or more

This game develops skill in spontaneously linking the parts of a sentence, finding transitional words and phrases, making connections, and imposing coherence on ideas. It gets children to verbalize and challenges each player's resourcefulness and ingenuity. It can be played with a child or with several children.

Cut out a few pages of printed matter from a magazine or a newspaper dealing with a story or a subject suited to the interest and maturity of the players. It might be about sports, a hobby, an interesting person, or an exciting adventure.

Next, cut each page vertically in the middle, shuffle the half-sheets, and distribute them among the players. (If only one child is playing, hold the other half of each sheet yourself.)

Each player now must study his half. Then, as his turn comes to read it aloud, he must try to bridge over the gaps in the story or article by filling in the words he thinks are missing. The results can often be hilarious.

Meanwhile, his counterpart—the player with the other half—checks the accuracy of his guess.

Other versions, more or less difficult, would involve cutting the page diagonally, snipping out odd shapes here and there, tearing it irregularly, and selecting passages dealing with history, geography, nature, science, famous people, etc.

Who's calling whom in the following sentence?
"James called John come here."
That all depends on how you punctuate it:
1. "James," called John. "Come here!"
2. James called, "John, come here!"

TEACHER: *How would you punctuate this sentence: I saw a five-dollar bill on the floor.*
PUPIL: *I would make a dash after it.*

Why is a door always in the subjunctive mood?
Because it is always wood, or should be.

What grammatical form is most distasteful to lovers?
The third person!

By proper punctuation, make sense of the following:
That that is is that that is not is not but that that is not is not that that is nor is that that is that that is not.
That that is, is; that that is not, is not; but that that is not, is not that that is; nor is that that is that that is not.

Punctuation can mean money in your pocket. How would you punctuate the following sentence to collect the largest sum?
"Give me twenty five dollar bills."
Placing a hyphen between "five" and "dollar" will be worth seventy-five dollars more than placing it between "twenty" and "five."

Can you think of a sentence whose meaning could be changed to its opposite simply by the addition of the article a?
"I expect little more than just a token from him." This means that a token is about all I can expect from him.
"I expect a little more than just a token from him." This means that I do expect more than just a token from him.

Can you match the miracle of the deaf-mute who picked up a wheel and spoke?
Yes, there was the case of the blind man who picked up a hammer and saw.

A proofreader, correcting the pages of a book written by a famous philosopher, disagreed with the following statement: "No man can be happy." Accordingly, he punctuated it as follows: "No. Man can be happy."

III. Group Games

Most of the games in this chapter can be played by two or more. But there are some grammar and sentence games that are best played with at least seven, though sometimes fewer may participate. Here are some games that are suitable for large families, children's parties, or social gatherings.

VERB CHARADES

INTERMEDIATE   *Blank cards (playing-card*
Large families or groups   *size)*

This is an active game that gives the players an opportunity to express themselves creatively as they learn various verbs.

Divide the group into two teams. Whisper a verb to each member of a team or hand out cards with the verbs written on them. The verbs should be such as can be acted out so that their meaning may be conveyed by an appropriate gesture or activity. The members of the other team must then infer the word being enacted.

Here are a few simple verbs to start with: *shrug, loll, lope, wring, saunter, smirk, flutter, peep, shave, snip, paint, exercise, steal, bake, flinch, munch,* and *guzzle.*

This is a good game for teaching synonyms too. The same pantomime that will do to express the meaning of *loll* can also signify *sprawl* or *lounge.* If one of these words is intended by the pantomimist, and another of them is named by a member of the opposite team, credit can be given to every player on his team who can think of additional synonyms.

When a librarian goes fishing, what does she use for bait?
Bookworms.

IN THE MANNER OF THE ADVERB

INTERMEDIATE-ADVANCED
Large families or groups

Like ALPHABETICAL ADVERBS WITH CHARADES (page 177), this game has many educational values. It introduces the players to a variety of adverbs and their meanings and so adds to everyone's vocabulary. It stimulates the imagination and encourages creativity, and it gives each member of the group an opportunity to do something inventive.

One player, the victim, is sent out of the room while the rest decide on some adverb. When the victim is called in, he asks each player in turn any question he likes, and the player must respond "in the manner of the adverb."

Thus, if the adverb is RUDELY, the first player might interrupt the victim in the midst of his question. A second player might turn his back on his questioner while answering his question. A third might give him a curt reply. A fourth might laugh at the victim, and a fifth might stick out his tongue.

By this time, let us hope, the victim should get the point and guess the adverb. Of course, he receives full credit for any synonym of the adverb he may think of, like *impolitely*.

Some good adverbs for this game are *elaborately*, *speedily*, *contrarily*, *furtively*, *obsequiously*, *incoherently*, *incompletely*, *doubly*, *repetitively*, *dilatorily*, *weakly*, *obliquely*, *noisily*, *eccentrically*, *hesitantly*, *unintelligibly*, *misleadingly*, *wordlessly*, and *dishonestly*.

As can be seen from this list of adverbs, the game can be made as difficult and baffling as one likes. It takes a rather clever victim, for example, to conclude that everyone is acting *deceptively*, *naturally*, or *helpfully*. And it takes an equally resourceful group to think of new ways of acting out adverbs like *wittily*, *tediously*, or *sociably*.

COFFEEPOT

ADVANCED
Large families or groups

This old favorite is a grammatical variation on the game
of TEAKETTLE (page 155). It teaches the players the correct use of different parts of speech, broadens their vocabulary, and stimulates imagination as well as much laughter.
The larger the group, the more fun it is to play.

One of the players volunteers or is chosen by lot to be the
"victim." While he is out of the room, the rest of the group
agrees on some verb, like *talk, sing, eat, dance, smile, loaf,*
etc., to be represented by the word "coffeepot."

When the victim returns, he asks questions of the players
in rotation, using "coffeepot" to stand for the verb, in an effort to find out what it is. It is his job to devise questions that
will lead him to the verb in the shortest possible time. The
players, for their part, must answer his questions truthfully
in accordance with the meaning of the verb they have chosen.

Suppose, for example, that the verb SING has been selected.
The interrogation might proceed as follows:

Q. Can everyone coffeepot?
A. Well, that depends on what you call coffeepotting.
Q. Can you coffeepot with other people?
A. Oh, yes.
Q. Can you coffeepot alone?
A. Yes, indeed.
Q. Do you need special equipment to coffeepot?
A. No special outfit is needed, if that's what you mean.

The game proceeds in this way until the victim guesses
what the verb is. He is penalized one point for every wrong
guess and for every question he has to ask before he guesses
right. The next victim is the one who has given the answer
that enabled the first victim to guess the correct verb.

One can make the game somewhat more difficult by requiring that questions be so phrased as to admit only of "Yes" or "No" or "I don't know" by way of answer.

The familiar game of TWENTY QUESTIONS is really a variation of COFFEEPOT in which the word chosen is a noun. Of course, the questions in that case would have to be phrased differently: "Is coffeepot animate or inanimate?" "Is coffeepot animal or vegetable?" "Are coffeepots expensive?" "Are coffeepots abundant?" This variation is a good exercise in logical division. (Incidentally, try at least once making "coffeepot" coffeepot!)

If "coffeepot" is an adjective (*beautiful, gruesome, fragrant, clumsy, repulsive, ill-mannered*, etc.), the questions have to be put something like this: "Can a person be coffeepot?" "Are you often coffeepot?" "Are coffeepot people in great demand?" "Is anyone present coffeepot now?" "Are coffeepot people likely to be successful in love?"

Finally, the game can be played by making "coffeepot" an adverb—*slyly, foolishly, graciously, glumly, hideously, gallantly, crudely*, etc. In that case, the victim may have to ask questions like "Do you often behave coffeepot?" "Do only women act coffeepot?" "Would behaving coffeepot help one in business?"

This is the COFFEEPOT way to good grammar!

Try punctuating the following:
Said I I said you said I said said said he who said I said you said I said said is said said said is not said as you said said.

Said I, "I said you said I said 'said.'" Said he, "Who said I said you said 'said'? I said ' "said" ' is said ' "said." ' 'Said' is not said as you said 'said.'"

What is the longest sentence in the world?
"Go to prison for life."

GRAMMAR ABC'S

ELEMENTARY-INTERMEDIATE   *Blank cards (playing-card*
Large families or groups   *size)*
                                                  Clock or timer

This game is a pleasant way of reviewing the parts of speech.

Prepare two decks of fifty-two cards each by attaching to them removable stickers. On each sticker write a letter of the alphabet according to the following plan: nine E's, seven each of A's, I's, O's, U's, and Y's, and three each of the consonants.

After shuffling the deck thoroughly, the first player says to the second, "I have a message for you from a friend of yours."

"Whom?" asks the second player.

Turning up the top card in the deck—say, the letter F— the first player answers, "I have forgotten his name, but he has a *funny* face," using an appropriate adjective beginning with the letter on the card drawn from the deck. Player 1 now keeps his F card.

Next, the second player draws a card from the top of the deck—say, M—and asks, "Did he have a *monkey* face?" or uses any other appropriate adjective beginning with that letter. He too keeps his card with M.

The game continues in this way until everyone has had a chance to draw a card and supply in the sentence an appropriate adjective beginning with the letter drawn. No duplication of adjectives is allowed. Thus, if another F is drawn, the player who turns up this card must supply some adjective other than *funny* to describe the friend's face—perhaps *freckled, fat,* or *florid.*

If all the players are able to supply appropriate adjectives the first time around, the first player, when his turn comes again, says, "Your friend brought with him a ————," and, drawing a card from the top of the deck—say, the letter B—

fills in a noun beginning with that letter—e.g., *basketball*. The next player, saying, "He also brought a ———," must do likewise with the letter he draws, and so must the rest of the players.

In the third round, adverbs are sought. So the statement may be phrased: "Your friend was dressed ———." Here a P might appropriately be used for *plainly*. In each round, the form of the statement or question is determined by the first player and is followed by the others.

In the fourth round, verbs are in demand. Hence, the statement may take the form: "Your friend ——— when he came." Here the letter Y might be used to form the verb *yawned*.

If a player cannot think of an appropriate word, within a given time, he is penalized one point and passes his letter to the next player, who tries to provide a word beginning with it. Each player accumulates in a pile in front of him the letters with which he provided suitable words.

There are a number of ways in which the game can be made more challenging. For example, players may be forbidden to introduce words that make sentences contradicting what has already been said by other players. Thus, if one player says that the friend's face was *kind*, it would be inappropriate for another player to describe it as *mean*, *cruel*, or *evil*.

Then too, for the sake of variety, the form of the questions or statements may be changed in order to encourage a broader range of possible sentences. It is a good idea to list beforehand questions and replies requiring different parts of speech, perhaps building up a story or situation to a climax. For instance, in one game a person met a *wicked* man who turned out to be a *robber* who laughed *sinisterly* and *stole* a bunch of jewels.

This game provides many opportunities for humorous or exaggerated use of language in the creation of sentences.

FOLLOW THE FORMULA

INTERMEDIATE-ADVANCED   *Blackboard and chalk*
Large families or groups   *Clock or timer*

Speaking and writing correct English means, to a considerable extent, following certain accepted patterns in the construction of sentences. Once these patterns have become a matter of habit, one is free to develop a personal style.

This game, by emphasizing the pattern or formula according to which sentences may be formed, helps the child to appreciate the function of the parts of speech in expressing meaning. While playing the game, he learns not only grammar but correct usage.

The formula is simply an arrangement of the names of successive parts of speech such that, when words exemplifying them are substituted in the same order, a meaningful sentence is formed.

For example, suppose the following formula is written on the blackboard:

Adjective, proper noun, verb, adjective, noun.

Each player, within a given time limit, must compose a meaningful sentence according to this pattern.

Here is how the game might proceed:

PLAYER 1: Crafty Albert cheats credulous fools.

PLAYER 2: Stupid Jack eats dead worms.

PLAYER 3: Irate Peter makes dreadful threats.

PLAYER 4: Shy Joan loses many opportunities.

The game may be complicated in a number of ways. In the first place, the formula may be expanded to include adverbs, prepositional phrases, subordinate clauses, participles, infinitives, and gerunds, according to the abilities of the group. Several such formulas can be strung together to make a single paragraph of related sentences. Step by step, children can be led in this way to vary their sentence structure—e.g., to begin with an adverb—and to express themselves in interrogative and exclamatory as well as declarative sentences.

Patterns may be taken from the paragraphs in a book or magazine article. After a while, players may be encouraged to propose their own patterns to one another.

Penalties are imposed for failure to think of a correct sentence, conforming to the pattern, within the time limit. This can be varied according to the difficulty of the formula and the abilities of the players.

TABOO

INTERMEDIATE   *Clock or timer*
Large families or groups

Playing this game will develop verbal facility, alertness, and an appreciation of the way the parts of speech are used in sentences.

First, a questioner is chosen. Then, it is agreed that a particular part of speech—say, the noun—is to be taboo for everyone but him. He may use as many nouns as he likes in asking questions of each of the players in turn, but they must avoid nouns in their answers. He is free to ask any questions he wants in an effort to trap a player into using the forbidden part of speech. Anyone who does so is "out."

Here is how the questioning might begin:

Q. How do you like this game?

A. I think it's a good game.

Q. You're out! You used the noun "game"!
   If you wanted to chop down a tree, what instrument would you use?

A. I'd use whatever I could find that was handy.

Q. What is that you're wearing around your neck?

A. Call it what you may, it's not knotted, but beaded. Haven't I identified it precisely?

Q. I'll ask the questions. Which do you like better, day or night?

A. Neither.

After one time around, a new part of speech may be made taboo: the adjective, the conjunction, the preposition, the pronoun. In each case the problem is different, and it takes quite as much proficiency to frame the questions as it does to find an appropriate answer.

Here is how a questioner might try to trap players into using verbs:

Q. What do you do when you are embarrassed?

A. Nothing in particular.

Q. How would you react if you saw a ghost?

A. Calmly, without fear or agitation.

Q. What must a person do to keep in good health?

A. Everything necessary for nutrition, exercise, and rest.

A time limit should be set on responses.

STUFF AND NONSENSE

ELEMENTARY-INTERMEDIATE

Large families or groups

This is a good game for teaching children the way the parts of speech are used in the construction of sentences. It is best played with a group of at least eight. More can join if the game is suitably modified.

The players are seated in a circle. One starts by whispering to his neighbor at his left an article (*a, an,* or *the*). The player thus spoken to then whispers to the one at his left an adjective (*sick, young, ugly,* etc.). The third player must whisper to his neighbor a singular noun (*fool, dog, song,* etc.). Each player, in turn, adds another part of speech and passes it along to the person at his left, in the following order thereafter: verb, adverb, a number, another adjective, and a plural noun.

When the eighth player has been reached, all take turns, in order, calling out the words they contributed, until the complete sentence is heard. The result can be very funny. For example, one group came up with the following: "The aggressive motorman carved morosely sixty-nine silly cats."

Naturally, the game can be complicated by changing the order of the parts of speech; adding conjunctions (*or*, *and*, etc.), prepositions (*by*, *from*, *with*, etc.), and interjections (*ouch*, *well*, *ah*); or specifying a particular kind of pronoun (personal—*he*, *me*, *us*; relative—*which*, *who*, *that*; or interrogative—*whose*, *whom*) or adjective (color, shape, size, etc.) to be used. In this way children can be taught the various kinds of sentences, clauses, and phrases.

A man received a telegram reading: SHIP SINKS!

When his wife read it, she thought the first word was a noun referring to the boat on which her daughter was sailing, and she fainted.

But her husband, who was in the plumbing business, knew that the first word was a verb, and he shipped the sinks.

Two men found part of a page of an old newspaper on which all that could be read was the headline: CONVICTS REBEL.

One man, interpreting the first word as a noun and the second as a verb, thought a rebellion had broken out in a prison.

But the other, interpreting the first word as a verb and the second as a noun, pronounced the two words differently and concluded that a rebel had been brought to justice.

They never did find out which one was right.

Can you think of a sentence in which the presence or absence of a comma could make the difference whether two people married or not?

"They did not marry because they wanted to live in comfort." This means that they did marry, but not because they wanted to live in comfort.

"They did not marry, because they wanted to live in comfort." This means that the reason they did not marry was that they wanted to live in comfort.

SENTENCE TREASURE HUNT

ELEMENTARY-INTERMEDIATE   *Paper and pencil*
Large families or groups   *Blank cards (playing-card size)*

This is an "action" game for a group of children who won't sit still for very long. It will develop their ability to see words and phrases as functional parts of the sentence, to connect and arrange them meaningfully, logically, and grammatically, and to recognize well-known expressions or sayings.

Take some famous quotation, nursery rhyme, proverb, advertising slogan, or poem, and divide it into a number of words and phrases.

Write these on separate slips or cards and hide them under pillows, behind picture frames, or in various nooks and crannies around the house.

Then, when the children assemble, send them out on a hunt to find the hidden "treasure."

If a player comes upon a word or a phrase, he is to leave it just where he found it, copy it on a sheet of paper, and move on without saying anything, in search of the other parts of the original quotation or poem until he has put them all together. The first to do so wins.

The difficulty of the game can be varied according to the length and complexity of the passage selected.

WORDS OF WIT AND WISDOM

INTERMEDIATE-ADVANCED   *Clock or timer*
Large families or groups

This is a game that places a premium on fluency and wit. Based on word association, it encourages alertness and mental celerity. The larger the number of players, the better.

The group is divided into two evenly matched teams.

First, the leader calls out a word. Within, say, a minute, a member of either team has to compose a humorous sentence or make a witty remark suggested by the *associations* called up by the word. If, within the time limit, a member of each team comes up with a witticism, the one who, in the leader's judgment, has made the cleverer remark scores the point. If two members of the same team can think of two different funny things to say in the allotted time, the team scores two points.

Here, for example, is how one such game began:

LEADER: Barber.

PLAYER 1: He trims everyone.

PLAYER 2: He gets in my hair.

LEADER: It's such a close shave, I think I'll cut this short. The first one to come up with another one wins the round.

PLAYER 2: I believe I won that round by a whisker.

LEADER: O.K. Astronaut.

PLAYER 3: He's out of this world.

PLAYER 4: And he's always up in the air.

LEADER: Mortician.

PLAYER 5: He's a grave fellow.

LEADER: Dentist.

PLAYER 6: He looks down in the mouth.

LEADER: Tonsillitis.

PLAYER 7: It's just a pain in the neck.

LEADER: Toreador.

PLAYER 1: He takes the bull by the horns.

LEADER: Woodpecker.

PLAYER 2: He doesn't give a rap.

LEADER: Batter.

PLAYER 3: He's often out of whack.

LEADER: Pitcher.

PLAYER 4: He keeps the ball rolling.

PLAYER 5: But he balls everything up.

PLAYER 6: He never gets to first base.

LEADER: Railroad conductor.
PLAYER 7: He tells you where to get off.
PLAYER 1: But he also puts you on the right track.
LEADER: Baker.
PLAYER 2: He takes the cake.
LEADER: Tailor.
PLAYER 3: He keeps me in stitches.
LEADER: Banker.
PLAYER 4: He certainly takes an interest in you.
PLAYER 5: What's more, he's a credit to his community.
LEADER: Janitor.
PLAYER 6: He makes a clean sweep.
LEADER: Author.
PLAYER 7: He's as good as his word.
LEADER: Yachtsman.
PLAYER 1: He keeps his head above water.
PLAYER 2: He takes the wind out of your sails.
LEADER: Tobacconist.
PLAYER 3: He's not up to snuff.
LEADER: Laundryman.
PLAYER 4: He's a complete washout.
PLAYER 5: And he often throws in the towel.
LEADER: Milliner.
PLAYER 6: I take my hat off to her.
PLAYER 7: She certainly makes you use your head.
LEADER: Shoe salesman.
PLAYER 1: I'm always treading on his heels.

In a similar vein, one can say of the construction worker that he's a tall-story man, of the cardsharp that he's just a joker, of the aviator that he is a high flyer, of the cashier that he's a teller of fortunes, of the printer that he's not one's type, of the fruit peddler that he has lots of dates, of the garbage man that he is often down in the dumps, and of the carpenter that he is a chiseler. Indeed, there is hardly a job, an object, or an activity about which one cannot say something witty if one puts one's mind to it.

The game can be played just for laughs, of course, but it does sharpen one's perception of the humorous oddities of language and common turns of phrase.

HOW'S BUSINESS?

ADVANCED
Large families or groups

This is a variation of the preceding game in which the witticism must in each case be made in response to the question, "How's business?" directed at people in different occupations or professions.

The dialogue might take the following form:

LEADER: How's business, Mr. Tailor?
PLAYER 1:   Sew-sew.
LEADER: How's business, Mr. Farmer?
PLAYER 2:   Growing.
PLAYER 3:   I'm not exactly making hay.
PLAYER 4:   I'm working for peanuts.
LEADER: How's business, Mr. Electrician?
PLAYER 5:   Rather light.
LEADER: How's business, Mr. Garbageman?
PLAYER 1:   Picking up.
PLAYER 2:   Rotten.
PLAYER 3:   It stinks.
LEADER: How's business, Mr. Dentist?
PLAYER 4:   Nerve-racking.
LEADER: How's business, Mr. Astronomer?
PLAYER 5:   Looking up.
LEADER: How's business, Mr. Carpet Salesman?
PLAYER 6:   Rugged.
LEADER: How's business, Mr. Author?
PLAYER 7:   All write.
LEADER: How's business, Mr. Butcher?
PLAYER 1:   I have no beef.

PLAYER 2:   I'm living off the fat of the land.
PLAYER 3:   I can't deliver fast enough.
LEADER: How's business, Mr. Cobbler?
PLAYER 4:   It's my sole support.
LEADER: How's business, Mr. Pillow Manufacturer?
PLAYER 5:   Down every day.

Similarly, a cowboy might be at the end of his rope, a munitions dealer might find business abominable, a bikini manufacturer might find the outlook bare, a pugilist may say it is about to improve, a mortician may find it dead, an acrobat may find it in full swing, a cattleman bullish, a bricklayer building up, a shipwright booming, a statistician average, a musician basically sound, and a pennant maker flagging. One player may say that the gardener finds his business no bed of roses, while another may say he is in the clover. A cutler may have the edge on his competitors, while a brassiere salesman may be just abreast of them. A vintner may find himself hard pressed, a ship captain in desperate straits, and a corset manufacturer pinched. A liquor dealer may find business spirited, while a bird merchant may be feathering his nest. In fact, the humorous possibilities of this game are virtually inexhaustible.

~~~~~~

Can you make sense out of this: It was and I said not but.
"It was 'and,' " I said, "not 'but.' "

A letter to a man was addressed in this way:
                    HILL
                    JOHN
                    MASS
Can you tell his full name and address?
John Underhill, Andover, Massachusetts.

FRANTIC SEMANTIC ANTIC

INTERMEDIATE-ADVANCED   *Paper and pencil*
Large families or groups

This popular game, also called MAD LIBS, provides much merriment at the same time that it familiarizes the players with various parts of speech as used in complete sentences. There are no winners or losers; the object is to add to the hilarity.

First, either write or find a lively paragraph of interest to the players. It might be about them or their friends—their habits, clothes, hobbies, etc.—or about any subject or persons likely to be well known to the players.

Next, substitute for certain key words in the paragraph or story—in particular, nouns, adjectives, verbs, and adverbs— spaces in which you write only the part of speech of the missing word, together with other necessary grammatical information—e.g., *past tense of active verb, plural noun, masculine proper noun, adverb of manner*, etc.

Now, reading only what you have written in the blank spaces, and taking them in the order in which they appear in your paragraph, ask each player, in turn, to supply a word that fits the required part of speech or grammatical form. Write the answers in the blank spaces.

Finally, you read aloud the full text, including the words that have been supplied. The results are usually comic in the extreme. Thus, in one instance, the account began like this: "An *odious* girl would like to *petrify* a *sniveling, succulent* boy in her *hideous* home. She invites him to a *second-rate* dinner with her *fiendish* parents, who behave *psychotically*. The first course consists of stuffed *pajamas* and sour *astronauts* served *guiltily* with a *ghoulish accent*."

Naturally, the more "far-out" the verbs, adjectives, nouns,

and adverbs are, the greater the merriment when the paragraph is finally read aloud to everybody.

Another way of playing the game is to give each player the entire list of parts of speech or grammatical forms in the order in which they appear in the story and to have each write down an appropriate word for every blank. Then let each in turn read the whole story with his own words inserted. Obviously, the zany possibilities are multiplied by the number of players participating.

APT ADVERBS or TOM SWIFTIES

ADVANCED   *Paper and pencil*
Large families or groups   *Blank cards (playing-card*
                               size)
                             Clock or timer

The object of this well-known game is to think up sentences in which an adverb is somehow—surprisingly, wittily, punningly, cunningly, but always funnily—used to describe the way someone said something or asked a question. An example would be: "Hello, father," he said sunnily.

The players are allowed five minutes of concentrated thought. Then, one by one, they read what they have produced. If anyone present thinks he can improve on someone else's sentence, he may try. The one with the greatest number of acceptable sentences wins.

Here are a few, just to get the snowball rolling.

"Start the engine," he said crankily.

"It's a great piano," he said grandly.

"Have some sardines," he said cannily.

"Don't be so hard," he said feelingly.

"You're not so pretty yourself," she said plainly.

"I'd like to get out of here," he said cagily.

"You'll find everything posted on the bulletin board," he said tactfully.

"Would you like some pie?" he asked mincingly.

"I'm glad I finally fixed that flat," he said tiredly.

"You've got a wound there, all right," he said touchingly.

With a more mature group, the game can rise to such heights as the following:

"I see you're sunburned, sir," he said tangentially.

"Don't you have enough hats already?" she asked captiously.

"I thought I heard a crow," he said cautiously.

"This looks like a good place to camp," he said tentatively.

"I can't seem to take off weight," she said fatuously.

"These violin strings are too tight," he said fretfully.

"Slip me that ermine wrap," he said furtively.

"This hatchet stinks," he said accentedly.

"This garret must be ventilated at all costs," he said fanatically.

"Why don't you try it?" he asked testily.

"I use a straw to do it," he said succinctly.

"I don't believe in the inheritance of acquired characteristics," he said genially.

"It's been quite a while since my last haircut," he said gruesomely.

Another way of playing the game is to write down on a set of cards a number of adverbs like *cattily*, *doggedly*, *sheepishly*, *craftily*, *airily*, *roundly*, *wryly*, *dryly*, *warily*, *movingly*, *saucily*, *cuttingly*, *winsomely*, *handsomely*, *grippingly*, *resignedly*, etc. After shuffling the cards thoroughly, lay them face down on the table. Each player, in turn, draws a card from the top of the deck and is given a minute to come up with an appropriate sentence. Other members of the group may then offer suggestions or improvements.

***

"Who shall I call?" asked a gentleman of his companion as he stepped to a telephone booth to invite some friends to a party.

"An English teacher," was the prompt reply.

VERB VIGNETTES

ADVANCED   *Paper and pencil*
Large families or groups   *Blank cards (playing-card*
                                      size)
                                  Clock or timer

This is a variation of APT ADVERBS, but the emphasis is on
the verb in each sentence. Players are encouraged to be creative and witty in matching verbs with statements. The procedure followed is the same as in APT ADVERBS.

Here are a few examples:

"Stop playing that violin!" he squeaked.

"Turn off that radiator!" he steamed.

"That looks like pork on your plate," the rabbi insinuated.

Here too, cards can be prepared with suitable verbs like
boomed, fumed, piped, grunted, panted, stormed, etc., and
then used, as in APT ADVERBS, to stimulate the players'
imaginations.

PARTICIPLE PATTER

ADVANCED   *Blank cards (playing-card*
Large families or groups   *size)*
                                  Clock or timer

After a few rounds of APT ADVERBS and VERB VI-
GNETTES, the players may be sufficiently warmed up to
carry on the hilarity with past participles—i.e., verb forms
used as adjectives—prefixed by *dis, de, im, re,* etc., like *de-
creased* (which might be said of a lady who had had her face
lifted).

Here is how the patter might begin:

PLAYER 1: How would you describe an alcoholic deprived
             of his drink?

PLAYER 2: Dispirited. How would you describe lovers in the dark?

PLAYER 3: Delighted, of course. What could be said of a divorced couple who later remarried?

PLAYER 4: First they were impaired, but later they were repaired.

Once again, the players' imaginations can be whetted if cards are prepared with suitable words like *debased, dissected, rebutted, disconcerted, defiled, reminded* (the result of a brain transplant, perhaps), *defeated, disjointed, derided, rebuffed, depressed, impressed, repressed, expressed, released, receded, dismissed, recouped, referred, defined, refined, regaled, rehearsed, relayed, remitted, relieved, dispatched, revamped, disgorged, reversed, discarded, explained, disinterested, reproved, improved, extolled, extended, distended, repealed, revealed, repulsed, delivered, distracted,* and the like.

What common noun is singular at the top and plural at the bottom?
TROUSERS.

Just as he was about to board a plane with a rare serum needed by a dying man in another city, a doctor received a telegram from the patient's wife: DON'T COME TOO LATE.

Reading it as two sentences, he concluded that he was too late, and he turned back. It was only when he arrived home that he read the telegram again, this time as one sentence, and concluded that he was being urged to make haste. But this time it really was too late!

Maria Fëdorovna accidentally caught sight of the following note appended, in the handwriting of her husband, Alexander III, at the bottom of a death warrant:
PARDON IMPOSSIBLE, TO BE SENT TO SIBERIA.
Maria transposed the comma, so that it read:
PARDON, IMPOSSIBLE TO BE SENT TO SIBERIA.
Whereupon the convict was released a free man.

TITLES AND AUTHORS

INTERMEDIATE-ADVANCED   *Paper and pencil*
Large families or groups   *Blank cards (playing-card
                                    size)*
                                Clock or timer

This is another one of those games that can be played just for
amusement, although it does have educational value in calling attention to the possibilities of punning with English
spelling and pronunciation.

The players are allowed five minutes to write down as
many titles and authors as they can think of. But any resem-
blance between the titles and authors in this game and actual
titles and authors is entirely coincidental. No, the fun in this
game consists in making up a title and an author's name that
somehow—by playing wittily on words or letters—go fit-
tingly together. A typical example might be: *Sing the Day
Through*, by Caroline Chirp.

When time is up, each player, in turn, reads what he has
produced. The one with the greatest number of acceptable
titles and authors wins the game.

It is an easier game than it seems. As a warm-up, you
might give the players the following "bibliography."

You're Smarter Than You Think! by O. Eugene Yus.

Carpeting, by Walter Wall.

I Made It! by Justin Time.

It Doesn't Matter Who You Are, by N. E. Body.

Porpoises I Have Known, by Adolf Finn.

Locusts and Grasshoppers I Have Known, by Kate E. Did.

Evils of Alcohol, by Bruno Beer.

Pleasures of Alcohol, by I. M. A. Drinker.

Pisan Memoirs, by Eileen A. Little (also appearing under
the name of I. Lena Lot).

Guide to Good Digestion, by Abel E. Ake.

Don't Make a Move! by Eustace Till.

I Can't Stay Out, by Inigo Again.

Atom Smashing, by Molly Cule.

Body Building, by Ophelia Muscles.

Story of the Alphabet, by A. B. See.

Nonsense, by M. T. Head.

Practical Optometry, by I. C. Well.

Into the Ocean, by I. M. Wet.

Jokes, by May Kem Laff.

Indian Wars, by Tom A. Hawk.

Ocean Days, by Saul T. C. Man.

Yours for the Asking, by Saul I. Have.

Cooking for Yourself, by Amelia Like.

Secrets of a Magician, by Ivan Ish.

I Can Do Anything, by Jesse F. I. Kant.

Telescopes and Binoculars, by Luke N. See.

Guide to Urban Parking, by A. Carl Ott.

Television and Radio Hookups, by Annette Work.

After You, Alphonse, by Hugo First (also written under the name of Inigo Last).

Life in a Madhouse, by Hugh O. Nuts.

I've Had My Fun, by Gail Adie.

Practical Chemistry, by Tess Toob.

Polygraph Testing, by C. F. Eliza Little.

Another way of playing the game is to write down on a set of cards a number of names like *U. Delia Cards, Celia Fate, C. U. Sune, Carrie Yon, Carrie Yerone, Fannie First, Jennie Delp, S. R. Dean, Q. T. Pi, Ruth Leslie Dun, F. Yolanda Plane, Jessie Fitt Israel, B. Jean Yal, Helen Highwater, Y. Dinah Lone, Ira Kant, F. I. Ada Man, Beatrix Ter* (and her sister, *Cynthia Ter*), *I. Hope Eliza Lone, Joan A. House, I. Mollie Fie*, and others equally zany. After shuffling the cards thoroughly, lay them face down on the table. Each player, in turn, then draws a card from the top of the deck, reads it to the others, and is given ten seconds to come up with an appropriate title. Other members of the group may thereupon offer suggestions or improvements.

GAMES TO IMPROVE YOUR CHILD'S ENGLISH

"Help Wanted" advertisements may no longer specify the sex of the person who is to fill a job vacancy.

Recently a young lady applied for a job as a maid, in response to an advertisement for someone to do "light housekeeping." Both she and her prospective employer were somewhat mystified, at first, until she realized that what he was really looking for was someone to do "lighthouse keeping."

Punctuate the following sentence to make it logical:
"Mary Queen of Scots wept bitterly an hour after she was beheaded."
"Mary, Queen of Scots, wept bitterly; an hour after, she was beheaded."

What words do not need an apostrophe when they express possession?
The pronouns OURS, YOURS, HIS, HERS, ITS, THEIRS, and WHOSE.

Just by adding the indefinite article "a" to a sentence, change it from an expression of praise to one of blame.
"There are few mistakes in your paper." (Praise.)
"There are a few mistakes in your paper." (Blame.)

When is "I is" good grammar?
In the sentence "I is the ninth letter in the alphabet."

Punctuate the following group of words in two different ways to correspond to two different meanings:
Mr. Jones the teacher is absent.
1. Mr. Jones, the teacher, is absent.
2. Mr. Jones, the teacher is absent.

PART THREE

Scoring the Games

8

KEEPING SCORE

I. Games to Score Games

Scores, grades, and marks act as motivating devices. Besides being signs of achievement and progress, they promote learning by setting goals to be attained and providing incentives for further effort. Children like a contest; they also like to beat their previous record.

You can make the scoring of any game a game in itself.

Some methods of keeping score penalize wrong answers; others reward right answers; and still others simply show the relative standing of the players. The method of scoring used can be adapted to the type of game being played.

JAILER

Blackboard and chalk

This amusing way of keeping score will heighten the fun and suspense.

Before the game begins, a simple box is drawn on the blackboard for each participant, like this:

This is the "jail"—or rather, its framework—that awaits the loser. The object is to "stay out of jail."

As soon as a player misses, a part of him is "put into "jail" —first his head (with eyes, nose, and mouth); then his body; next a leg; with his fourth mistake, the other leg; and, with successive misses, each arm. After seven errors, he is "locked up" with a succession of bars, until he finally looks something like this:

Needless to say, you can add as many parts of the body (ears, hands, feet, etc.) and as many bars to the jail as desired to suit the length of the game. Each line drawn counts as one miss.

_____

The following advertisement appeared in the classified section of a newspaper:
"Piano instruction. Special pains given to beginners."

A sign outside a delicatessen reads:
OUR TONGUE SPEAKS FOR ITSELF.

HANGMAN

Paper and pencil

This is a variation of JAILER, equally graphic and droll. Each player draws a frame scaffold, like this:

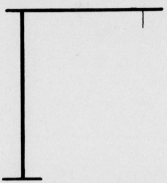

With each miss, he takes a step toward "hanging" himself: first, his head, and then, in turn, his body, each arm, each leg, each ear, each eye, his mouth, and his nose. The object, of course, is to avoid being "hanged."

The loser's paper looks like this:

HUMBUG

Paper and pencil

This method of keeping score can be used either to reward correct answers or to penalize mistakes.

Suppose it is used to keep track of errors. Then, as soon as a player makes one, he must draw the body of the humbug, marked below with a *B*. For his next mistake, he is penalized by having to add its head, *H*. Then, if he persists in making errors, he must add its eyes, *E*. Next, he will have to add feelers, *F*, as well as legs, *L* (one at a time until six are filled in), and a tail, *T*.

A complete humbug—the loser's paper—looks like this:

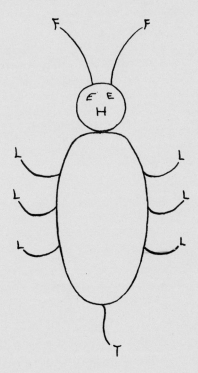

To show the relative standing of the players as the game proceeds, you can use a number of simple devices, as follows:

FIREMAN UP THE LADDER

Blackboard and chalk

Draw a ladder with as many rungs as there are gradations in the score. The bottom line represents zero; the top line, the highest possible score; and the other lines are marked accordingly.

If the ladder is drawn on a slate, each player's standing can be marked on it either with his initial or with chalk of a distinctive color, and any change can easily be made with the aid of an eraser.

FILL 'ER UP!

For this method of scoring you will need a few drinking glasses—one for each player.

Mark each glass, from top to bottom, by means of a crayon, lipstick, or eyebrow pencil, with a series of equally spaced dots running up the side. These represent the successive gradations in score from zero to the highest.

All glasses are empty at the start. As a player scores points, he is rewarded by having his favorite beverage poured into his glass to the level attained.

At the end, of course, the players enjoy the fruits of their success in proportion to their merits.

THE LAST LAP

This is simply the reverse of FILL 'ER UP! Instead of starting empty, each player's glass begins full of his preferred drink.

For each point scored, a player is entitled to remove and drink one tablespoonful from his glass. The player who empties his glass first wins.

COAST TO COAST

Map
Colored tacks

This way of scoring also teaches geography.

First get a large map of the United States of the kind that is readily available from a gas station or a travel agency. Mark on this map a number of places between the city in which the game is being played—say, New York—and a city on the most distant coast. Possibly ten major cities along the way may be circled in red.

For each point gained, a player moves his distinctively colored tack to the next town on the route. For each penalty incurred, he has to move back one town. The one who gets to the final destination first wins the game.

Of course, this method of scoring admits of many different variations—for example, to include the scaling of mountains, the crossing of rivers, visits to national parks and historic sites, etc.

How would you describe an electrician who had lost his job?
Discharged.
But would you say he had been refused if he got another?
More likely he might be revolted.

MAKING A PILE

This method of scoring appeals to the child's desire to accumulate.

The objects to be accumulated may be marbles, checkers, pennies, bottle caps, playing cards, stamps, beans, sticks of gum, candy balls, buttons, golf tees, beads, nuts, tickets from a roll, or whatever else the children would like to play with.

After the tokens have been equally divided among the players, the game begins. As points are scored, the players win tokens from one another. The object is to accumulate the biggest pile.

KEEPING OUT OF THE RED

Red and blue crayons

A red and a blue crayon are needed for this method of keeping score.

Each player has his own "account." Credits are marked in blue, debits in red.

The results are easy to read. The object, of course, is to "keep out of the red."

GROWING UP

Blackboard and chalk

Here the successive gradations in score are represented by differences in people's size. The object is to "grow up."

The lowest score places a player among the Mites. Next, he becomes a Squirt, then a Midget, and, in order, a Runt, a

Dwarf, a Pygmy, a Shrimp, a Peewee, a Featherweight, a Lightweight, a Boy, a Man, a Giant, and a Titan or a Superman. If girls play, other names can be substituted—e.g., Elf, Gnome, Brownie, etc.

The names should be written in a vertical column, to represent graphically the differences from the shortest to the tallest, and the initials of the players can be added and erased as they "grow" from one stage to the next.

PROMOTION

Blackboard and chalk

As players score points, they can be "promoted" to a higher position, likewise shown on an ascending scale. Boys, for example, can move up the ranks in the Army from private, corporal, and sergeant to second lieutenant, first lieutenant, captain, major, lieutenant colonel, colonel, brigadier general, major general, lieutenant general, and general. Or the promotion can be scholastic: from preschool, kindergarten, first grade, second grade, etc., through the various years of high school, college, and postgraduate degrees.

How might a sea captain order you to the rear of his ship?
Sternly.

Can you think of a sentence with five and*'s in succession?*
Well, the story goes that when one sign painter saw the work of his competitor, who had painted MacDonald and Goldberg, *he remarked, "The spaces between 'MacDonald' and 'and' and 'and' and 'Goldberg' are too small."*

What popular television game might an electrician enjoy playing?
Watt's My Line?

ENJOYABLE PUNCHES

Star punch
or box of stars
Blank cards

To make punches enjoyable, you will need the kind of star punch or hole puncher that can be purchased in any stationery store.

Each member of the family has his permanent punch card. For every point scored, he gets a punch—i.e., a hole punched in his card. The punching may be continued over a period of time for several games.

An alternative is to purchase a box of stars in gold, silver, and other colors and to distribute these on a point basis to be pasted by each player on his own card.

TENNIS SCORE

The object here is to complete the word LOVE by gradually filling out the letters of the word as points are scored. The first point would permit the player to make the horizontal stroke in the letter L; the second point would be equivalent to the completion of the letter. A square consisting of four strokes will make the letter O; and so on. The completed word would look like this:

Toothpicks can be used to form the strokes.

WATCH THE CLOCK!

This is a good method of keeping score when there are only two players.

All you need is a paper plate, a pin, two strips of paper of unequal length, and a pencil.

Make a "clock" of the plate by writing in the numbers of the "hours" around its face and inserting the "minutes" between the numbers. Pin to the center an "hour hand" and a "minute hand" so that they are both freely movable.

Set your clock at "twelve midnight."

The older child then shows his score by moving the hour hand, and the younger by moving the minute hand.

Keeping score, in this case, is also "telling time."

HIGH MAN ON THE PYRAMID

Colored tacks

This is really the inverse of "low man on the totem pole."

Draw a large pyramid, with a number of horizontal lines across its face.

The base line represents zero; the apex, the highest attainable score.

Each child is given a differently colored tack, and, as he wins or loses points, he moves his tack up or down on the pyramid, so that his standing in relation to the other players can be seen at all times.

If you asked the letters of the alphabet to an afternoon party, which ones could not come until later in the evening?

The last six, because they cannot come until after tea.

SQUARE YOURSELF

Paper and pencil

Each player draws on his paper a square marked off into eight, ten, or as many boxes as are needed to keep track of points won or lost.

Then, a checker, a bean, a penny, or any other small counter is placed in an empty box for each point scored, or removed for each point lost. The object is to fill all the boxes in one's square.

Other ways of keeping score involve the use of an abacus; marking degrees on a thermometer; cutting notches around the rim of a paper cup or plate or on a stick; adding beads to a string, or tying knots in it. Children love stars, tickets, or coupons that indicate gradations of progress.

A man who had sent a handsome birthday present to his son, a freshman at college, was astonished to receive the following telegram from him: YOU ARE A GRANDFATHER!

But everything was finally cleared up when the old man found that the message his son had told the telegrapher to transmit was supposed to read: YOU ARE A GRAND FATHER!

How would you correct the punctuation of this sentence so that it makes sense? "Caesar entered on his head, his helmet on his feet, his sandals in his hand, his sword on his forehead, a frown and sat down."

"Caesar entered—on his head, his helmet; on his feet, his sandals; in his hand, his sword; on his forehead, a frown—and sat down."

II. Scoring Group Games

Games involving groups of children lend themselves to still other methods of scoring.

If the less capable players are easily discouraged, they can best be given a sense of achievement if you "accentuate the positive." One way of doing so is to link the scorekeeping with some other game, like baseball or football, which the children already know and enjoy.

BASEBALL SCORING

This adds the excitement of baseball to the process of keeping score for any other game.

First, divide the players into two teams as evenly matched as possible.

Next, arrange the chairs in the form of a baseball diamond. At the center stands the "pitcher," who will toss the questions to the members of the opposing team as they take their turns "at bat" according to a "batting order" previously agreed upon.

A correct answer counts as a "hit" and puts the batter on "first base." If the next batter also gets the answer right, he advances his team to "second base." His team moves ahead one base with each right answer. A run is scored by four consecutive correct answers.

Three wrong answers put the other team at bat. With each missed or wrong answer the opportunity to score is transferred to the opposite team.

The game should last for nine innings, but its length may vary according to the time available.

FOOTBALL SCORING

Blackboard and chalk

Draw a football gridiron on the blackboard.

Each team starts on its own twenty-yard line.

Every correct answer advances a team four yards.

No gain is recorded for an incorrect answer.

If a team fails to advance ten yards in four chances, it must relinquish the ball to the opposite side, which then begins where the first team ended.

A team correctly answering three out of four questions nets twelve yards and thus scores a "first down."

Penalties for various types of "fumble"—talking out of turn, for example—can also be imposed.

HOCKEY, BOWLING, GOLF, ETC., SCORING

The methods used in keeping score in these games can be similarly used or adapted in tallying the results of a word game, according to the experience, maturity, or interests of the players.

Who is the author of The Pleasures of Banking?
Cassius Good.
And who wrote In the Good Old Days of Yore?
Dinah Saur.

If a chicken could talk, what kind of language would it speak?
Fowl (foul) language, of course.

The following sign was posted conspicuously in a store:
Our Best Is None Too Good.

III. Matching the Players

It is important, of course, that arrangements be made for every player to participate in the game. Here are two systems of setting up matches in games in which individual players are pitted against one another. Both methods will ensure that no player is left out.

ROUND ROBIN

This method of matching the participants is suitable for games in which every player must compete with every other player.

Draw a square with as many boxes in each direction as there are players. Thus, for a game with five players, you will need a square with twenty-five boxes, as shown below.

	A	B	C	D	E
A		AB	AC	AD	AE
B			BC	BD	BE
C				CD	CE
D					DE
E					

Now write the name or initial of each player above one of the vertical columns and, in the same order, from top to bottom at the left of each horizontal row, as shown.

Then draw a diagonal line passing from the first box at the left in the top row to the last box at the extreme right in the bottom row, as in the illustration.

Finally, above the diagonal line, fill in each box with the names or initials of the two players listed above it and to its left.

In this way, you will have provided a match for every player with every other player. Rematches between any two players can be indicated in the blank space below the diagonal line, if desired.

ELIMINATION

This method of pairing players ensures that everyone is matched against another player and that, after the first round, he will meet his match.

The essential principle can best be represented by the diagram below, which, of course, can be extended indefinitely for any number of players.

$$L\,1—\begin{cases} L\,1—\begin{cases} 1 \\ 2—W\,2 \end{cases} \\ L\,4—\begin{cases} 3—W\,3 \\ 4 \end{cases} \end{cases}—W\,3$$

Each number (1, 2, 3, 4) represents a different player. The winners (W 2 and W 3) of the first round (represented in the diagram as two matches, one between 1 and 2, the other between 3 and 4) are themselves matched against each other in successive rounds until only one winner remains (shown in the diagram at the extreme right as W 3). In the same way, the losers of the first match (here L 1 and L 4) play against each other in the following rounds until only one loser remains (shown in the diagram at the extreme left as L 1).

In the final match the one winner and the one loser may compete against each other.

PART FOUR

Word Lists,
Bibliography,
and Indexes

COMMON HOMONYMS

adds, adz
aid, aide
ail, ale
Air, e'er, ere, heir
aisle, I'll, isle
all, awl
allowed, aloud
altar, alter
ant, aunt
arc, ark
ascent, assent
ate, eight
auger, augur
aught, ought
autarchy, autarky
aye, eye, I
bad, bade
bail, bale
bait, bate
baize, bays, beys
bald, balled, bawled
band, banned
bard, barred
bare, bear
baron, barren
base, bass
bay, bey
be, bee
beach, beech
beat, beet
beau, bow
been, bin
beer, bier
bell, belle
berry, bury
berth, birth
better, bettor
bight, bite
billed, build
blew, blue
bloc, block
boar, bore
board, bored
boarder, border
bolder, boulder

born, borne
borough, burrow
bough, bow
bouillon, bullion
boy, buoy
braid, brayed
braise, brays, braze
brake, break
breach, breech
bread, bred
brewed, brood
brews, bruise
bridal, bridle
brows, browse
but, butt
buy, by, bye
calendar, calender
callous, callus
cannon, canon
cant, can't
canvas, canvass
capital, capitol
carat, caret, carrot
cask, casque
cast, caste
cause, caws
cede, seed
ceiling, sealing
cell, sell
cellar, seller
censer, censor
cent, scent, sent
cents, scents, sense
cere, sear, seer, sere
cereal, serial
cession, session
chased, chaste
check, Czech
chews, choose
choir, quire
choler, collar
choral, coral
chord, cord
chute, shoot
cite, sight, site

clause, claws
climb, clime
coarse, course
coign, coin, quoin
colonel, kernel
complement,
    compliment
core, corps
correspondence,
    correspondents
council, counsel
coward, cowered
creak, creek
crews, cruise
cue, queue
currant, current
cygnet, signet
cymbal, symbol
dam, damn
Dane, deign
days, daze
dear, deer
dependence,
    dependents
descent, dissent
desert, dessert
dew, due
die, dye
dine, dyne
dire, dyer
discreet, discrete
doe, dough
done, dun
draft, draught
dual, duel
dyeing, dying
earn, urn
ewe, yew, you
eyelet, islet
fain, fane, feign
faint, feint
fair, fare
fate, fete
feat, feet
filter, philter

find, fined
fir, fur
fisher, fissure
flair, flare
flea, flee
flew, flue
floe, flow
flour, flower
for, fore, four
forbear, forebear
forego, forgo
fort, forte
forth, fourth
foul, fowl
franc, frank
frays, phrase
frees, freeze, frieze
gait, gate
gamble, gambol
gild, guild
gilt, guilt
gnu, knew, new
gorilla, guerrilla
grate, great
grease, Greece
grisly, grizzly
groan, grown
grocer, grosser
guessed, guest
guise, guys
hail, hale
hair, hare
hall, haul
handsome, hansom
hart, heart
hay, hey
heal, heel, he'll
hear, here
heard, herd
heroin, heroine
hew, hue
hide, hied
hie, high
higher, hire
him, hymn

hoard, horde
hoarse, horse
hoes, hose
hold, holed
hole, whole
holy, wholly
hour, our
idle, idol, idyl
in, inn
indict, indite
invade, inveighed
its, it's
jam, jamb
joust, just
key, quay
kill, kiln
knave, nave
knead, need
knight, night
knot, not
know, no
knows, nose
lacks, lax
lain, lane
laps, lapse
lead, led
leak, leek
lean, lien
lessen, lesson
liar, lyre
lie, lye
limb, limn
links, lynx
literal, littoral
lo, low
load, lode, lowed
made, maid
mail, male
main, mane
maize, maze
manner, manor
mantel, mantle
marshal, martial
massed, mast
mean, mien
meat, meet, mete
medal, meddle
metal, mettle
mewl, mule
mews, muse

might, mite
mince, mints
miner, minor
missal, missle
missed, mist
moan, mown
moat, mote
mode, mowed
morning, mourning
muscle, mussel
mustard, mustered
naval, navel
nay, neigh
necklace, neckless
none, nun
oar, o'er, or, ore
ode, owed
one, won
packed, pact
pail, pale
pain, pane
pair, pare, pear
palate, palette, pallet
passed, past
patience, patients
pause, paws
peace, piece
peak, peek, pique
peal, peel
pedal, peddle
peer, pier
penance, pennants
pidgin, pigeon
plain, plane
plait, plate
pleas, please
plum, plumb
pole, poll
populace, populous
pore, pour
praise, prays, preys
precedence,
     precedents
presence, presents
pries, prize
prince, prints
principal, principle
profit, prophet
quarts, quartz
rack, wrack

rain, reign, rein
raise, rays, raze
rap, wrap
rapped, rapt, wrapped
read, red
read, reed
real, reel
reek, wreak
rest, wrest
retch, wretch
rheum, room
rhyme, rime
right, rite, wright,
     write
ring, wring
road, rode, rowed
roe, row
role, roll
roomer, rumor
root, route
rose, rows
rote, wrote
rough, ruff
rung, wrung
rye, wry
sac, sack
sail, sale
scene, seen
scull, skull
sea, see
seam, seem
seas, sees, seize
serf, surf
serge, surge
sew, so, sow
shear, sheer
side, sighed
sighs, size
sign, sine
slay, sleigh
sloe, slow
soar, sore
soared, sword
sold, soled
sole, soul
some, sum
son, sun
staid, stayed
stair, stare
stake, steak

stationary, stationery
steal, steel
step, steppe
stile, style
straight, strait
straightened,
     straitened
succor, sucker
suite, sweet
summary, summery
sundae, Sunday
tacked, tact
tacks, tax
tail, tale
taught, taut
team, teem
tear, tier
teas, tease
tern, turn
their, there, they're
threw, through
throe, throw
throne, thrown
thyme, time
tide, tied
to, too, two
toe, tow
told, tolled
ton, tun
tracked, tract
troop, troupe
vain, vane, vein
vale, veil
vial, vile
vice, vise
wade, weighed
waist, waste
wait, weight
waive, wave
waiver, waver
war, wore
ward, warred
way, weigh, whey
weak, week
weather, wether
who's, whose
wont, won't
wood, would
yoke, yolk
you'll, yule

COMMON PREFIXES

a, an—not, without
ab, abs—from, away from
ac, ad, af, ag, al, an, ap, at—to, toward, thoroughly
ambi—both, around, on both sides
ante—before
anti—against, opposed to
bi—two, twice, double, doubly
circum—around
co, cog, col, com, con, cor—with, together
contra, contro—against, opposed to
de—off, away, freeing from, depriving of, completely
di—twofold
di, dif, dis—from, not, apart
e, ec, ef, ex—out of, off, from, without, thoroughly
eph, epi—over, upon
equi—having equal, equally
eu—good, well, advantageous
extra—beyond, outside
extro—outward
ig, il, im, in, ir—not
il, im, in, ir—in, into, toward, thoroughly, completely
inter—between, among

intra—within, in the interior
intro—inward, toward the interior
mis—wrong, ill, bad, incorrectly
multi—many
non—not
ob, oc, of, op—against
per—through, by, thoroughly
peri—around
poly—many
post—after
pre—before
pro—for, forward, in favor of
pseudo—false, fictitious
re, red—back, again
retro—back, backward
se—aside, apart, without
semi—half
sub, suc, suf, sug, sum, sup, sur, sus—under
super, supra—above, higher, over, beyond the usual
syl, sym, syn—along with, like, together
ultra—excessively, exceedingly, beyond, on the other side
un—not, without, lacking, reversed, removed

COMMON ROOTS

ag, act—do, drive
alter—another
am, ami, amic—friend
ama, amor—love

ambul—walk
anim—life, mind
annu, enni—year
anthrop—man

338

apt—fit, fitted
aqua, aque—water
aud, audi, audit, aur, aus—hear
ben, bene—good, well
bio—life
can, cant, chant—sing
cap, capt—take, seize
capit—head
card, cor, cord—heart
ced, cess—go, yield
chrom, chroma, chromo—color
chron, chrono—time
cit—arouse
clam, clamat—cry out
clin, cline—bend
clud, clus—close
corp, corpor, corps—body
cred, credit—believe
cresc, cret, crete, crue—grow
culp—fault
cur, curat—care, cure
curr, curs—run
dic, dict—say
doc, doct—teach
duc, duct—lead
dur—hard, lasting
equ—equal, just
fac, fact—make, do
fer—bear, carry
fin—end, limit, boundary
flect, flex—bend
flu, flux—flow
form—form, design
fort—strong
frac, fract, frag, frang—break
grad, gress—go, move
gram, graph, graphy—write
greg—group
ject—throw
junct—join, bind
lect, leg, lig—read, choose
liber—free
locu, loqu—speak

logue, logy—word, discourse, study
luc, lum—light
mal, male—bad, evil
medi—middle
micro—small
migr—move, travel
miss, mit—send
moni—warn
mono—one, alone
mort—death
mot, mov—move
mut—change
nomin—name
not—know
nov—new
omni—all
oper—work
path—feel, suffer
pel, pulse—drive, urge
pend, pens—hang, weigh
phon, phone, phono—sound
pon, pos, pose—place, put
popul—people
port—carry
pot—power
press—press
prob—prove
rec, rect, reg—rule
rid, ris—laugh
rupt—break
sci—know
scop, scope—look, see
scrib, script—write
sect—cut
sist, sta, sti—stand
spec, spect, spic—look, see
spir, spirit—breath
strict, string—bind, draw tight
tact, tang—touch
tele—far
tempor—time
ten, tent—hold, have

tend, tens—stretch
ter, terr—land, earth
the—God
tor, tors, tort—twist
tract—draw
trib—pay, grant
uni—one

vad, vas—go
ven, vene, vent—come
vers, verse, vert—turn
vid, vis—see
viv—live
voc, voke—call
volt, volu, volv—turn, roll

COMMON SUFFIXES

able, ible, ble—worthy of being, fit to be, capable of being
ac, ic—pertaining to, consisting of, in the nature of, characterized by, like, in the manner of, belonging to
acy—state or quality of being
al, ial—belonging to, pertaining to, characteristic of, appropriate to, act of
an—belonging to, pertaining to
ance, ancy, ence, ency—state, act, quality, process, condition of being
ant, ent—one who, tending toward
ar, ary—belonging to, relating to, like, of the nature of
ar, er, or—one who
ate—act, condition of being, having the function or office of, characterized by, possessing, making
ation, ion, ition—state, condition, process of being
cle, cule—small
cy—state, quality, office, rank, condition of

ee—one to whom an act is done or a right is granted
eer—one who conducts, manages, or produces professionally
ery, ry—character, behavior, conduct characteristic of; art, trade, occupation; place where something is done
esque—in the manner or style of
ette—small
fic—causing
fold—multiplied by
ful—abounding in, characterized by, full of
fy—make, cause
hood—state, condition, character, quality of being; those having the quality of being
il, ile—pertaining to, appropriate to, suited for, capable of
ine—pertaining to, like, characterized by, of the nature of
ious, ous, uous—abounding in, having, possessing the qualities of, in the nature of
ise, ize—render, make into, subject to, put into conformity with, make like, act in the

manner of, practice, carry on

ish—of the nature of, belonging to, characteristic of, suggesting, showing the undesirable traits of, resembling

ism—act, process of being, conduct characteristic of, condition of being, doctrine or practice of, peculiarity of, addiction to

ist—one who practices, does, professes, advocates, adheres to; one skilled in or professionally occupied with; one who operates on

ity—state, condition, quality, degree of being

ive—having the quality or nature of; given or tending to

less—without, free from, lacking, beyond the range of, unable or without power to

like—resembling

ly—characteristic of, like, befitting, in the manner of

ment—result, means, act, process, art, method, state, quality of; manner of being; degree of being

ness—state, quality, or degree of being

oid—in the shape of

ory—serving for, pertaining to, that which serves for or pertains to

ship—state, condition, or quality of being; office, dignity, or profession; art or skill; one entitled to a rank, dignity, or title

tude—state, quality, degree of being

ward—motion or direction toward

y—characterized by, having, full of, tending or inclined to, somewhat

OTHER BOOKS OF WORDS AND WORD GAMES

Adams, Franklin P., *Innocent Merriment*. Whittlesey House (McGraw-Hill), 1942. An anthology of light verse, with examples of novelties in rhyme and humorous oddities.

Allen, F. Sturges, *Allen's Synonyms and Antonyms*, T. H. Vail Motter, ed. Harper and Brothers, 1938. (There is also a paperback edition.) A thesaurus arranged like a dictionary.

Borgmann, Dmitri A., *Language on Vacation*. Charles Scribner's Sons, 1965. Advanced diversions involving technical word play with codes, ciphers, panagrams, etc.

Devlin, Joseph, *A Dictionary of Synonyms and Antonyms*. Popular Library, 1961. A paperback listing Latin and Greek prefixes, suffixes, and roots, in addition to synonyms and antonyms.

Ernst, Margaret S., *Words: English Roots and How They Grow.* Alfred A. Knopf, 1964.

Fuller, John G., *Games for Insomniacs.* Doubleday & Co., 1966. Strictly adult and sophisticated word games. Excellent, original, and stimulating.

Kaufman, Gerald L., *New Word Puzzles.* Dover, 1957. A paperback containing original word games of the "fill-in" type.

Krevisky, Joseph, and Linfield, Jordan L., *The Bad Speller's Dictionary.* Random House, 1967. In this dictionary you look up the word as you think it may be spelled—e.g., "farmasy" or "sinnic"—and you find the correct spelling immediately opposite. At the end of each list under a letter of the alphabet are words that look alike or are often confused. These are correctly spelled and defined.

Lear, Edward. *The Complete Nonsense of Edward Lear.* Holbrook Jackson, ed. Faber and Faber, 1947. This is a classic nineteenth-century book of limericks.

Mersand, Joseph, *Spelling Your Way to Success.* Barron, 1959. This book by an extraordinarily gifted teacher and trainer of teachers is an excellent practical aid to spelling improvement.

Morris, William and Mary, *The Word Game Book.* Harper and Brothers, 1959.

Ostrow, Albert A., *The Complete Card Player.* McGraw-Hill, 1945. Hundreds of card games, from the simplest to the most complex, clearly described.

Rand, Ann and Paul, *Sparkle and Spin: A Book about Words.* Harcourt, Brace and World, 1957.

Redfield, Bessie G., *Capricorn Rhyming Dictionary.* Capricorn Putnam, 1965. An encyclopedic paperback dictionary of rhymes.

Schwartz, Robert J., *Complete Dictionary of Abbreviations.* Crowell, 1955.

Shipley, Joseph T., *Playing with Words.* Prentice-Hall, 1960. Excellent collection of word charades, oddities, limericks, and games.

Smith, Samuel S., *How to Double Your Vocabulary.* Crowell, 1964. Adult games, quizzes, and word lore.

Sola, Ralph de, *Abbreviations Dictionary*, rev. ed. Duell, Sloan and Pearce, 1964. Standard work.

Wells, Carolyn, *A Nonsense Anthology*. Charles Scribner's Sons, 1902, 1919. (There is also a paperback edition.)

Wood, Clement, *Poets' Handbook*. Greenberg, 1940. A classic text on the different types of verse forms and rhythmic patterns, with a rhyming dictionary.

In addition, you can find more material under the following headings in game books and library catalogues. These are the words to conjure with for more fun with words!

ACROSTICS	PALINDROMES
ALLITERATIONS	PUNS
ANAGRAMS	QUIZZES
BONERS	REBUSES
CHARADES	SCRABBLEGRAMS
CROSSWORD PUZZLES	SPOONERISMS
CRYPTOGRAMS	TONGUE TWISTERS
LIMERICKS	WORD SQUARES
MNEMONICS	

COMMERCIAL WORD GAMES

ANAGRAMS. A word-building game for four to six players. Selchow & Richter Co., Bay Shore, N.Y. (Parker Brothers also puts out this game.)

CHARGE ACCOUNT. Using letters called out by a moderator, players must place them in a sixteen-box square to build as many words as possible. Two to four may play. Milton Bradley Co., Springfield, Mass.

CLOCK-A-WORD. When a player presses a lever, a group of letters appears—say, AIELTROGO—and the clock starts ticking. All the players then race one another against the clock to make the longest possible word in the shortest possible time with the given letters. De Luxe Reading Corp., Elizabeth, N.J.

DIAL-A-WORD. A beautiful plastic set of concentric movable circles with wedges indicating prefixes, roots, and suffixes, making it possible to form thousands of words. An attractive color key with the suffixes calls attention to their function as grammatical signals. Boston Educational Research Co.

JOTTO. A paper-and-pencil game using special pads, similar to SECRET WORD. The Jotto Corp., New York City, N.Y.

PASSWORD. This game for four is made by Milton Bradley Co., Springfield, Mass.

PDQ. Key letters are used as clues to sentences. Milton Bradley Co., Springfield, Mass.

PERQUACKEY. This is essentially a dice game with the alphabet. Lakeside Toys, Minneapolis, Minn.

SCRABBLE. A board marked off in squares is used for the letters, which vary in point value according to the frequency with which they occur in forming words. The same game "for juniors" has pictures, in the letter squares, of objects beginning with the appropriate letters—e.g., a tiger for *t*. Two to four can play. Selchow & Richter, Bay Shore, N.Y.

SCRABBLE CROSSWORD CUBES. The object of the game is to build words in crossword style, using letters tossed up by alphabetical dice. Two or more can play. Selchow & Richter, Bay Shore, N.Y.

SCRAMBLE. The object of the game is to be the first to unscramble the letters of a word shown to all players. Two to four can play. Lakeside Toys, Minneapolis, Minn.

SCRIBBAGE. The object of the game is to form words within a definite time limit, using letters tossed up by alphabetical dice. The words must be formed in crossword fashion. Any number can play. E. S. Lowe Co., New York City, N.Y.

SPILL AND SPELL. This is another alphabetical dice game. Parker Brothers, Salem, Mass.

VOCABLECARDS. These are playing cards for vocabulary-building. Vocablecard Co., Dept. B, 1137 S. Westmoreland Ave., Los Angeles, Calif.

Index of Skills Taught

Within each of the four categories under which the games in this book have been broadly grouped by chapter—rhymes, vocabulary, alphabet and spelling, and grammar and sentence—you can select the specific skill you wish to have your child develop and the game or games best suited to teach it.

345

Noting the Difference in Spelling Between Words Spelled Similarly

Likes and Dislikes 251, Similarity War 278, Spelling Concentration 217, Spelling Rummy 220, Word Ladders 202

Noting Differences Between Spelling and Sound

Blends and Ends 37, Blends and Ends Casino 39, Brain Strain 127, Fishing for Rhymes 52, Hink Pink 48, Rhyme Concentration 44, Rhyme Dice 43, Rhyme Dominoes 46, Rhyme Grab Bag 62, Rhyme Ping-Pong 32, Rhyme Time 33, Rhyme Wheel 36, Rhyme Whirl 33, Rhym-o 54, Sillygism Rummy 124, Sillygisms 121, Similarity War 278

Pronouncing Words Correctly

Blends and Ends 37, Brain Strain 127, Fishing for Rhymes 52, Hink Pink 48, Match My Rhyme 52, Rhyme Climb 64, Rhyme Concentration 44, Rhyme Dominoes 46, Rhyme My Name 66, Rhyme Ping-Pong 32, Rhyme Wheel 36, Sillygism Rummy 124, Sillygisms 121, Similarity War 278, What's My Rhyme? 49

Recognizing and Using Adjectives

Adjective Match 256, Adjective Rummy 257, Adverb Match 260, Adverb Rummy 262, Alphabetical Adjectives 174, Coffeepot 294, Everyday Grammar 263, Follow the Formula 298, Grammar ABC's 296, Modifier Rummy 262, Stuff and Nonsense 300, Taboo 299

Recognizing and Using Adverbs

Adverb Match 260, Adverb Rummy 262, Alphabetical Adverbs with Charades 176, Coffeepot 294, Everyday Grammar 263, Follow the Formula 298, Grammar ABC's 296, In the Manner of the Adverb 293, Modifier Rummy 262, Stuff and Nonsense 300, Taboo 299

Recognizing and Using Antonyms

Antonym Match 147, Antonym Rummy 145, Antonym War 154, Concentration 151, Word War 155, Word-y 168

Recognizing and Using Different Parts of Speech

Alliterative Add-a-word 177, Alphabetical Add-a-word 175, Backward Sentence Ghost 283, Coffeepot 294, Everyday Grammar 263, Follow the Formula 298, Frantic Semantic Antic 307, Grammar ABC's 296, Grammar Dominoes 267, Grammar Ghost 286, Grammar Pyramid 271, Grammar Rummy 264, Grammar Solitaire 275, Gram-o 265, Modifier Rummy 262, Sentence Dice 289, Sentence Ghost 281, Sentence Superduperghost 285, Sentence Superghost 284, Similarity War 278, Stuff and Nonsense 300, Suite Words 273, Taboo 299

Recognizing and Using Synonyms

Antonym War 154, High-brow Proverbs 160, Putting On the Dog 159, Similarity War 278, Synonym Match 146, Synonym Rummy 144, Synonym War 153, Verb Charades 292, Word War 155, Word-y 168

Recognizing and Using Verbs

Adverb Match 260, Adverb Rummy 262, Apt Adverbs *or* Tom Swifties 308, Coffeepot 294, Everyday Grammar 263, Follow the Formula 298, Grammar

Using a Thesaurus

Using Transitional Words and Phrases

Versifying

Visualizing the Spelling of Words

Index of Games